GAME OF MY LIFE:
DALLAS COWBOYS

Jean-Jacques Taylor

SportsPublishingLLC.com

Publishers: Peter L. Bannon and Joseph J. Bannon Sr.
Senior managing editor: Susan M. Moyer
Acquisitions editor: Mike Pearson
Developmental editors: Elisa B. Laird and Mark Newton
Art director: K. Jeffrey Higgerson
Dust jacket design: Dustin J. Hubbart
Interior layout: Dustin J. Hubbart
Photo editor: Erin Linden-Levy

Printed in the United States of America

Sports Publishing L.L.C.
804 North Neil Street
Champaign, IL 61820
Phone: 1-877-424-2665
Fax: 217-363-2073
SportsPublishingLLC.com

Library of Congress Cataloging-in-Publication Data

Taylor, Jean-Jacques.
   Game of my life, Dallas Cowboys : memorable stories from Cowboys Football / Jean-Jacques Taylor.
      p. cm.
   ISBN 1-59670-036-X (hardcover : alk. paper)
   1. Dallas Cowboys (Football team)—History. 2. Dallas Cowboys (Football team)—Biography. 3. Football players—United States—Biography. I. Title.

GV956.D3T39 2006
796.332'64097642812—dc22

2006015696

To my parents, Doris and Henry. I thank God for you every day.

And to Lorraine, Jasmine, Ashton-Jude, and Allanah

CONTENTS

PREFACE

There are pictures of me wearing a red uniform—complete with helmet and shoulder pads—lugging a football under my arm as a five-year-old on a snowy day in Buffalo, New York. Boxes filled with notebooks from years of playing electric football as a youth sit in my garage, a reminder of how football has always been at the epicenter of my life.

My fervor for football only intensified when I moved to Dallas as an eight-year-old in 1975. What kid wouldn't prefer to root for the Dallas Cowboys as opposed to the Buffalo Bills?

When the Cowboys beat Denver to win Super Bowl XII, I reveled in their victory. And when they lost to Pittsburgh, the despair felt overwhelming.

My relationship with the Cowboys changed in 1995, when I started covering them daily for the *Dallas Morning News*. No longer could I be a fan. I had to become an objective observer who informed fans why the Cowboys were winning and losing. That wasn't too difficult, because the players I had idolized as a kid, such as Tony Dorsett and Roger Staubach, had long since retired.

As an adult, the Cowboys remain inextricably linked to my life. I can identify defining moments in my life by what was going on during the Cowboys' season at that particular time—like in 1997, when I missed a 20-17 loss to the New York Giants because my mother died unexpectedly from complications caused by lupus. The afternoon she died, I had been so excited because I had gotten an exclusive interview with Nate Newton concerning his poor performance against Chicago, and I couldn't wait to write the story.

I missed a 2003 game against Philadelphia, a 36-10 loss, because my pregnant wife was due any day, and I didn't want to be a three-hour flight away in case she started having the baby. Our son arrived four days later, but I made the next game. I even scheduled my marriage around the Cowboys, squeezing it in three weeks before the start of training camp, which gave us time to honeymoon and ensured football season would never affect my anniversary.

I'm not alone. Others can easily make similar timelines of their life that coincide with various points in Cowboys history, in part because the franchise has had so many memorable games and has impacted the lives of so many people.

This book tells the stories of 24 players and a coach and recounts their most memorable games with the Cowboys. There are so many great players in franchise history that aside from the Hall of Fame players, it was difficult to pare the list to 25. Because the book relies on first-person accounts, however, some natural choices were eliminated from consideration, such as Bob Hayes, Harvey Martin, and coach Tom Landry.

I tried to link the players with pivotal moments in franchise history, such as the Ice Bowl, the Hail Mary game, and the Super Bowls. There are also chapters on players such as James Washington, who never played in a Pro Bowl but turned in one of the most memorable performances in Super Bowl XXVII. Then there's Paul Palmer, who played half a season in Dallas but had a 100-yard game against Washington in Jimmy Johnson's only win in 1989.

This book is also about stars such as Emmitt Smith, Tony Dorsett, Troy Aikman, Roger Staubach, Deion Sanders, and Mel Renfro and their most memorable games. Some of their choices I expected, such as Smith's 1994 game against the New York Giants. Others, such as Renfro's performance in the 1970 Pro Bowl, caught me completely by surprise.

My hope is that you'll enjoy these snippets of Cowboys history as much I enjoyed compiling them and they'll make you relive some of the best times of your life.

ACKNOWLEDGMENTS

No project like this can ever be completed without the help of many people, some of whom probably don't realize how much they helped me complete it. Sometimes, their help came in the form of providing a phone number; or babysitting my two-year-old son, AJ, so I could work deep into the night; or convincing a reluctant subject to talk. All the support from family, friends, and coworkers is deeply appreciated and played a role in the completion of this project. That said, I have a few special thank-yous to hand out.

To God, who makes all things possible, and my pastor Rickie G. Rush, whose teachings guided me during the process. And to the men of IBOC, who made me realize just how much I cherish our Friday night gatherings.

Thanks to Mike Pearson of Sports Publishing, who brought the project to me, and Elisa Bock Laird for guiding me through it.

To my editors at *SportsDay*: Bob Yates, Garry Leavell, and Noel Nash, who supported this project from start to finish. And to my partners on the Cowboys beat, Todd Archer and Matt Mosley, who worked a little harder some days during football season so I could slip away for interviews.

To Rich Dalrymple and Brett Daniels of the Dallas Cowboys public relations staff, who provided phone numbers, contacts, and anything else I needed. To Mary Knox for helping me set up interviews with Tony Dorsett and Roger Staubach.

To former *Dallas Morning News* colleague Frank Luksa, who started covering the Cowboys in the 1960s and happily shared his insight on players, and to Bob St. John, whose game stories from the 1960s brought those teams to life nearly half a century later.

To the staff at DallasNews.com, who labored to put every game story in Cowboys history online, making my research infinitely easier.

To former Cowboys personnel director Gil Brandt, who was never too busy to answer my questions about how players were acquired or what the franchise was thinking when it made a decision.

To Brad Sham, the team's radio voice for most of the past four decades, for telling me everything he could about the Cowboys in the 1970s and 1980s.

Finally, to men who helped make the Cowboys one of the world's most successful, recognizable, and popular franchises. Without them, this book isn't possible. So I want to thank Troy Aikman, Bill Bates, Larry Brown, Calvin Hill, Tony Hill, Chuck Howley, Jimmy Johnson, Ed Jones, Lee Roy Jordan, Bob Lilly, Paul Palmer, Drew Pearson, Preston Pearson, Don Perkins, Mel Renfro, Deion Sanders, Emmitt Smith, Roger Staubach, George Teague, Everson Walls, James Washington, Randy White, Darren Woodson, and Rayfield Wright for their time and their memories.

"Next Year's Champions"

CHAPTER 1

DON PERKINS

The self-doubt never left Don Perkins. It didn't matter whether he was one of the best running backs in Iowa at Waterloo West High School. Or one of the best in the nation at the University of New Mexico. Or one of the best in the National Football League with the Dallas Cowboys.

Perkins never convinced himself that he was good enough to take his talent for granted. The doubt made him work harder and longer than most. The doubt drove him to succeed.

"Humility was an admirable quality when I grew up. Now, it's seen as the attitude of a loser," Perkins said. "There were a lot of us who played as hard as we could and as well as we could with no presumption of how great we were.

"I never wanted that type of pressure. If you say that, then it kind of scares me because I have to live up to those words and people expect something from me. I'm just a little kid from Waterloo, Iowa, and people are counting on me. I didn't like that feeling."

People counted on Perkins whether he liked it or not because he was one of the best athletes to ever come through Waterloo, starting three years on the varsity and leading his team to an undefeated season as a senior.

He received plenty of interest from Iowa State and Drake University, but University of Iowa coach Forest Evashevski never called. Some suggested it was because the Hawkeyes didn't think the 5-foot-10, 164-pound running back could thrive in the Big Ten.

West coach George Dutcher gave him another story.

"I was dating an Anglo girl in high school, and word got out even though we were trying to be covert," Perkins said. "My coach told me that Iowa thought that would be bringing trouble to their campus."

It wasn't the first time race relations had impacted Perkins' life. In fact, race relations brought his parents together.

"My dad and his brothers grew up in Waxahachie, Texas, which is pretty close to Dallas," Perkins said. "As teenagers, they got into a fight with some soldiers, and somebody cut somebody. I don't know all of the details, but they weren't going to stay around and discuss it with the law because it probably wasn't going to matter. They ended up in Fargo, North Dakota, because one step out of Fargo puts you in Canada."

Two of his brothers later moved to Minneapolis, while Perkins' father found work at a meat packing plant in Waterloo. His mother, an only child, was born in Chicago, but her parents moved to Waterloo.

"We grew up as poor kids. We used water from a well and outhouses, and we had unpaved streets," Perkins said.

Although he was a member of the All-State team as a senior, Perkins had doubts that he would succeed on the college level.

"I figured I'd give it a shot and see what happened. I played OK in high school, but these guys were from all over the country," Perkins said. "New Mexico was as far as I could get away from home, so I figured I'd see a different part of the country until they cut me and sent me back to Iowa."

As usual, Perkins starred. He led the Skyline Conference in rushing as a sophomore and became one of nation's best all-around offensive players.

After college, his route to the pros was unconventional. The city of Dallas was going to receive an expansion franchise, but it wasn't going to be operating in time to participate in the 1960 NFL draft. So the league allowed the Cowboys to sign a limited number of players to personal services contracts. The Cowboys signed Don Perkins and Don Meredith under the arrangement.

"[The Cowboys] could pick any five players—and if they could sign them—that would be the league's concession since they couldn't pick in the draft," Perkins said. "I was one of the five. I signed a two-year contract worth $10,000 each season, and I got a $1,500 bonus.

Don Perkins finds a gap in the 1967 "Ice Bowl." © *Vernon J. Biever Photo*

"I'm from Waterloo, Iowa, and New Mexico, and they've got all these guys from big-name schools like Illinois and Notre Dame. I was going to give it my best shot, but I had a wife and a kid, so when I didn't make the team, at least I was going to be $1,500 richer when I got home."

A recurring foot injury forced Perkins to miss the 1960 season, but he quickly became an impact player in 1961 with 851 yards rushing and nearly 1,600 yards in total offense.

"He was an explosive runner," said Lee Roy Jordan, the Cowboys' middle linebacker from 1963 to 1976. "He got to the hole faster than just about anybody I've ever seen, and he was through it just as fast."

At 5 feet, 10 inches and 204 pounds, Perkins was also an exceptional blocker. He generated tremendous power in a small area with his powerful hips and thighs and drove through opponents.

"He was a tough, tough competitor," said Cornell Green, a safety from 1962 to 1974. "He would block anybody."

The Cowboys no longer feared the mighty Green Bay Packers, and they were no longer going to be happy simply competing against them.

They wanted to win championships.

A 34-27 loss to Green Bay in the 1966 NFL championship game had convinced them of that. In 1966, Dallas posted a 10-3-1 record, second only to the Packers. They had averaged a league-high 27.8 points per game and had outscored their opponents by 206 points.

The year before, they had fallen behind Green Bay 14-0 before their offense ever took the field, but they had the ball on the Green Bay 2-yard line in the waning moments with an opportunity to force overtime, when Don Meredith threw an interception.

"In 1966, we were just happy to be there," Green said.

That's understandable, considering where the Cowboys had come from.

Clint Murchison, who had failed in his attempt to purchase at least two other teams, was awarded an expansion franchise in 1960. A month earlier, he had signed New York Giants defensive coordinator Tom Landry to a personal services contract with the intention of naming him head coach. Murchison already had hired Tex Schramm to oversee the expansion process.

It didn't go smoothly.

In their first five seasons, the Cowboys went 18-46-4 and never won more than five games, including a 0-11-1 record in their inaugural season. After a 5-8-1 finish in 1964, Landry received a 10-year contract extension.

Suddenly, no coach in professional sports had more security.

Dallas responded with a 7-7 record in 1965. The next year, the Cowboys played for the championship.

"Tom Landry and Murchison were getting a lot of young talent," Perkins said. "Many of us had been there since 1960 or 1961, and we knew what it was like to be the laughingstock of the league, which we were in the early years, [and then] to become a contender.

"I think we felt that we could play with anybody. We believed in ourselves, and we could give anyone a run for their money."

Dallas played with an attitude, starting the season 7-2. Don Meredith and Craig Morton directed a balanced offensive attack that was equally efficient running or passing.

Perkins led the team with 823 yards and six touchdowns, and Dan Reeves added 603 yards and five touchdowns. Lance Rentzel had 996 yards receiving with eight touchdowns, and Bob Hayes had 998 yards and 10 touchdowns.

"It was statistically an OK year, but there were a lot of emotions involved that year," said Perkins, who signed a two-year deal before the season. "We were making some progress, but I was determined above all else not to stay too long. That was real important to me because I didn't want to put Tom in a bad position and I didn't want to put Tex in bad position."

Dallas struggled near the end of the regular season, losing three of its final five games. Still, the Cowboys had earned the right to host the first playoff game in franchise history.

Rookie running back Craig Baynham, who carried the ball three times for six yards in the regular season, scored a franchise-record three touchdowns as Dallas blasted Cleveland 52-14 to set up a showdown with Green Bay.

"I thought we were a much better football team," Green said. "We had a lot of speed and athletes, and if not for the bad weather, we would've kicked their butts."

Perkins gained 51 yards on 17 carries, but Bart Starr's 1-yard plunge in the final seconds lifted the Packers to their second consecutive championship.

"They were a really fine team," Starr said. "They had a lot of athletes and great players. It said a lot about them that they could play in that weather, given where they were from, and almost beat us."

GAME OF MY LIFE
By Don Perkins

The day before the game, they had heating coils on the field to warm the field. When we practiced on Saturday, it was 26 or 28 degrees, and that was fine. We could handle that. We could get traction, which was important because we had a fast team. We felt good because the playing conditions were OK.

The next morning, I remember the operator calling our room with a wake-up call. Mel Renfro picked up the phone and the operator said, "Good morning. It's 8 a.m. and it's 27 below zero."

We were like, "There's no way that's right. She doesn't know what she's talking about."

So Mel and I went to the window and pulled the curtain back, but we couldn't see anything because the window was frosted.

We both said, "Oh, my God."

I don't think I felt overly intimidated by the weather because everyone had to play in it, so I was like just shut up and do it. I don't think you get used to playing in weather like that, but I grew up playing in cold weather in Iowa. In New Mexico, we played teams up and down the

Rocky Mountains and we played schools in Montana, so I knew about cold weather.

They had heaters and blowers on the sideline, but the guys not playing were really freezing because we all know you get colder standing around than when you're running around and moving. We'd come off the field, and the biggest battle we had was getting all of the backups away from the heaters because they weren't giving up their spaces.

We were slipping and sliding all day, and I didn't pick up a whole lot of yards. It really didn't matter what I did because we lost the game. As an athlete and competitor, that's how you feel after the game. The object is to win the game, and if we didn't do that, then what I did didn't matter.

We were up 17-14 in the 4th quarter, but we knew the Packers. The whole country knew the Packers and their capabilities. We didn't think the game was over.

The game went right down to the wire. It all came down to digging a little hole and getting some traction and trying to win the game on one play. You can't see much from the sideline. There are better views from the press box and on TV, but I was glued to the action.

I think it's certainly a disservice to my buddy Jethro Pugh that he became infamous and people called him a goat because he was the one wedged out on that play. It's always been a team game.

It was like a morgue in the locker room after the game. I can still see Bob Lilly and Jethro Pugh with their heads down. I don't remember any comments from Coach Landry. I just remember that long plane ride. Everybody was trying to be somewhere else and wishing they were someone else.

———————————

The losses hurt too much. More than the joy Don Perkins ever experienced from the victories.

Frankly, he couldn't take it anymore. He didn't want to take it anymore, so he decided to move on.

The game had been good to him. And he appreciated it. But he didn't want to play anymore.

So he decided the 1968 season would be his last. He would fulfill the final year of his contract and say goodbye to professional football.

"The emotional aspects of football are so hard on you. It takes a couple of days to get over the bumps and bruises, but the emotional aspect is major," Perkins said. "The Ice Bowl took a lot out of me.

"Part of why I quit was the emotional intensity involved in the game. We had gone the last two years to the wall—the championship game—only to lose to the Packers, and emotionally I didn't feel like I could take that again. There's something about building your hopes up to a high level and never getting there."

Perkins was also weary of fighting his own paranoia.

Every year, it seemed, the Cowboys added another running back capable of taking his job. Dan Reeves arrived in 1965, Walt Garrison and Les Shy came in 1966, and Craig Baynham, a "futures pick," showed up in 1967. In the 1960s, teams could draft players when they still had college eligibility and retain their rights until they could be added to the draft pool.

Perkins viewed Garrison, who was playing on third down most of the time, as a bigger, stronger, faster player with better hands.

Perkins didn't want to be reduced to a part-time player like Green Bay's Jim Taylor at the end of his career or be informed that he was no longer good enough to warrant a roster spot. He wanted to leave the game while he was still a good player, and he didn't hide those feelings from Tex Schramm or Tom Landry.

"Garrison was a good friend and a good football player, but it was time for me to find another line of work. They tried to talk me into reconsidering, but it wasn't a matter of money," Perkins said. "I never sat on the bench. I think it would've killed me to do that. I didn't even know if I could do it. I knew that if I couldn't figure it out, they would figure it for me—and I never wanted that to happen.

"Every year I went through the same thing. I showed up for camp and worked out, but I always wondered which running back they had drafted was going to replace me. I thought about those things, but I never played that way. I never played with less than full intensity."

And he played well in 1968.

With Reeves injured much of the year, Perkins became the Cowboys' primary ball carrier. He rushed for 836 yards—the second-highest total of his career—and a 4.4-yard average with four touchdowns and earned a sixth straight trip to the Pro Bowl.

The Cowboys won their first six games before a 28-17 loss to Green Bay ended their streak. But the Cowboys finished the season 12-2 with a five-game winning streak. It was the best season in franchise history, and they won the Capitol Division by five games.

They owned the Eastern Conference's best record and had easily handled Cleveland, the Century Division champions, 28-7 in week two of the regular season. The year before, Dallas had routed Cleveland 52-10 to claim the Eastern Conference championship.

A victory and the Cowboys would meet the Baltimore–Minnesota winner for the right to play the New York Jets in Super Bowl III.

But Don Meredith turned in one of the worst performances of his nine-year career, completing only three of nine passes with three interceptions before being benched in favor of Craig Morton. Cleveland shocked the Cowboys 31-20.

After the Pro Bowl, Perkins knew he had played his final game.

Perkins, who scored 45 touchdowns, had gained a franchise-record 6,217 yards, while catching 146 passes for 1,310 yards. He was the Rookie of the Year in 1961 and an All-Pro in 1962.

"It caught everybody by surprise when he retired because of his age and because he was still a good player," Green said. "We missed his leadership and competitiveness after he left."

After he left professional football, Don Perkins never met a job he wouldn't try if the timing were right.

He has been a television broadcaster, a radio show host, and a truck driver. Perkins, who resides in New Mexico, spent years in law enforcement as well as starring in a play based on the life of Frederick Douglass, the 19th-century abolitionist and politician.

"I never had any great notions of being in the theater," he said. "The one-man show was fun, and it was pretty good. The broadcasting was pretty interesting, too. There were also some things that I had to do. My truck-driving thing occurred because I was going through a marriage that had not worked out and I just needed to get away.

"But a lot of those things I did are like playing sports. There's a bit of an adrenaline rush and a little bit of fear."

The Cowboys honored his contribution to the franchise by placing him in the Ring of Honor in 1976. Fittingly, he went in with Don Meredith.

"I was flattered and I was pleased," he said. "When you consider all of the players that have gone through this organization, it's kind of funny to see my name is up there. I didn't plan on this type of stuff happening to me.

"It's humbling because I'm from Waterloo and I think they're going to find out they got the wrong guy because I wasn't very fast and I wasn't big and tough. They're going to wonder why my name is up there, but it's a very nice tribute."

Perkins is enjoying retirement these days and spending time with his children and grandchildren.

"My day-to-day life is important," he said. "The relationships with my kids and my grandkids and my relationships with acquaintances and friends are the most important things to me."

CHAPTER 2

CALVIN HILL

Calvin Hill's father didn't learn to read or write until after he got married, but he understood the importance of knowledge. And he made sure his son understood education was the key to avoiding a life in the steel mills, where many people in the Turner Station section of Baltimore worked.

"On my parents' marriage certificate my father made his mark," Hill said. "He believed in education and felt like that was the one thing that was going to make a difference in my life.

"My mother went to school to the 11th grade. She taught him to read and write, and she taught a bunch of her sisters to read and write."

Soon after their only child was born, Hill's education began. Although Calvin wasn't even walking yet, Hill's father purchased a set of encyclopedias—"knowledge books" he called them—because he wanted them available as soon as his son learned how to read. When Hill reached elementary school, Hill's father took an active role in the Parent-Teacher Association and devoted quiet time each evening for his son to complete his homework.

The summer before Hill entered the ninth grade, his father made a life-altering decision based on getting him the best education possible. The Hills' family physician wanted to know if Calvin was interested in attending a prep school in upstate New York that was looking for more cultural and regional diversity.

"My father asked me if I was interested in going to prep school and I told him no," Hill said. "The next day he informed me that I was going to try for this scholarship that would send me to Riverdale Country School."

Hill received the scholarship, and the boy who had lived his entire life in a segregated section of Baltimore was headed to prep school.

"It was a culture shock. I had not dealt with any white people in my life except the ice cream man and the pharmacist," Hill said. "I had never heard of atheists or agnostics. I didn't realize there were different nationalities among white folks, like Italians and Germans. I didn't realize there were other religions, like Judaism."

Hill, who preferred basketball and baseball, decided to try out for the football team. Success came quickly—he scored four touchdowns in his first game—and by the time his career was over he was receiving scholarship offers from virtually every football powerhouse in the nation. UCLA, Notre Dame, Michigan, and Syracuse all wanted his name on a national letter of intent.

"I wanted to go to a big school," Hill said, "and I wanted to play in front of a big crowd."

Hill had just about settled on attending UCLA, when one of his assistant coaches suggested he visit Yale.

"The weekend I visited Yale, they played Dartmouth in front of about 70,000, and it was a beautiful day," Hill said. "I had never envisioned Ivy League football being like that.

"Harvard had had a black quarterback, but Yale never had had a black quarterback, and I wanted to be the first one."

So he signed with Yale.

His dream of being the first black quarterback lasted two days before the coaching staff moved him to running back and linebacker. Hill considered transferring, but opted to stay. By the time his career ended he was recognized as one of the finest players in the nation.

Several teams worked him out, and the Cowboys notified him that they wanted to take him early in the draft. On draft day, Hill thought it might be funny to play a joke on tight end Bruce Weinstein.

"I pretended to be from the New York Football Giants and proceeded to tell him that we had taken him in the second round," Hill said. "I could hear him put his hand over the microphone and tell his friends that he had gotten drafted. I started laughing, and it gave me away."

A little while later, Hill's phone rang.

"It was Gil Brandt essentially telling me the same thing I told this guy. Then he put [Tom] Landry on the phone, and he had a distinctive voice," Hill said. "Then the press got on the phone, and it dawned on me that, perhaps, this was not a joke.

"I was still trying to digest all of this when a columnist from the New Haven [Connecticut] paper wanted to come over and interview me. It was a shock to me."

Calvin Hill, a star running back at Yale who was selected with the 24th pick of the first round in 1969, spent his first few days with the Cowboys at linebacker.

Then they tried him at tight end.

"They drafted me as an athlete. I was a quarterback before I went to Yale, and they moved me to running back," Hill said. "I threw the ball, I ran the ball, I caught the ball. When I got to the pros, I was delighted just to be in the pros. It was something I had done for years for nothing, and now I was going to get paid to do it."

There was nothing unusual about the Cowboys' experiment.

Rayfield Wright moved from tight end to tackle. Mel Renfro shifted from running back to free safety. Cornell Green was a star basketball player at Utah before becoming a cornerback with the Cowboys.

Tom Landry wanted athletes on both sides of the ball. Landry wasn't really that interested in a player's football skills because he figured the coaching staff could help a player improve.

But he knew no amount of coaching was going to make a player faster or more athletic. So personnel director Gil Brandt scoured college campuses looking for athletes who might be able to play football.

"Tom wasn't looking for football players," Brandt said. "He wanted athletes that fit into his offensive and defensive schemes because he wanted players who were athletic enough to adapt to different situations."

Green was one of the first.

He had never played football—not even in high school—but the Cowboys signed him as a free agent, and he became one of the finest players in team history. Green intercepted 31 passes in his 12-year career and led the team in interceptions four times.

"I couldn't even put on a uniform when I first got there," said Green, who played in five Pro Bowls, "but it only took me about two weeks to figure it out. I started the first preseason game, so I figured I was doing OK.

"The Cowboys' philosophy at the time was to get as many athletes on the field as possible. They wanted speed and quickness. Bob Lilly wasn't fast, but he was one of the quickest players in the game over a 10-yard distance. Chuck Howley was one of the fastest linebackers in the game. He had speed and instincts that allowed him to make plays others couldn't.

Running back Calvin Hill heads upfield during a game on September 16, 1973, against the Chicago Bears at Soldier Field. The Cowboys beat the Bears, 20-17. *Diamond Images/Getty Images*

"Mel Renfro might have been the best athlete on the team, and Rayfield Wright played safety in college," Green said. "That tells you all you need to know about his athleticism."

Wright was a star basketball player at Fort Valley (Georgia) State who was going to training camp with the Cincinnati Royals—if he hadn't made the Cowboys' roster.

"Landry was looking for athletes because they're different than football players," Wright said. "Athletes can make a play to win a game that a football player might not. Athletes play football in football season, basketball in basketball season, baseball in baseball season, and then they run track and start all over again."

Hill wasn't sure where the Cowboys were going to use him when he left training camp for a few weeks to participate in the College All-Star Game. Although Don Perkins, the fourth-leading rusher in NFL history had just formally announced his retirement, veteran Dan Reeves was the starter and Craig Baynham was the backup.

When Hill returned from the all-star game, Reeves was struggling to find his form after off-season knee surgery and Baynham had bruised ribs. That meant Hill was going to start against San Francisco.

"I was so nervous, you would've thought I was going to the electric chair," Hill said, "but I gained more than 100 yards. It gave me a lot of confidence because I had a certain amount of doubt the first week. There was pressure because I was the first-round pick, and I didn't want to be a guy from Yale who flubbed.

"Once we put on the pads, I realized a guy from a big school wasn't any different from me. I was a high school All-American as a senior, so why shouldn't I be better than all of these other guys because I was better than them when we were in high school."

Hill never relinquished the starting job and earned Player of the Week honors when he rushed for 70 yards and threw a 53-yard touchdown pass to Lance Rentzel in a 24-3 win over St. Louis to start the season.

In his second start, he tied Don Perkins' single-game rushing record with 138 yards and two touchdowns in a win over New Orleans. He was even better the next week with 91 yards rushing on 10 carries and 202 yards in total offense.

Hill was leading the league in rushing in 1969 when the Cowboys met Vince Lombardi's Washington Redskins in a game that would probably determine the Capitol Division champion.

GAME OF MY LIFE
By Calvin Hill

We were playing Washington and it was a big game. It was *the* game.

They had hired Vince Lombardi, and he had sort of turned their team around. Lombardi had brought in a new attitude and gave their fans hope. I had friends who were big Redskins fans, and they talked about how Lombardi had installed curfews and all of these other things that were going to make the Redskins a winner.

We were 7-1 and playing really well, but the game was essentially Landry versus Lombardi. They hadn't met each other on the field since the Ice Bowl, and there was a lot of hype about the game. Plus, if they beat us, they had a chance to make it a race in the division. If we won, we were going to run away with it.

I was excited to be playing in Washington because it was close to Baltimore where I grew up and my folks were at the game.

I ran back the opening kickoff 50 yards, and Bob Wade, who later became the basketball coach at the University of Maryland, tackled me, so the game got off to a good start. The game plan was designed to run the ball because we wanted to keep the ball away from Washington because they had a really good offense. They had Sonny Jurgensen at quarterback, Charlie Taylor at receiver, tight end Jerry Smith, and running back Bobby Mitchell, so we wanted to keep them off the field.

There were a lot of moments from that game I remember. Seeing Frank Ryan—he was Jurgensen's backup—before the game and being surprised that he had so much gray hair. And I remember getting knocked out of bounds on the Redskins sideline one time and when I looked up, I was looking at Lombardi and he had a smile on his face. I remember thinking, "That's Vince Lombardi."

I scored a touchdown in the end zone near the dugout where we came out of our locker room and onto the field. We were running to the left, and I jumped over someone trying to cut me. I jumped four or five feet—I couldn't believe I had done that—and I saw my old man sitting right there as I was coming down. That was cool.

It's like I got into a zone and everything I did was working, and I felt good. The bottom line as a runner is to keep the chains moving and keep the other team's offense off the field. I felt like I did that because we controlled the ball most of the game. I set a team record for carries [25] and yards [150] that day.

I wasn't even aware of the rushing record. At some point, somebody told me I had a chance to get 1,000 yards, but that didn't mean anything to me. In high school and college the only time you were aware of records was when somebody said something. The only records I was aware of as a kid were when somebody was talking about Jim Brown.

I grew up a Colts fans, and I was never aware of how many yards Lenny Moore and Alan Ameche had. The only thing that was important was to win.

I also hurt my toe that game, and it was never the same after that. We used to do a lot of quick shifting, and sometime during the third quarter when I landed in a three-point stance, my foot felt awkward. When I pushed off, I realized I was hurt. I just didn't realize how badly

I was hurt. That was my last play because I couldn't go anymore. They said it was a jammed toe, but it turned out to be worse than that.

Hill, who had been among the league's leaders in rushing when he jammed his toe, missed the next two games.

"They tried to shoot it up the next week against Los Angeles, but I couldn't play," Hill said. "Then I tried to play against the 49ers and couldn't. It was supposed to be a jammed toe, but nothing worked. I couldn't understand why it continued to hurt, and I started to doubt myself."

Not healing the problematic toe wasn't from a lack of effort.

People from around the state and the country sent home remedies. He tried a few, but none worked. Then teammate Lance Rentzel, who was married to entertainer Joey Heatherton, recommended his wife's podiatrist.

Her doctor quickly diagnosed the problem.

"He looked at an X-ray and said my toe was fractured. [The Cowboys' doctors] either hadn't seen it or didn't tell me about it. I remember the relief of knowing there was some reason I couldn't play."

Hill played the last two games with the broken toe, which required an injection at the fracture site before every practice and game. He also had to wear a size 16 shoe on his right foot because of a steel bar doctors inserted in that shoe to immobilize the toe.

"I had so much novocaine in my foot I couldn't feel it when I touched the ground because it was numb," Hill said. "If you can't feel your foot, it's hard to run. Feel is important to communicate to the brain as to how far you should put it down on the ground. Sometimes, I jammed it too far down. I had to look at the ground while I was running."

He also developed a silver dollar-sized blister that became infected and kept him in the hospital for more than a month after the season.

It was a miserable end to a season that started with such promise.

He recorded three 100-yard games and finished the year with 942 yards, a 4.6-yard average and eight touchdowns. He was named Rookie of the Year.

Hill didn't view it as a coincidence when the Cowboys drafted Duane Thomas, a Dallas native, from West Texas with the 23rd pick of the first round.

"It took me about a year to recover," Hill said. "They told me my foot wasn't a big issue, but they drafted a running back, and two years later they drafted two running backs, and a year after that they drafted another running back.

"My foot hurt a little in 1970, and I couldn't do certain things. I couldn't push off on it hard. I couldn't make hard cuts."

It affected his ability to be the player who burst onto the scene in 1969. Still, Hill was playing well when he suffered a back injury in week nine of the 1970 season.

"I was 12 yards behind [St. Louis running back] MacArthur Lane, when I got hurt," Hill said. "When I was ready to play, Duane had gotten rolling, and I didn't play much the rest of the year. Duane helped me through that period. It was like I had been forgotten."

He finished the season with 577 yards while averaging 3.8 yards per carry.

In the off-season, Hill got married and devoted himself to training. He led the NFL in rushing in the preseason and proved it was no fluke. Against Buffalo in the opener, Hill rushed for 84 yards on 22 carries, caught four passes for 43 yards, and scored a franchise-record four touchdowns.

He rushed for 145 yards in the next two games.

"I felt sensational. I had the spring back in my legs back and I was going to have a good season," Hill said, "then I tore my right knee."

New York Giants defensive back Spider Lockhart wrecked Hill's season with a submarine tackle in the third quarter of a 20-13 Dallas win over the Giants. He suffered a torn anterior cruciate ligament on the play.

"Initially I was told I sprained it, and I missed six games. I hurt it again scoring a touchdown in the NFC championship game against San Francisco," Hill said. "I really had to change my gait. If I was running to my right, I couldn't cut laterally. I was a long jumper in high school, and I could jump off both legs. I couldn't do that anymore."

But he proved he could still run the football in 1972 after Dallas traded Thomas to San Diego. Hill became the first running back in franchise history to surpass the 1,000-yard mark with 1,045 yards and a 4.2-yard average and six touchdowns. He followed that up with 1,142 yards and six touchdowns in 1973.

"I was frustrated heading into 1972 because I just wanted to show what I could do," Hill said. "To get 1,000 yards was important because there weren't a lot of guys who did it. It was a big deal."

A year later, he left for the riches of the World Football League.

———————————

Football never defined Hill. He never let it.

If he hadn't been drafted, Hill would have gone to divinity school in New York City.

"My hope was that I could go somewhere to play football and get $8,000 or $10,000, which would tide me over for two to three years at divinity school because I had a fellowship," Hill said. "I wasn't training to be a preacher, but I wanted to further my own theological and spiritual understanding.

"I thought the black church was the most established institution, and I saw it as an opportunity to continue my evolution and study the isms—racism, sexism, etc.—that held people back."

Even while he played professional football, Hill was always thinking outside the box. That approach led him to an eclectic mix of jobs in the sports world, from vice president of the Baltimore Orioles to his current position as a consultant with the Cowboys.

Hill joined the Cowboys as consultant for player development and assistance nearly a decade ago. It's a role he values because he's seen how the pressure of performing and the pain of playing drive players to use drugs. And he has seen players who earned millions lose it all through bad investments.

Owner Jerry Jones hired Hill and his wife, Janet, to create a program in the wake of nearly three years of off-the-field issues that helped turn the Cowboys from an elite team that won three championships in four seasons into a club that didn't even make the playoffs in 1997.

More importantly, the issues tarnished the reputation of a franchise that had always been viewed as pristine when Tom Landry was coach from 1960 to 1988. From October 1995 to November 1996, the Cowboys had five players suspended by the National Football League a total of seven times for violating the league's substance abuse program, including stars such as receiver Michael Irvin and defensive tackle Leon Lett.

Hill devised a plan for the Cowboys based on drug programs he had helped formulate for the NFL's Cleveland Browns and the Rand Corp.

"Calvin was uniquely qualified for the position because he had first-hand knowledge of what it's like to be a professional athlete for this franchise and what it entails, because we're one of the most visible organizations in the country," said Cowboys public relations director Rich Dalrymple, who joined the organization in 1990.

"He's been very valuable to this organization when it comes to helping young men make the transition to highly paid athletes and as a sounding board for players, coaches, and executives regarding a range of social issues."

CHAPTER 3

MEL RENFRO

Mel Renfro was always the fastest kid. At the park. On the football field. On the track. The venue didn't matter. He had speed. And he loved to run.

Maybe it's because he was always chasing his three older brothers around their north Portland neighborhood, so he would be included in the games they played. Or, maybe, he just figured if he ran fast enough and long enough, good things would eventually happen.

"I was always a runner," Renfro said. "As a little kid in the park, I'd tell four or five guys to try to catch me, and they could never do it.

"My teachers were always telling me I had something special. I was always the captain. Always the leader. I was always the quarterback. I had a little following. My fifth-grade teacher told me to keep doing what I was doing because one day I was going to be something special."

As he matured, Renfro's athletic endeavors advanced from playing tag in the park to dominating the local track and football scene at Jefferson High School.

Renfro once helped Jefferson win a track meet with a victory in the pole vault. It was the first time he had ever competed in that event. As a senior, he essentially won the state track meet by himself by finishing first in four events.

On the football field, Renfro and Terry Baker, who later won the Heisman Trophy at Oregon State, helped Jefferson win 34 consecutive games and three straight state championships.

Although he was one of the most sought-after players on the West Coast, Renfro ultimately decided between Oregon and Oregon State. He chose Oregon State; his father chose Oregon.

"I was a quiet, shy, introverted kid, who didn't want to go far from home," Renfro said. "I felt a little bad because I had told Oregon State I was going with them, but I got over it after a few days."

At Oregon, Renfro continued to excel on the football field. By the time his career ended, he was one of the finest all-purpose players in the nation. He rushed for 1,540 yards and a 5.5-yard average while catching 41 passes for 644 yards. He averaged 26.7 per kickoff return and 12.9 yards per punt return. He scored 23 touchdowns.

Fate helped make him a member of the Cowboys.

On the day President John F. Kennedy was assassinated, Renfro slammed his fist into a mirror in rage and suffered a deep wound that prevented him from playing in the Orange Bowl. Renfro needed surgery to repair his wrist, and the Cowboys, desperately in need of athletes to upgrade their talent level, spread rumors about the nature of the injury.

Their smoke screen worked, and Renfro was available in the second round. Oakland, playing in the rival American Football League, didn't draft him until the ninth round, which made negotiations pretty easy for the Cowboys.

Then, of course, coach Tom Landry had to find a position for him. Renfro's explosive speed and elusiveness suggested he would be a terrific kick returner and halfback, especially for a team looking for a player who could complement Don Perkins.

But his slender frame couldn't withstand the pounding the position demanded his body take. So the Cowboys tried him at safety, while letting him return kicks.

Renfro averaged 25.4-yards per kickoff return as a rookie and 30.0 yards in his second season.

"I enjoyed my short time on offense," Renfro said. "You got more attention, more press, and more money."

Renfro played free safety from 1965 to 1969, then Landry moved him to cornerback in 1970.

"I got out there and got comfortable to the point where you know receivers, the game, and what's happening; you can function well," Renfro said. "I studied my opponent and their mannerisms, and I had a great backpedal. I kept receivers in front of me without turning my shoulders.

"I would look at the guard's, the back's, or the quarterback's body, and I'd break it down in my head what was going to happen. At a certain point, he could only do so many different things, and I'd be ready for it."

A few weeks before the 1970 season began, the Cowboys made a trade that gave them the NFL's best secondary. As usual, it didn't cost them much.

The Cowboys dealt backup defensive end Clarence Williams and backup center Malcolm Walker to Green Bay for cornerback Herb Adderley, a key starter on the Packers' five championship teams in the 1960s. Defensive ends Larry Cole and George Andrie made Williams expendable, and center Dave Manders made Walker easy to trade.

Adderley, considered among the game's top cornerbacks, preferred a gambling style that tended to annoy by-the-book coaches such as Landry and Green Bay's Vince Lombardi. In an era of bump-and-run technique, where defensive backs tried to maul receivers at the line of scrimmage, Adderley preferred to play off of the line.

He'd give the illusion that a receiver was open and accelerate toward the ball when it was thrown, either intercepting it or knocking it down.

"When I heard about the trade, I figured Green Bay either had the best set of cornerbacks in the league or they were the biggest fools in the league," said Cornell Green, a Cowboys safety and cornerback from 1962 from 1974.

"It took me about two weeks to see he could still play at a high level. We just played basic man-to-man defense and locked teams down."

Renfro and Adderley were now the cornerbacks, and Green moved from cornerback to strong safety. Cliff Harris, Charlie Waters, and Richmond Flowers manned the free safety position. At the time, Adderley, Green, and Renfro had combined to play in 14 Pro Bowls.

"He brought a lot of attitude with him," Renfro said of Adderley. "He knew how to win. They won when they weren't even that good. But Lombardi knew how to win, and he brought a little of that attitude with him.

"He screamed at us in the locker room a couple of times, and no one had ever done that. Coach wouldn't scream at us, but Herb did, and he got our attention."

That's because he was used to winning championships with Green Bay. Nothing less than a championship was acceptable.

"Green Bay wasn't always the best team, but they had guys who made plays," Green said. "Herb was a guy who made plays for us. He gave us confidence because he knew how to play and win big games."

Cornerback Mel Renfro. *Focus on Sport/Getty Images*

Coach Landry's Flex defense was designed to stop the run and put teams in long-yardage situations on second and third down. Now, the Cowboys were going to snuff their opponents' passing attacks, too.

The Cowboys struggled early as all of the parts worked to fit together. They started the season 5-4, including blowout losses of 54-13 to Minnesota and 38-0 to St. Louis.

"People had written us off. The season was over," Renfro said. "Coach Landry relaxed his practices a little and kind of threw out the playbook and said, 'You guys have some fun the rest of the year.' We started to dominate people. That was the highlight of the Doomsday Era.

"We were good in 1967, 1968, and 1969, but we were even better in the early '70s. Lee Roy Jordan was our captain and our leader, and we believed in him. He talked all of the time about not letting our opponents get in the end zone—and we didn't."

The loss to St. Louis forged a bond between the players, especially on defense.

"We had a saying on defense. They may drive all the way down the field, but they're not getting in the end zone," Cowboys defensive lineman Bob Lilly said. "We developed a lot of confidence on defense."

In winning their last five games, the Cowboys allowed 36 points. The pass defense finished third in the NFL, limiting opposing quarterbacks to a 48.4 percent completion rate with 10 touchdowns and 24 interceptions. Only the 1977 Cowboys played better pass defense.

The Cowboys streaked into the playoffs as Renfro was playing some of his best football.

In the NFC divisional playoff game, the Cowboys led 5-0 with 35 seconds left. On second-and-9, quarterback Billy Munson threw a pass that bounced off Earl McCullough's hands and into the arms of Renfro, clinching the victory and extending the defense's streak without allowing a touchdown in 21 quarters.

"If they score, we lose for the fifth year in a row," Renfro said, "and don't make it to the 'Big Dance.'"

Green, who had never played strong safety until that season, shut out Pro Bowl tight end Charlie Sanders, who averaged 13.6 yards per catch and scored six touchdowns. Waters recovered two fumbles.

Then came a visit to San Francisco for the right to play in Super Bowl V.

Lee Roy Jordan's interception had set up a touchdown run by Duane Thomas, giving Dallas a 10-3 lead. On its next possession, San Francisco quarterback John Brodie threw deep to Pro Bowl receiver Gene Washington. Renfro out-jumped Washington and intercepted the pass, returning it 19 yards and setting up another Dallas touchdown for a 17-3 lead.

"We shut [John] Brodie and [Gene] Washington down," Renfro said. "He might've caught one pass, but I kept knocking them down. That series of games highlighted my career."

Now, the Cowboys were going to get an opportunity to win the championship that had eluded them since 1966.

Jim O'Brien's 32-yard field goal as time expired provided the Colts with a 16-13 victory. After the game, though, the hot topic was whether John Mackey's 75-yard touchdown on a deflected pass should've counted.

At the time, it had tied the score at 6-6.

Johnny Unitas' high pass grazed receiver Ed Hinton's fingertips. Officials said it touched Renfro's fingers before settling into the arms of Mackey, who sprinted the rest of the way for a 75-yard touchdown.

Had the officials ruled that Renfro didn't touch the pass between the time it bounced off Hinton's fingers and Mackey caught it, the touchdown would have been negated. According to the rules at that time, two offensive players couldn't touch a pass consecutively.

"They said it went off my fingers. At the time I had no sensation of touching it, so to me I didn't touch it," said Renfro, who later intercepted a pass for the third consecutive game. "They made such a commotion about the pass and its significance, but it had no bearing on the game.

"We were leading and we had had control of the game. It's obvious to me that if you throw two interceptions in your territory in the fourth quarter, you're giving the game away."

Rayfield Wright said fate seemed to conspire against the Cowboys that day.

"There was no instant replay or anything we could do about it," he said. "It was a bad call, but it was one of those things."

Another controversial play occurred in the fourth quarter.

Thomas fumbled into the end zone, and Dave Manders apparently recovered.

"But Bill Ray Smith grabbed the ball, started yelling that it was their ball and the referees gave it to them," middle linebacker Lee Roy Jordan said. "It was a good play by him, but it should've been a touchdown for us."

When the game ended, the teams had combined for 11 turnovers. Dallas linebacker Chuck Howley was named MVP, the only player on a losing team to ever earn that honor.

"They called the game a comedy of errors," Renfro said, "and they were exactly right."

Renfro tried to find solace the next week at the Pro Bowl, where he was named MVP after fourth quarter punt returns of 82 and 59 yards in the NFC's 27-6 victory.

GAME OF MY LIFE
By Mel Renfro

That whole week was quite an experience. There was an emotional letdown from the week before because we had lost the Super Bowl, and it was especially tough for me because of all the controversy about the tipped pass. People were talking about it every day. It made me infamous.

The week was miserable. The press was all over me. "Did you touch that ball?" They must have asked me that a jillion times. I told them a jillion times that I had no sensation of touching the ball.

I was pretty much a loner, so I didn't have anyone with me. I stayed in my room the whole week, and I didn't really talk to anybody. I didn't go anywhere. The whole off-season was kind of bad, although the Pro Bowl took some of the sting out of it.

It was the first AFC–NFC Pro Bowl, so it was significant. It wasn't the carnival atmosphere that the Pro Bowl is today. Nobody wanted to get hurt, but guys played hard. It was competitive. We wanted to win.

I didn't want to field the first punt return. It bounced a couple of times and I said, "Oh, heck, I might as well get it." Finally, it bounced right into my hands. The coverage team kind of relaxed because they didn't think I was going to pick it up. I split the middle, and I didn't have to put a move on anybody until about the 30. I made a little move and went into the end zone for an 82-yard touchdown.

A couple of series later, I got the second one. I was still tired, and I didn't want the ball. Dick Nolan was the coach. He had been my defensive coach with Dallas, but now he coached the 49ers. We had beaten them in the playoffs, which is why he was coaching the Pro Bowl. He told me to get out there and field the punt.

You have to understand that I hadn't even returned punts in three years because I had foot problems and the Cowboys wanted me healthy and on the corner.

That second punt was a short kick, and I just came up and fielded it on the run. I kept right on going, and it kind of surprised them again. I never got touched, and I was back in the end zone with a 59-yard touchdown.

I remember being so tired in the end zone. I was gasping for air, and a guy was trying to stick a microphone in my mouth, but I was so tired I couldn't speak. It was the end of the year after playing every game, the playoffs, the NFC championship game, and now the Pro Bowl. I was worn out.

They must have thrown my way 15 times. Oakland quarterback Daryle Lamonica was the "Mad Bomber," and he liked to throw to his teammate, Warren Wells, on left side. Miami's Paul Warfield was over there, too. They were both speedsters, and Lamonica liked to throw deep, so they just kept coming after me.

It was pretty easy to read because they were either gonna go deep or run the turn in, so I kept my position and waited to see what they were going to do. They ended up playing like defensive backs because a lot of times I was in better position to catch the ball than they were. I remember late in the fourth quarter how tired I was.

I didn't have an interception, but I got my hands on a lot of balls. I would've had one, but I didn't want Chicago's Dick Butkus to knock my head off. I was coming in to intercept a ball, and there came Butkus.

I was going to intercept it, but I had to let the ball go or Butkus would've killed me.

Personally, I thought I had a great year capped off with a great Pro Bowl. It was funny because I was a defensive back, but I was named Offensive Back of the Game.

The obsession reporters and fans had with the tipped pass in the Super Bowl drove Mel Renfro even harder to succeed.

"When I got home after the Pro Bowl, the people in Portland rolled out the red carpet. My family was ecstatic," he said. "My off-season was fairly good, but the tipped pass kept coming up—and it was a bitter pill to take.

"Everybody wanted talk about the tipped pass. Nobody wanted talk about Craig Morton's two interceptions in the fourth quarter."

Renfro was also learning how to adapt his game.

After intercepting 10 passes in 1969, teams no longer challenged him. Opposing quarterbacks played as though they had a patch on one eye and couldn't look at his side of the field.

He intercepted only four passes in 1970 and four more in 1971.

"It was a little frustrating," Renfro said, "because you want to feel like you're contributing. It also got a little boring because I didn't see many balls, so I had to work harder to stay focused."

While the defense had made a name for itself—Doomsday, they called it—the offense had no identity. That was about to change.

Roger Staubach started the Cowboys, first two games in 1970. He made only one other start the rest of the season.

And he didn't like it. The competitor in him wouldn't allow it.

Not after starter Craig Morton guided the Cowboys to only three touchdowns in three playoff games. Each of those scores was set up by a turnover.

And certainly not after Morton had completed 12 of 26 passes for 127 yards with three interceptions and a touchdown in the Cowboys' 16-13 loss to Baltimore in Super Bowl V.

"Craig was hurt in the Super Bowl, and Roger was ready to play," Lilly said, "but Coach Landry went with Morton."

On the plane back to Dallas, Staubach and coach Tom Landry talked about the quarterback's future.

"Coach Landry sat down with me, and I told him I really felt like I need to be traded," Staubach said, "and he said, 'You're gonna get a chance to play.'"

"I didn't come in the NFL to be a backup, but I understood. Craig Morton was a heck of player, but he had some injuries. I started the first game and beat the Eagles, and we were losing to the Giants in the second game and Coach Landry was going to take me out, but I told him I really thought I needed to stay in the game, and we won that one.

"In the third game, Craig was kind of ready and he took me out when we got behind in the second quarter, and he explained his decision at halftime."

At the end of the season, Staubach had thrown just 82 passes. A naval commitment had forced him to spend four years in the service. At the time he was nearing 30 and he still wasn't sure just how good he could be.

The news from Landry that he was going to get an opportunity to win the starting job buoyed his spirits and encouraged him to work even harder in the off-season.

Staubach and Morton competed for the starting job during the preseason in 1971. Each played so well that Coach Landry announced he had two starting quarterbacks. That lasted for seven games. Staubach took over and guided the Cowboys to 10 consecutive wins, including a victory over Miami in Super Bowl VI, where he was named Most Valuable Player.

The nucleus of the team had been created with the drafts from 1962 to 1966, which were responsible for adding players such as Renfro, middle linebacker Lee Roy Jordan, defensive end George Andrie, receiver Bob Hayes, defensive tackle Jethro Pugh, guard John Niland, running back Walt Garrison, and Morton.

"We wanted to win it because this same group of players had come along together and we weren't boys anymore. We were men," Lilly said. "We were very focused on going back to Super Bowl and winning it. There was a lot less joking around, and we were a lot more serious. We knew we were good enough."

They simply needed to get over the hump in the postseason. Although the Cowboys had finished in first place five consecutive seasons, their postseason record had been 1-5 entering 1970. Although they didn't win the Super Bowl, they did double the number of playoff wins in franchise history.

"When I was a rookie, the Cowboys were touted as the team of the future in the Eastern Division," Renfro said. "In 1966, we started winning games, but we couldn't win them in the playoffs. At least we got to the big one in 1970, but we didn't win it.

"We always had a positive attitude about what we could do, but we just couldn't get it done in the big games. We had the players and the talent and the coach. We just had to get over the hump. We finally did in 1971 because everyone was in their prime and playing well."

Life after Mel Renfro's 14-year NFL career ended hasn't always been pleasant.

There have been failed business decisions. And numerous personal issues. And a bout with prostate cancer.

But Renfro has persevered. Now, he finds himself at a good point in his life.

"I always had a strong spiritual base. I grew up in the church, and my parents made sure I knew right from wrong," Renfro said. "I became a Christian in the '80s, and I felt a strong sense of God, and I knew eventually I would rise above whatever was going on.

"I questioned my faith a lot because I couldn't seem to get where I thought I should be or where I wanted to go."

The exclusion from the Pro Football Hall of Fame hurt more than any of the issues he had because football had always been his security blanket. When all else failed, he had the game and his accomplishments.

No one could ever take that away. The Cowboys had immortalized him by placing him in their exclusive Ring of Honor in 1981.

He deserved it after playing in the Pro Bowl each of his first 10 NFL seasons. He held the franchise record for interceptions (52) and kickoff return average (26.4). Five times, he was named to the All-Pro team as one of the NFL's two best cornerbacks.

"I think I was hurt a lot by the Hall of Fame thing," he said. "I would see guys go in that didn't have half of my credentials, and I couldn't understand it. I was frustrated by it. Bob Lilly told me to relax because I was going to get there. He told me it wasn't a matter of if, but when.

"I was angry and bitter, but there was nothing I could do about it. Then the Lord told me not to be angry anymore. He told me to let it go."

Renfro finally received the call he had been waiting for in January 1996.

"I didn't have to go through that mental anguish any more," said Renfro, "of wondering whether I would get in or not."

Life is good now.

He's working with fellow Hall of Fame players Tony Dorsett and Rayfield Wright at First Team Lending, a Dallas-based mortgage company, and he makes several promotional appearances a year either as a member of the Hall of Fame or the Ring of Honor.

"I grew up with somewhat of an inferiority complex," Renfro said. "I just didn't think I was smart enough or good enough to compete in the world. I knew I could do it in football and athletics, but I didn't know if I could do it in the world and that bothered me.

"After my career, I found out I was good enough. I realize now that I can compete with anybody on any level. People just achieve differently. My achievements were in the athletic arena; others achieve in other arenas. I can live with that."

CHAPTER 4

CHUCK
HOWLEY

Chuck Howley's professional football career had seemingly ended a year after the Chicago Bears made him the seventh selection in the 1958 draft, but he wasn't disappointed.

He didn't like the hustle and bustle of Chicago with its high-rise apartment buildings and fancy nightclubs. He preferred a place like his hometown of Warwood, a suburb of Wheeling, West Virginia, nestled along the Ohio River.

Warwood was the kind of place where street fairs and festivals marked the seasons and family picnics were a way of life. It was the kind of place where generations were buried side by side in well-manicured cemeteries and fathers taught their sons to hunt squirrels and rabbits.

Howley enjoyed football and reveled in the competition, but the game never defined him. How could it? He wasn't even good enough to make the freshman team at Central Catholic High School.

Besides, Howley also liked gymnastics, especially when the YMCA sponsored a program for one of the neighboring towns and he had an opportunity to do flips on a trampoline. Basketball and wrestling were fun, too.

"Your last period of the day was your practice period," Howley said. "After football season, it became a study period unless you had another sport, so that's what I did—I found another sport."

Howley improved enough to make the football team at Warwood, where he starred at linebacker and center after gaining 45 pounds between the end of his sophomore and junior years of high school. He earned a scholarship to West Virginia and became one of the finest athletes in school history.

Not bad, considering former NBA star Jerry West, whose silhouette is part of the National Basketball Association logo, is the most famous athlete to wear the Mountaineers blue and yellow. Howley, the Southern Conference's Athlete of the Year in 1957, lettered in diving, wrestling, gymnastics, track, and football.

At West Virginia, Howley played center and linebacker well enough that the Bears drafted him in the first round.

"I did not realize what the pro draft was until one of our coaches—Bob Snyder—called me out of class and told me I was drafted No. 1 by the Bears," Howley said. "I really didn't know what professional football was all about at that time."

Howley, accompanied by Snyder, visited the Bears that weekend, and the rookie signed a contract.

"I just wanted to prove I could make the club. That's what I did," Howley said. "There was some real satisfaction in making the team."

Howley played 12 games at center as a rookie and then moved to linebacker. Three games into the 1959 season, a crack-back block resulted in a torn knee ligament, ending his season.

"You know it when it snaps," Howley said of his knee ligament. "I tried to get back. I went to training camp the next year, but they put me on injured reserve."

A year later, Chicago released him. Howley returned home and started running a Sunoco gas station to support his family.

"I had proven I could play pro football, so I decided I was going to stay home," Howley said. "You can make a living in the service station business, but I wasn't going to get rich, that's for sure.

"It was an available business that I knew a little bit about. We made a small profit, which I thought we could."

Hard work never bothered Howley.

His father drove a Wonder Bread truck for nearly 40 years making daily deliveries to local grocery stores throughout Warwood to support his wife and his five children—four boys and a girl.

And he learned to drive on his grandfather's produce truck. Each morning about 4:30, Howley and his grandfather would fill the truck with baskets of fresh fruits and vegetables before driving through various neighborhoods in nearby Willoughby to sell the produce.

Although he was content running the gas station, Howley didn't like the way his career ended. He decided to use the annual West Virginia alumni game in the spring of 1961 to test his knee.

"I just wanted to see if my knee would hold up," he said. "I didn't even tape my knee."

The knee was fine, and Howley considered playing pro football again. The Cowboys—0-11-1 as an expansion team in 1960—were scouring the country for players.

Don Healy, a former teammate in Chicago, now working for the Cowboys told Tex Schramm that Howley might consider playing again. The Cowboys traded second- and ninth-round picks in 1963 to the Bears for Howley's rights.

"Tex Schramm called me and asked me if I would be interested in playing some football, if they could acquire my rights," Howley said. "I told Tex that since he was calling me, he probably already had my rights.

"I told him I'd like to come to Dallas, so I got on a plane headed there and signed a contract worth a whopping $7,500."

It was one of the best trades the Cowboys ever made. Howley played 14 seasons, tying him for the second longest tenure in franchise history. He played in two NFL championship games and two Super Bowls, made six Pro Bowl teams, and was inducted into the club's exclusive Ring of Honor in 1977.

"I don't know that I've ever seen anybody better at linebacker than Howley," Tom Landry once said.

———

It had taken a decade, but the triumvirate of coach Tom Landry, president and general manager Tex Schramm, and personnel director Gil Brandt had finally built a powerful team with a talent-laden roster that gave the franchise staying power.

From 1966-69, Dallas went 42-12-2 and won four consecutive division titles. No NFL team won more games or had a better winning percentage. In fact, only Baltimore (41-12-3) and Los Angeles (40-13-3) were in the same class as the Cowboys.

Dallas, though, had nothing to show for its dominance.

Green Bay had beaten the Cowboys in the Cotton Bowl 34-27 in 1966 and triumphed again in the Ice Bowl 21-17 in 1967. Leroy Kelly and the Cleveland Browns had beaten Dallas in the playoffs in 1968 and 1969.

Still, there was optimism heading into the 1970 season because Landry had offensive firepower in receiver Bob Hayes, running backs Calvin Hill and Duane Thomas, fullback Walt Garrison and a defense led by Bob Lilly, cornerback Mel Renfro, safety Cornell Green, and linebacker Chuck Howley.

Linebacker Chuck Howley (54) helps George Andrie (66) stop the ball carrier during Super Bowl V on January 17, 1971, against the Baltimore Colts.
Diamond Images/Getty Images

"We knew we had a good ballclub," Howley said. "We'd been together for 10 years and Landry had molded a pretty strong team together."

Controversy and injuries nearly ruined the season.

Craig Morton, the starter at the end of the season, had off-season shoulder surgery and wasn't ready to start the season. Roger Staubach, the 1963 Heisman Trophy winner, had joined the Cowboys in 1968.

Staubach, who played in the fourth quarter of the Cowboys' 38-14 playoff loss to Cleveland in 1968, started the first two games of the season, guiding Dallas to a 2-0 record. But after he threw two early interceptions against the Cardinals, Morton replaced Staubach, who was not pleased with the move.

Leg and shoulder injuries kept Hill on and off the field, and Hayes didn't catch a pass in four of the first five games. The result: Dallas was 5-4 in the middle of November after a 38-0 loss on *Monday Night Football* to St. Louis in which it committed six turnovers. It remains their worst defeat ever on the show.

Earlier in the season, Minnesota had beaten Dallas 54-13, the worst loss in franchise history. The loss to St. Louis dropped the Cowboys into third place, two games behind the Cardinals.

They did not lose again.

Landry decided Morton, a six-year veteran, was putting too much pressure on himself, so the coach took over play-calling responsibilities. The move worked, and Dallas averaged 30.6 points per game and stormed into the playoffs.

A defense led by Howley, middle linebacker Lee Roy Jordan, and defensive tackle Bob Lilly started to suffocate opposing offenses. They allowed 34 points in their last five games and pitched a shutout—a 5-0 win over Detroit—in the first round of the playoffs. Then came a 17-10 win over San Francisco in the NFC championship, propelling Dallas into Super Bowl V.

The game did not live up to the hype, which is why it has been referred to as the Blooper Bowl. The teams combined for 11 turnovers, and Howley became the first and only player on a losing team to be named Most Valuable Player after he intercepted two passes and recovered a fumble.

GAME OF MY LIFE
By Chuck Howley

The Baltimore Colts were probably second to the Green Bay Packers, especially when Johnny Unitas was there, as far as being my favorite team to play against. You always want to compete against the best—and that's what they were. The Colts were a great ballclub, and they had as good of players as the Packers did.

Back then, the Super Bowl was nothing like it is now with all the glamour and TV ads that make the game last so long that I can hardly stand to watch it. It was the Super Bowl and we knew we had to play a good game to win it and become world champions, but I don't think—at that time—we really understood the importance of what the Super Bowl was all about.

We acted like it was just another game, but it wasn't. It was the Super Bowl. We wanted to win it, but I don't know if we had the urgency we needed in a game of that magnitude.

We were really down after the game, which is natural. We were all upset with ourselves because we lost a game that we really believed we should've won.

I look back on that game and the one thing I remember is that when Jim O'Brien lined up to attempt the 32-yard field goal that would win the game or send it to overtime, I remember thinking they can't beat us with a field goal. It wasn't until that ball went through the uprights and they started celebrating that I really understood that we lost the game. It was an odd, weird feeling. The way the game was played, I probably shouldn't have been surprised.

The game was a mixture of mistakes, but I was fortunate enough to be in the right place at the right time. I had two interceptions, a fumble recovery and forced a fumble, but I didn't think about winning the MVP. I didn't know what it meant to be the MVP.

I was standing in the shower, thinking about the game, and one of the guys said, "Chuck, you're the MVP."

Once I got dressed, the media said, "What do you think?"

What do you do in a situation like that? There were 44 other players around me, and it's a fantastic honor, but please, forgive me for not jumping up and down. It was an individual deal, and we just lost the biggest game of the season. It was hard to rejoice because we lost the ballgame. The award didn't mean as much to me at that point as it did later in my life.

I was actually surprised they picked me as MVP out of all the players on the field that day. Usually, someone stands out enough on the offense or the winning team to earn the MVP. The ball seemed to find me a lot that day, and I was happy about it. I don't know if I was in position or out of position, but any defensive player likes to see the ball coming toward his hands.

On my second interception, I was sitting on my butt in the end zone when it came to me. I was covering a down-and-in, and the ball was right there. I couldn't help but catch it. I was just having fun. That's what I did when I played the game.

A team with a different mind-set reported to training camp in Thousand Oaks, California, on the picturesque campus of California Lutheran with its brisk mornings and cool evenings, which provided some comfort during the tough two-a-day practices that seemed more like military boot camps than football practices.

"After losing to Baltimore, there was a fixation with everyone to win the Super Bowl," Howley said. "We knew we had to get back to the Super Bowl, and this time we were going to win it. It wasn't something we all talked about. We just knew we had 'X' amount of games we had to win before we could get back to the Super Bowl.

"We all knew what we had to do, but it wasn't something we were going to remind each other of every day. In the first one, we questioned whether we should be there. That season, we didn't have any doubt. We knew we were going to make it to the Super Bowl."

Dallas started the season 4-3 to fall two games behind Washington in the NFC East as coach Tom Landry used Roger Staubach and Craig Morton to shuttle the plays into the game. Then Landry decided Staubach gave the Cowboys the best opportunity to win games.

Staubach started the next week against St. Louis, completing 20 of 31 passes for 199 yards. He guided the Cowboys to seven consecutive regular-season victories as Dallas won its second consecutive NFC East title.

After beating Minnesota (20-12) and San Francisco (14-3) in the playoffs, Staubach led the Cowboys to their first championship 24-3 over Miami.

"That's the ultimate goal for every athlete who plays professional football. Everyone wants a Super Bowl ring," Howley said. "It's a great achievement when you get one. It's something you never forget."

Howley played only one more full season. He retired in 1973.

"I started thinking about retirement because my wife wanted me to do it from a family standpoint," he said, "but I just enjoyed the game. The year I did retire we were at a charity function, and Coach Landry was also there, and my wife bought my jersey for $6,000 or $7,000 and she said, 'I told you Tom, I am retiring this number.'

"It was time, Tom wanted me to play a backup role. I didn't feel D.D. Lewis was any better than I was."

But the Cowboys had some injuries at linebacker, and Landry asked Howley to come out of retirement to help the team. Howley agreed with one stipulation: If he wasn't playing full time, he would retire for good.

"I didn't want my last year to be on the bench," Howley said. "It came a point where the linebackers were all healthy again. I was waiting to go to my ranch, but I wasn't told I was deactivated and we came in from the practice field and they told me I had been deactivated. I headed straight to my ranch."

In today's NFL, a player of Chuck Howley's caliber would earn millions in salary before the end of his career. When Howley was a star, most players needed a second job to make ends meet.

That's how Howley became involved in the uniform-rental business. Howley established the company—Chuck Howley Uniform Rental—with two partners in 1968 and bought them out a few years later when his partners tried to talk him out of retiring.

"They didn't think the business would be as profitable if I wasn't still playing football," he said. "Plus, I wanted a raise over the $100 a week they were paying me. I didn't think that was going to be enough when I retired from football."

Howley owned that company, which rented, cleaned, and leased uniforms, for nearly 25 years before selling it, though he stayed another six years to run the company for the new owners. Howley continues to run a subsidiary, Uniforms Inc., that sells and leases uniforms. A contract with the City of Dallas provides a chunk of business.

"I enjoy taking care of customers, and I want to do things right," Howley said. "This is my livelihood. The customer owes me nothing. My job is to give him the best service possible."

When he's not running his uniform business, Howley spends much of his time with his wife, Nancy, on his ranch in Canton, Texas, about an hour east of Dallas. The father of two—43-year-old Scott, and 38-year-old Robin—raises quarter horses and spends time with his five grandchildren.

"I enjoy it. It's fun to get away from the city sometimes," Howley said. "I enjoy working outdoors and working with the animals."

CHAPTER 5

RAYFIELD WRIGHT

For as long as he can remember, basketball was Rayfield Wright's passion. It came naturally.

His father was a 7-footer. An uncle was 7 feet, 6 inches. A brother was 7 feet.

"My brother, Lamar, taught me the game. We built a basketball goal in our backyard, and the whole neighborhood would come and watch us play," said the man who opened running lanes and protected quarterbacks with his 6-foot-6, 255-pound frame during an NFL career. "I used to sit there because I was young, tall, and skinny, and they wouldn't let me play because they were bigger boys.

"My brother played above the rim. That's why I loved to play above the rim. That's the way the game was supposed to be played. We were basketball players."

So it didn't really matter that he wasn't that good at football. In fact, he didn't play football at Fairmont High School in Griffin, Georgia. Coach Hiram Whitaker wouldn't put him on the team. It seems he worried that the gangly youngster might get hurt.

As he prepared for high school graduation, Wright did have scholarship offers to play basketball, including one at Loyola University in

Chicago. But his family didn't have the money to make up the difference between the scholarship and the full cost of tuition.

He decided to join the Air Force and was just a few weeks from attending basic training, when his cousin, John Willis, suggested he play basketball at Fort Valley State in Georgia. It took some coaxing from L.J. Lomax, the football coach at Fort Valley State, but he won over Wright and his family and ultimately helped young Rayfield get out of his military commitment.

So, finally, Wright had an opportunity to play football.

Wright's scholarship, however, called for him to play football and basketball for the Wildcats. Once he got his chance, Wright was everywhere on the football field—playing free safety, punter, defensive end, and tight end. He took to the game naturally and earned All-Conference honors.

Gil Brandt, the personnel director for the Dallas Cowboys, had started sending Wright questionnaires, an indication the team was interested in him. A few days before the NFL draft, Brandt phoned and told Wright the Cowboys might be interested in selecting him.

The Cowboys wanted the best athletes; they figured coach Tom Landry could teach them football techniques. The Cowboys drafted him in the seventh round and promptly told him they weren't sure whether he would play tight end, defensive end, or somewhere else.

Wright signed a three-year contract with the Cowboys, which included a $10,000 signing bonus, but he wasn't giving up on his basketball dream.

"My heart was set on basketball, but football represented an opportunity," Wright said. "Coming from the Deep South there weren't many opportunities for blacks in the '60s. I told my mother and grandmother that if it didn't work out, I was going to Cincinnati and play basketball for the Royals.

"That's where my heart was. Sometimes in life you think you're set to go a certain way, and you end up going a different way. I wanted to play basketball, but those skills made me a good football player."

But it took time for the Cowboys to find a position for Wright. In two seasons as a tight end, he caught one pass—a 15-yard touchdown.

Before his third season, Landry informed him that he was moving to offensive tackle. Landry assured Wright that his physical skills and athleticism would serve him well at the new position.

The coach had no idea Wright's basketball skills were going to make him a star football player. Initially, Wright struggled as he tried to imitate players like Bob Brown and Forrest Gregg, who were among the best offensive linemen in the game.

Offesive lineman Rayfield Wright. *Bruce Bennett Studios/Getty Images*

"I struggled with the position," Wright said. "I got the game film and studied all night, but I couldn't do what they did. I'd get knocked down at practice. I needed my own style."

One morning at 3 a.m., Wright had a revelation. Football, he thought, was no different than basketball. Playing tackle was no different than playing defense in basketball. The quarterback was the basket. All he had to do was stay between the defender and the quarterback.

It was a simple concept, but it worked.

"When I defend you as a basketball player, I don't care where you go as long as I stay between you and the basket. I do that by shuffling my feet quickly from side to side," Wright said. "It doesn't matter which way you go because you can't get by me. I went out on the field the next day, and I was fine.

"The only thing I had to do was develop my upper-body strength. When a guy came in close, I'd give him a quick punch—like a karate chop—to his shoulder. If you hit him with enough force, he turns. You can't run forward if you're turned sideways. While he was straightening back up, I'd hit him on the other shoulder."

Practice, however, is one thing. Games are another. Wright's first NFL start came in week 10 of the 1969 season against the undefeated Los Angeles Rams and their legendary defensive line, nicknamed "The Fearsome Foursome." He would be matched up with Deacon Jones, who had been named to the Pro Bowl each of the previous four seasons.

On the first play, Jones barreled over Wright. It didn't happen again. Los Angeles won 24-23, but Jones wasn't much of a factor. Wright received a game ball for his effort. He started the last six games, including the playoffs and received some All-Pro consideration.

"I never worried about football after that game," Wright said. "I knew I could play."

The 1972 Cowboys entered the season with their heads held high. No longer were they "next year's champions."

They were defending Super Bowl champions. World champions.

A dominating 24-3 victory over the Miami Dolphins in Super Bowl VI had legitimized the franchise's success, which had been shrouded by its inability to win a title. President Tex Schramm, coach Tom Landry, and personnel director Gil Brandt were building one of the NFL's most consistent teams.

The Cowboys, who began playing in 1960, didn't post their first winning season until 1966. In the next six seasons, Dallas compiled a record of 63-19-2 with six consecutive first-place finishes. None of it meant much until they won a championship.

"We had been labeled for so many years as the team that couldn't win the big game. It seemed like we always got close to the top, and little things would happen to keep us from winning," Wright said. "Then we came back and got to the Super Bowl again through our determination and dedication and defeated Miami.

"We kind of let out a sigh of relief. The stigma of losing that had bothered us was gone. The team that couldn't win the big game was gone, too."

The Cowboys entered the 1972 season with no pressure. Their demons had been exorcised.

There weren't any significant defensive changes, and the biggest offensive change involved Calvin Hill becoming the team's featured running back instead of Duane Thomas.

Dallas selected Thomas with the 23rd pick of the first round in 1970, and he responded with 803 yards and five touchdowns on 151 carries. He was Rookie of the Year and helped the Cowboys advance to Super Bowl V against Baltimore.

There had been problems, though. Landry said Thomas could've only thrived on a veteran team like the club he had in 1970.

"It wasn't that I was accepting him. I would just as soon had gotten rid of him," Landry once told the *Dallas Morning News*. "As long as I saw the team could operate with him, and he could contribute to them, then I would let it go. But once that season was over, I knew it would never happen again. The team would never tolerate the same thing another season. So we got rid of him."

At least they tried to trade him.

When the Cowboys refused to restructure his contract after his rookie season, Thomas called a news conference before the 1971 season and ripped the triumvirate that ruled the Cowboys. He referred to Schramm as, "sick, demented, and totally dishonest." Landry was "a plastic man." Brandt was "a liar."

The Cowboys dealt him to New England before the 1971 season, but the Patriots voided the trade and returned Thomas to Dallas. It appeared Thomas wasn't any happier with New England, either, and the Patriots weren't going to tolerate that kind of attitude. For the rest of the season, Thomas rarely spoke to his Dallas coaches, teammates, or the media.

Still, he led the team in carries (175) and rushed for 783 yards and 11 touchdowns. He had 95 yards in the Super Bowl win over Miami.

"It was a love-hate relationship," he told the *Dallas Morning News* in 2003, "and I finally said I don't really enjoy those types of relationships. They're impossible."

Dallas traded him to San Diego before the start of the 1972 season, paving the way for Hill.

The 1969 first-round pick responded by becoming the first running back in franchise history to gain more than 1,000 yards. He finished the season with 1,036 yards on 245 carries and six touchdowns for the Cowboys, who finished 10-4.

But that wasn't good enough to win the NFC East. Coach George Allen, in his second year as Washington's coach, guided the Redskins to an 11-3 record that guaranteed them home-field advantage, if the teams met in the playoffs.

"We had a great opportunity to win the Super Bowl that year," Wright said, "because we were back in the playoffs again."

And when the Cowboys scored two touchdowns in the final 1:30 to rally past San Francisco, he knew the label "next year's champions" was gone forever.

Staubach saw that too.

As long as Staubach had the ball, Wright said the Cowboys believed they could win. No deficit was too great.

"Roger had 'it.' He knew how to take charge without saying he was in charge," Wright said. "His leadership was based on performance."

Like an improbable 30-28 victory over San Francisco in an NFC divisional playoff game that changed an entire franchise's mind-set.

GAME OF MY LIFE
By Rayfield Wright

Football is played for 60 minutes. It's not played for 59 and one-half minutes. The 49ers forgot that.

When we scored that touchdown to win the game, Larry Cole started rolling around on the ground like a bouncing beach ball. We came back and scored two touchdowns in the last 1:30 to win, and you just don't do that in the National Football League.

Roger Staubach came in the game in the third quarter, but he had played so much over the previous few years that we didn't think it was a big deal. Craig Morton had played really well for us during the course of the year to help us get into the playoffs, but Roger came in and did a tremendous job to help us win the game. That's just the kind of player he was.

We scored a touchdown to get close, but we still needed to recover an onside kick to have a chance to win the game. We worked on onside kicks every week because we knew how important special teams were to winning games. A lot of teams didn't recognize how important specials teams were, and a lot of players didn't want to play on special teams.

When we had to kick that onside kick to have a chance to win the game, we had the confidence that we were going to get the ball. Toni Fritsch used to kick onside kicks behind his back and all that kind of stuff because he was a soccer player from Austria, and he could do a lot of different things with the ball.

But if you believe in something and you believe you can get it done in your heart, then you really go after it. It doesn't happen all of the time, but in that particular case, we needed an onside kick, we believed we could get it, and we got it.

The fans in the stands were so obnoxious and hurt that they came out of the stands after the game and a big fight broke out. Gil Brandt was trying to get off the field, and everyone was fighting. The players were trying to get off the field, but the fans wouldn't let us off so we basically had to fight our way off the field. I never will forget. Gil was running around like he was a karate man just kicking everybody.

Once we got in the locker room, it was like winning a Super Bowl. Now, it wasn't that good, but it was comparable because of how we won it. That's why Larry Cole was rolling all over the field. He was so excited. Coach Landry was excited, and it excited me because you don't see that passion much in the professional ranks. You see it in college, but not the professional ranks.

I was really elated about that ballgame.

After the emotional high of beating San Francisco, the Cowboys didn't have long to celebrate.

They had to travel to the East Coast and play archrival Washington—"The Over The Hill Gang"—which had been invigorated by Allen. Taking an aggressive approach by spending freely to add and retain players and readily trading draft choices for proven veterans, Allen quickly turned around a moribund franchise.

When he replaced Bill Austin in 1971, he guided Washington to a 9-4-1 record. It was only the second time since 1955 that Washington had completed a season over .500. He was also their sixth coach in 13 seasons. That type of instability doesn't breed winning.

Allen, though, changed the team's attitude, and he revived a lackluster rivalry by making the Cowboys public enemy No. 1.

"George demonized the Cowboys and made us the target," said Calvin Hill, who played five seasons with Dallas and two with Washington. "He did a great job of helping to create the real rivalry. George galvanized his players and team by telling them the Cowboys were the bad guys and the guys they had to beat to accomplish their goals.

"He created a completely different ideology based on how much he disliked the Cowboys. The Cowboys used the drafts, so he said we're not giving unproven rookies money. I give the money to veterans. The

Cowboys were tough negotiators, so he paid top dollar to free agents. He pooh-poohed shifting and the multiple offense. He thought you could beat the Cowboys by being physical."

The rivalry began in 1958, when Clint Murchison was looking to buy an NFL franchise. He nearly bought Washington owner George Preston Marshall's franchise, but the deal fell apart at the last minute.

When Murchison tried to buy a franchise for Dallas, Marshall didn't want that to happen because he thought it would cut into the Redskins' fan base. At the time, no NFL franchise was farther south than Washington. The Redskins regularly played exhibition games throughout the South and were a popular team in that region.

Murchison gained support from NFL expansion committee chairman George Halas, who agreed to put a proposal for a franchise in Dallas before the league's owners. Halas told Murchison he needed 100 percent approval from the other owners to get a franchise.

Marshall had no intention of voting in favor of Murchison's expansion franchise. That changed when he learned Murchison's lawyer, Tom Webb, had bought the rights to "Hail to the Redskins" from Barnee Breeskin, the Redskins band director who had written the music to the team's fight song. Marshall's wife wrote the lyrics. Breeskin had sold the song after a dispute with Marshall. Murchison told Marshall that unless he voted in favor of the expansion team, he wouldn't allow Washington to use its fight song.

Marshall voted for the new franchise, and the rivalry was under way.

Hosting a playoff game for only the second time since 1942, the RFK Stadium crowd was whipped into a frenzy. The teams split their regular-season games, each winning in its home stadium. And in the playoffs, Dallas didn't play nearly well enough to beat Washington on the road.

Roger Staubach, the hero of the divisional playoff win over San Francisco, failed to direct even one touchdown drive. Dallas managed just 169 total yards in the 26-3 loss as it failed in its bid to play in the Super Bowl for the third consecutive season, a feat no other team had ever accomplished.

"I don't think the travel or the emotions had anything to do with the loss," Wright said. "We were professionals, and we had a job to do no matter where the games were played.

"Every year, I felt that we had the team and the players and the talent to get to the Super Bowl and win it. It was no different in 1972."

Rayfield Wright's father left when he was three years old. He never knew why. Still doesn't.

"I wonder sometimes what life would've been like if he had been there, but you have to remember what it was like in the '40s on the racial side of things," Wright said. "I never understood why he left, and my mom said sometimes there are things you just don't talk about.

"My mind often wonders. I know how things were at that time in the South. My dad was from Cuba, and he didn't take anything from anybody. I don't know what caused him to leave. I do know a lot of wives told their husbands to leave if they wanted to live."

Wright has four children—two boys and two girls. He prays often to be the father he wanted as a youth. The lack of a father in the home, however, should not be confused with a lack of father figures. Or role models.

Wright had plenty: His scoutmaster, David Walker. His pastor, O.H. Stinson. And his college football coach, L.J. "Stan" Lomax.

Their impact on him is one reason Wright has devoted much of his life after football to youth. He helped found a program in Phoenix called Kids for Tomorrow, which was designed to help at-risk youth. And he's written an autobiography, *Wright Up Front,* which deals with his travails as a child in Griffin, Georgia, and his successes and failures as an adult.

"I've always worked with young people, because this world is not getting better, it's getting worse. I've always believed that you go back and what you say or how you act might help another young child trying to get out of a difficult situation.

"My only prayer for [*Wright Up Front*] is that it will find its way into the hands of a little boy or a little girl in some community around the world who doesn't feel as though they can get out of their environment," Wright said. "I pray they'll read it and say if this guy can come out of the situation that he came out of and become the person that he did, then maybe I have a chance. Maybe I can straighten my life out and stay in school and succeed."

That's the reason he returned to Griffin every off-season that he played in the NFL. He wanted to inspire the children from his hometown to dream big.

Wright was the first player from Griffin to play in the NFL. Since him, there have been 27 others, including receiver Willie Gault, who won a Super Bowl ring with the 1985 Chicago Bears, and linebacker Jesse Tuggle, the Atlanta Falcons' all-time leading tackler. It is no coincidence.

"I wanted the kids to be able to see me. And touch me. And feel me. And know me," he said. "I wanted them to know anything was possible if they worked hard enough. I wanted to encourage them."

He helped create Kids for Tomorrow because he believes children are our nation's foundation. Educate and train them, he believes, and America will stand strong for generations. Fail to do that, and there are no guarantees about the future.

"It doesn't do any good to go and make a speech to kids if there's no follow-up," Wright said. "If you motivate a child, but don't have a way for him to change his environment, he'll revert right back to what he was doing because of peer pressure."

After the Cowboys released him following the 1980 season and he retired, Wright spent much of his post-football career in anonymity. Although he made the 1970s' All-Decade team, played in eight NFC championship games, six Pro Bowls, and five Super Bowls, Wright never received the accolades for a player with his accomplishments.

Somehow, he got lost in the shuffle. Perhaps, it was the result of playing tackle, hardly a glamour position.

But Cowboys owner Jerry Jones placed him into the Cowboys' exclusive Ring of Honor in 2004, and he was inducted into the Pro Football Hall of Fame in 2006.

Now, he's busier than he's ever been with book signings and other football-related ventures. He's the CEO of Wright's Sports Nutrition, a company that provides nutritional supplements, and is a partner in First Team Lending, a Dallas-based mortgage company.

Life has never been better for Wright.

"You have to stay in position to receive your blessings," he said. "You can't move around and lose patience because they don't happen when you want them to. You have faith in God and let him work."

CHAPTER 6

LEE ROY JORDAN

This is all you need to know about Excel, Alabama, a farming community that produced one of the finest football players in Cowboys history.

"We had a four-way blinking stoplight," Lee Roy Jordan said. "Then they put in stoplights, with red, yellow, and green lights, but that burned too much electricity so they took it down and put back the blinking four-way light.

"They said we had 250 people, but that must have included a two-mile radius around Excel. It was a town that had a lot of interest in football, and all of the guys were farm guys and working guys, and we were hard and tough kind of guys, and all of us liked being tough guys on the field."

There were long days and short nights on the farm. The fields had to be tended, and the animals needed feeding. Everyone contributed because the farm provided everything the family needed.

It yielded cotton and vegetables and sugar cane, which was turned into syrup that was traded with the local store for groceries. The hogs, turkeys, cattle, and chickens provided food and money for the family of nine.

Hard work was a way of life.

"I didn't have to learn how to work hard. I grew up knowing that from the way we lived," Jordan said. "My mother and dad grew up in the Depression, and it was a tough life for them.

"Work ethic was real important to my daddy. He was a right-and-wrong kind of guy and he taught his children that. He also had a razor strap that he used to discipline us, but after you got a whipping, he'd sit you on his lap and tell you how much he loved you and cared about you and how he wanted you to teach your children the same types of things.

"My mother was a hard-working woman who could cook a meal in 15 minutes and feed 20 people. She'd work the fields with us and pick more cotton and corn than anybody."

When he wasn't working on the farm or riding steers or playing with the animals, Jordan was either watching his older brothers—Walter Jr., Carl, and Ben—play or he was on the field as a safety or running back, so they would have enough players to practice.

Jordan started on the varsity in the eighth grade. He became a force as a junior after growing four inches and adding 30 pounds over one summer.

"I went away a little-bitty guy," he said with a chuckle, "and came back a big bully."

The scouts noticed, and Alabama recruited him hard his senior year. Jordan wanted to play for Paul "Bear" Bryant at Alabama, so it wasn't hard to convince him that Tuscaloosa was the place to go to college.

"I loved his type of football. He used a lot of guys who were smaller in stature because he wanted quickness, pursuit, and endurance, and I thought I could play well in his system," Jordan said. "He became like a second father to me.

"He was hard and demanding, but he always knew how to put that arm on your shoulder and get you to do some more. I was going to give him my best shot every day. Knowing how to handle people was his greatest gift. He knew what it took to motivate people, whether it was yelling at somebody or patting them on the back."

In three seasons, Jordan's Alabama teams lost two games. The 1961 Tide went 11-0 and won the national championship, while allowing just three touchdowns all season.

"Right off the bat, he was a man on the football field," said Larry Lacewell, Jordan's freshman coach at Alabama. "He was tougher than other players, and he stood out from the crowd.

"He had great explosion, which is why he was such a hard hitter, and he gave great effort on the field. He also had uncommon leadership skills."

After his junior season, Jordan began thinking about playing pro football because he had earned some postseason awards. The Cowboys spoke with Bryant because they weren't sure he was big enough to handle the rigors of the NFL.

After Jordan left Alabama, the "Lee Roy Jordan Headhunter Award" was given to the standout hitter in spring practice.

"He didn't have great size," said Gil Brandt, the Cowboys' personnel director from 1960 to 1989, "but I don't know of any football player more competitive than Lee Roy Jordan."

Dallas drafted him with the sixth pick overall in 1963. The Boston Patriots of the American Football League drafted him in the second round. A $17,500 signing bonus and a brand new Pontiac Bonneville secured his services for Dallas.

In his autobiography, Bryant wrote, "I never had another one like Lee Roy Jordan. He was a center/linebacker, going both ways at 190 pounds, playing against guys like Jackie Burkett of Auburn, who was 6-3, 235 pounds.

"It's a wonder I didn't foul him up, because I tried him at two, three different positions as a sophomore, including offensive tackle, before he became a linebacker—the best linebacker in college football, bar none. He would have made every tackle on every play if they had stayed in bounds.

"I can remember nothing bad about Lee Roy: first on the field, full speed every play, no way to get him to take it easy."

The Cowboys entered the 1971 season with a single-minded focus. They were weary of the moniker, "next year's champion," following a 16-13 loss to Baltimore in Super Bowl V the previous season.

After five consecutive years of ending their season in disappointing fashion—only a championship removed their burden. After all, the disappointment of losing had driven quarterback Don Meredith into retirement following the 1968 season.

"Don mostly got the blame for all of the losses, and he didn't get much credit for all of the winning," Jordan said. "It's kind of sad when individual players take so much of the public abuse. It wasn't spread around like it should've been."

When Meredith left, Roger Staubach and Craig Morton battled for the starting position each of the next three seasons. In 1971, coach Tom Landry couldn't decide which player to start, so he used them both. First by series, then by play.

Neither helped Dallas win. The Cowboys won only four of their first seven games when Landry made Staubach the starter following a 23-19 loss to Chicago.

The Cowboys did not lose again.

"We had a team meeting and made a commitment not to continue playing that way," Jordan said. "We decided we wanted to get back to the championship game and have an opportunity to get to the Super Bowl again and redeem ourselves because we felt like we should've beaten Baltimore."

It helped that Staubach brought stability to the quarterback position. He finished the season with 126 completions in 211 attempts for 1,882 yards with 15 touchdowns, four interceptions, and a passer rating of 104.8. Morton completed 78 of 143 passes for 1,131 yards with seven interceptions, eight touchdowns, and a passer rating of 73.5.

"The quarterback situation was difficult on the team, but Coach Landry thought that was the best opportunity for the offense to succeed," Jordan said. "You always had a group of guys who pulled for one guy or the other, but the important thing was that we got it together during the latter part of the season. It didn't matter who was playing quarterback. We just had to win."

While Staubach was improving, so was the defense. The Cowboys allowed more than 14 points just once in their last 10 games, including three victories in the playoffs. Four times, they allowed a touchdown or less.

They allowed a total of six points—two field goals—in the NFC championship game and the Super Bowl.

GAME OF MY LIFE
By Lee Roy Jordan

The lowest we had ever been as players is after we had lost to Baltimore in Super Bowl V. We were extremely hurt by that loss.

We had lost the two championship games to Green Bay and two Eastern championship games to Cleveland, but losing to Baltimore was far more disappointing than those games because we were so close and we had a lot of opportunities to win it.

So the NFC championship was a big game, even though we had beaten them the previous year in the championship game. We felt extremely confident going into the San Francisco game that we could hold San Francisco to a low number. But we also felt like we had to force some turnovers to give our offense a chance to score some points.

They were a pretty explosive offense with Gene Washington at receiver and Ken Willard and Vic Washington at running back, but we felt like our matchup against their offense was extremely good. We felt like we could stop their running game and force them to throw the football. If we did that, we believed we would get some turnovers.

John Brodie had a great touch on the football and a strong arm. He was like Roger Staubach without the scrambling, but he read defenses well and made good throws down the field. They used a lot of formations, and they had a pretty wide-open offense.

It meant extra work for me, but it was fun. I loved making calls that would influence the ballgame. The coaches gave me the ability to audible, and I felt like I could affect the game because we could change our looks in the secondary and confuse John and affect his decision-making.

We played extremely well that day.

Defensive end George Andrie rushed the passer real well, and John had to throw some balls when he didn't want to. In fact, George intercepted a screen pass and ran it back to the 2-yard line to set up our first touchdown. That was a big, big play because it gave us the lead.

In the fourth quarter, John threw me an interception. The big thing that interception did was derail the momentum and clinch the game for us because a touchdown by them would've made it 14-10 with a couple of minutes left.

I saw John a few months after the game, and he asked me what I was doing in that spot, and I just laughed and told him that I always tried to read his eyes, and I would fake like I was going one way and then run back the other way.

I worked on intercepting the ball every day in practice. My thought was that I wasn't going to get many opportunities to catch the football, so I didn't want to drop one when I did. Gene Stallings, one of our defensive coaches, stayed out with me every day after practice. He would throw me passes as hard as he could and from a lot of different angles to make me catch the football.

Duane Thomas scored a touchdown early in the fourth quarter, and I thought that wrapped up the game for us because I didn't believe they could score two touchdowns to beat us because we had thoroughly dominated the game on defense. It wasn't one of those games where they had lots of chances to score points; they didn't have hardly any.

In fact, they gained most of their yards in the fourth quarter when we were playing a prevent defense.

What I liked is that after the game our attitude was that we hadn't accomplished anything. We won the NFC championship game in 1970, but we didn't accomplish what we had wanted so we talked about maintaining our concentration to make sure we won the Super Bowl.

Coach Tom Landry and defensive coordinator Ernie Stautner found the perfect symbiotic relationship between talent and scheme in 1971.

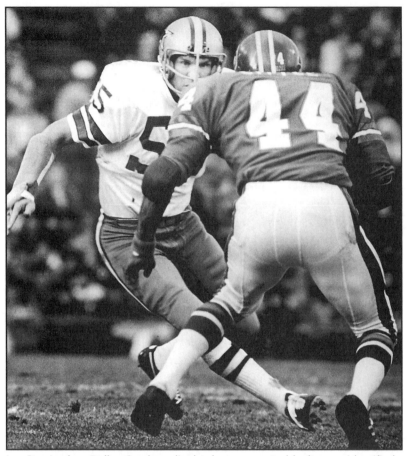

Lee Roy Jordan, Dallas Cowboys linebacker, moves to block an unidentified opponent. *Bruce Bennett Studios/Getty Images*

The Cowboys' 11 starters that season combined for 51 Pro Bowl appearances in their careers. Defensive tackle Bob Lilly and cornerbacks Herb Adderly and Mel Renfro are in the Pro Football Hall of Fame. Lilly, Renfro, and safety Cliff Harris and linebackers Lee Roy Jordan and Chuck Howley are also in the Ring of Honor.

"We had a lot of outstanding players, but we also had a system that we thoroughly understood," Jordan said, "and we realized that if we executed, Coach Landry's defense could win football games."

By the time the Cowboys played Miami in Super Bowl VI, they had mastered Landry's Flex defense, a gap-control, read-and-react scheme designed to stop the run. Dallas finished third in the NFL in total defense and second against the run, yielding 81.7 yards and just 3.2 yards per carry.

For perspective, the 1985 Chicago Bears, one of the best defenses in NFL history, allowed 3.7 yards per carry.

"The Flex didn't leave any holes for runners to go through. We didn't run to the football. We held our gaps, no matter what, until we made the ball carrier commit. It was an unbelievable concept," Jordan said. "It took us a while to learn the system because you couldn't run to the ball, which is what all of us had been taught since we started playing football.

"It was difficult to control that urge to run to the ball and make tackles, but you had to be patient and control your area. We learned that if we did that, we could control even the great runners."

Miami had one of the NFL's most potent rushing attacks in 1971 with Larry Csonka, Jim Kiick, and Mercury Morris. The Dolphins averaged 173.5 yards per game and 4.9 yards per carry with Csonka doing much of the damage.

He had gained 1,054 yards, while averaging 5.4 yards per carry. Kiick and Morris had combined for another 1,053 yards and a 4.8-yard average.

"We felt like we could attack their running game," Jordan said, "and really put pressure on Bob [Griese] and their receivers to really throw into our pass defense."

On Miami's second possession, Jordan helped force a Csonka fumble at the Dallas 46. The Cowboys recovered and drove for a field goal and a 3-0 lead. Csonka fumbled only 21 times in 1,891 carries, spanning 11 seasons.

"[The media] had talked all week about how Csonka didn't fumble," Jordan said. "When we caused that fumble, we felt like we could control them the rest of the game."

Dallas won 24-3, limiting the Dolphins to 80 yards on 20 carries. Csonka finished with 40 yards on nine carries.

"We had a party and all of that," Jordan said, "but everyone was exhausted because we had been focused on winning the Super Bowl since the end of the Baltimore game."

Staubach said he felt more relief than exhilaration after the game.

"I never saw New Orleans because I was in Coach Landry's hotel room every night studying and going over the game plan," Staubach said. "At one point, even his wife, Alicia, said he should let me go back to my room and take a break.

"There were two games in my life where I couldn't fall asleep the night before the game. The 1962 Army–Navy game and Super Bowl VI because we had been labeled next year's champions and we couldn't win the big one. I was a nervous wreck."

Five years later, Jordan retired as the Cowboys' all-time leading tackler with 1,236. The record stood until Darren Woodson broke it in 2003. Jordan also intercepted 32 passes and scored three touchdowns.

Jordan retired after a fine 1976 season in which he started 16 games and helped Dallas win its first NFC East title in three seasons. Los Angeles beat Dallas 14-12 in a divisional playoff game.

"I was 36 years old and played 14 years. For a guy who was supposed to be too small to play, I had a miracle career," Jordan said. "The year before, I made the decision to retire because I was working out 12 months a year to stay in shape against these 20-year-olds.

"I still wanted to make the plays as well as I could in the past, and that's the way I wanted to retire."

Football had been Jordan's passion for as long as he could remember. And he had played for two of the best coaches—Bear Bryant and Tom Landry—the game has ever known.

Since he was always a player who had relied on guile and preparation as much as athleticism to succeed, it seemed logical for Jordan to become a coach once his playing career ended.

"It was really hard to give up football because I loved it," he said. "I thought I would coach and be able to stay in the game. I talked to Coach Landry and Coach Bryant, and they were paying their assistant coaches about $20,000 a year. I knew I needed to make a little more than that to make ends meet."

That's because he had a wife, Biddie, whom he'd met on the Alabama campus, and three children.

First, he looked into buying a car dealership, but the deal fell through. But the banker he was working with knew a man on the bank's board of directors who owned 28 lumber yards that he might be willing to sell because he wanted to scale back his business.

"Would you like to meet him?" the banker asked.

"I'm unemployed," Jordan replied. "I'd like to meet anybody."

Three weeks later, Jordan had agreed to buy Redwood Lumber Company of Dallas. Three months later, the deal was completed.

Jordan renamed the company, which specialized in California Redwoods, Lee Roy Jordan Lumber. As president, he's run the company for nearly 30 years.

"I owned two lumber yards—one in Dallas and one in Austin—and then I had to learn how to run them," Jordan said. "Having grown up on the farm, I knew what a two-by-four was and a two-by-six was, but that was about all. I didn't know anything about the lumber business, but I wanted to run my own deal—no matter how small—to see if I could make it work.

"I wanted to be the head coach. I wanted to call the signals, decide who was on the team, how they worked together, and what the rules were. I'm a team player. I love my people, and I try to show them that in how I handle the business."

CHAPTER 7

BOB
LILLY

Bob Lilly's legendary strength came naturally from hard work on the West Texas farm where he grew up. He didn't take supplements or drink protein shakes to build strength; he baled hay and lifted machinery.

"I was 6-foot-4 and about 185 pounds as a freshman, and I worked with some heavy equipment on the farm," Lilly said. "One of the machines my dad rigged up had a long pipe through the front. I had to lift that up every day, and it was like doing squats every day.

"I didn't think I was particularly strong, but one day a friend and I were riding in his car when we had a flat. We didn't have a jack, so I picked up the car so we could take the tire off and change it. I didn't think it was a big deal until the next day at school I saw some guys trying to lift a similar car, and they couldn't do it."

Lilly used that strength and natural quickness to become one of the best defensive linemen in the history of pro football.

"He was so strong and so quick that you just couldn't block him," said Lee Roy Jordan, the Cowboys' middle linebacker from 1962 to 1976. "It was great playing behind him because it took those guards a long time to get to me.

"He wasn't that fast over 40 yards, but he had burst and quickness in a short area that allowed him to beat guards and centers and make plays in the backfield."

Lilly initially developed those skills at TCU, which recruited him out of Pendleton, Oregon. Although Lilly had grown up in Throckmorton, a small town about four hours from Abilene, a drought had destroyed the farm and forced his father to move his family west.

"I had a wonderful time growing up in Throckmorton," Lilly said. "I went quail hunting with my father, we had a movie theater that cost a quarter, and we could do a lot of things outside like fishing and boating. But we had to move. My dad had to feed the family."

Although he was being recruited by most of the schools in the Pacific 8 Conference, including UCLA, Washington, and Washington State, Lilly received a postcard from TCU inquiring about his interest in the Horned Frogs. He returned the postcard and informed the TCU coaches that he wanted to play for them.

Lilly played well as a sophomore and junior—freshmen didn't play on the varsity—and TCU promoted him heavily before his senior year as one of the top players in the country. His confidence had swelled, and he began to consider playing professional football.

It helped that the American Football League had been established, and the Dallas Texans of the AFL, which became the Kansas and the Dallas Cowboys of the NFL gave him two options close to home to play football.

"The leagues were competing for players, and there was a lot going on," Lilly said, "but I wanted to play in Texas, and I made it pretty clear.

"I'm pretty sure some of my coaches at TCU knew I wanted to stay in Texas. They told me that the NFL had been around a long time and they weren't sure the AFL was going to make it. That made a lot of sense because the AFL could've folded. Either way would've been fine because [the Chiefs] actually won the Super Bowl before we did."

None of the Cowboys thought Baltimore was a better team. Just like they hadn't been convinced Cleveland was better in 1968 and 1969.

Their thoughts really didn't matter, though, because each time they had lost. And each time they had been favored. The odds makers in Las Vegas made Dallas a 2.5-point favorite over Johnny Unitas and the Colts in Super Bowl V.

"It was a game we felt we could've won with a few bounces," Lilly said. "We were determined to go all of the way in 1971."

That's the attitude the players took with them during off-season workouts when they lifted weights and ran four days a week.

In 1970, the Cowboys had been 3-4 at the halfway point of the season, and coach Tom Landry had loosened the reins on the team.

Laughter had filled the meeting rooms. Practices had been hard, but less intense. The focused, diligent work ethic that had allowed the Cowboys to go from a moribund franchise to one of the NFL's elite returned a year later. The players had grown weary of disappointment and were determined to emerge as champions.

"We were working very hard. We knew we were good enough to win a championship," Lilly said. "We suspected it the first year we played Green Bay and the second year we still thought we could beat them. We had a couple of setbacks against Cleveland, but we certainly felt good enough to win a championship. We wanted to go back to the Super Bowl, and this time we wanted to win it."

They won with defense, while Landry sorted out the offense and decided whether Roger Staubach or Craig Morton would be the starting quarterback.

The Doomsday Defense finished third in the NFL in total defense, including second against the run. Lilly, linebacker Chuck Howley, cornerback Mel Renfro, and safety Cornell Green earned trips to the Pro Bowl.

The Cowboys allowed just 15.8 points per game and held six of their last seven opponents to 14 points or less. They were even better in the playoffs, allowing 18 points in three games.

"Me, Mel, and Herb had all played cornerback, so we didn't let the formation dictate what we did on defense," said Green. "If they came out in a formation that left one receiver on my side of the field, I'd cover him.

"We didn't do a lot of moving around or disguising what we were going to do. We played man to man and dared teams to beat us. We could play with anybody."

A dominating 24-3 victory over Miami for the world championship validated the team—and Lilly.

"To be part of a new team, all wide-eyed, and then finding out it's not very easy, and having to improve every year, and get tougher mentally and smarter and better and jell as a team … and finally win. It was rewarding to win a championship."

GAME OF MY LIFE
By Bob Lilly

We knew how to handle the Super Bowl this time.

Tex Schramm and the coaches protected us a lot more. The year before we got calls in the hotel all of the time from people wanting tickets, whether it was family and friends in Dallas or strangers. The Cowboys took over all of that.

They cut off phone service to our rooms after 10 p.m. and took the phone calls themselves. They had security around the hotel, so we didn't have people beating on the windows and screaming. Everything was all organized in terms of practice, and we had one press day on Monday and spent a half-day with them. Any other interviews granted during the week happened after practice or some other convenient time after we were through with football, so we didn't lose focus.

They kept us out by the airport, so we had to take a bus to go anywhere. Coach Tom Landry also did something really smart. The first three days he let us stay out until midnight so we got to explore all of New Orleans and get that out of our system.

They also changed the practice schedule. The year before, we played our game the first week of practice since there were two weeks between the championship game and the Super Bowl. This time, we had light practice the first week. We wore shoulder pads and helmets for three days before putting on full pads and going pretty hard for a couple of days. Then we didn't go hard again until the following Tuesday. Coach Landry made it a lot more normal for us than it had been the year before.

I watched more film of the Dolphins than any other game. They were a fine football team, and they had the best team I had seen since the Packers, especially offensively. They had three fine running backs—Larry Csonka, Jim Kiick, and Mercury Morris—and Paul Warfield was a great receiver. They had good interior linemen and tight ends, and they ran over people. They were scary to watch because nobody had really stopped them.

We were a mature team, and we realized it was their first Super Bowl, and we thought we might be able to take advantage of that. We had a feeling of invincibility, and we played that way. We had a lot of guys make a lot of big plays. It was amazing. There were no fluke plays. Everything we got we deserved.

There were also a lot of things that nobody noticed, like Cornell Green was double-covering Warfield when he tripped. He got back up and caught up to Warfield and jumped high to tip a ball away from Warfield that probably would've been a touchdown that made it 10-7.

Calvin Hill was playing at about 60 percent, but he made some good runs for us. Walt Garrison had a lot of effort plays that turned into first downs, Duane Thomas was running well, and Roger Staubach made some really key passes.

We beat them up front on defense. We didn't let them run the football and they wanted to run it bad. We forced them to pass, which

Defensive lineman Bob Lilly. © *Vernon J. Biever Photo*

wasn't their strength. We just didn't make any mistakes. After the game, Don Shula said, "You just saw a team play a perfect game."

One of the plays that set the tone was my sack of Bob Griese just before the end of the first quarter. He lost almost 30 yards, and it might have set a little tone that we could rush the passer.

Jethro Pugh and Larry Cole stunted, and George Andrie and I stunted. What I always tried to do is go first and take my guard with me. I also tried to grab George's tackle and that would make the center pick up George. I don't know what happened, but two of Miami's linemen ran into each other, and all of a sudden Larry Cole and I were both free.

I was in Griese's face first. Then Larry had him going the other way. Larry couldn't catch him, but I finally did. I had no idea it was almost 30 yards down the field. It was just before the first quarter was over.

Even when it was 17-3, we didn't let down because I never took anything for granted. After we scored the last touchdown to make it 24-3, defensive lineman Bill Gregory came into the game because we were in a nickel defense. That gave me a chance to sit on the bench and really enjoy the moment. George Andrie and I were shaking hands, and I hugged Jethro.

When it was over, Jethro jumped right into the air. I headed straight to Coach Landry, but two to three guys beat me. Rayfield Wright was on one side, and somebody else grabbed his other leg. I was holding his rear up. The next day in the paper Coach Landry had a big, wide grin on his face. It was wonderful.

It was unbelievable. When Pat Summerall and Tom Brookshier were interviewing us after the game, we were all talking really fast because our adrenaline was flowing so much.

The relief was incredible. A lot of the older guys had been called "next year's champions" and "bridesmaids." The headlines always talked about the Cowboys finding ways to lose. It was like a huge weight had been lifted off our backs. We were champions, and we had worked a long time to get there.

To celebrate the Cowboys' first championship, owner Clint Murchison set up a huge tent in the hotel parking lot and hosted a party for the players, coaches, support staff, and their families.

There was barbecue and cold beer and soft drinks. There was a dance floor and country music star Charlie Pride provided the entertainment.

The party lasted deep into the night.

"The next day, I got up to go to the Pro Bowl. I woke up about 7 a.m., and the sun was just coming up," Lilly said. "The tent and everything was gone except the bags of garbage. I'm thinking I just played the biggest game of my whole life and it's all over. Ten years from now no one will probably even remember the game. It was a letdown."

Lilly's emotions were understandable.

The Cowboys had been one of the league's elite teams since 1966, but had never won a championship. Lilly, the first draft pick in franchise history, had been through the 0-11-1 expansion season in 1960. He had been there when fans and media called for Landry's firing after the 1964 season. And he was there when the harsh criticism and emotional losses drove Don Meredith out of the game in 1968.

Already Lilly was trying to figure out how the Cowboys were going to find the intensity to defend their championship.

It didn't get any better at the Pro Bowl, where Lilly and his seven other teammates found out how much other star players around the league were making. As they moved into the 1972 season, the players had captured the elusive championship they had been chasing.

Now, they wanted to get paid.

While the off-season was full of distractions, the one thing players didn't have to worry about was a quarterback controversy.

Roger Staubach had passed for 1,882 yards with 15 touchdowns, four interceptions, and a 104.8 passer rating—and earned his first trip to the Pro Bowl. He had led Dallas on a 10-game winning streak to end the season and coach Tom Landry had promised Staubach an opportunity to wrest the starting job from Craig Morton.

He was in the process of doing that in the preseason, when Staubach's courage superseded his common sense in a preseason game against the Los Angeles Rams.

"He was running down the sideline, and Marlin McKeever, a linebacker from the Rams was chasing him," said Frank Luksa, who has covered the Cowboys since their inception for the *Fort Worth Star-Telegram,* the *Dallas Times Herald,* and the *Dallas Morning News.* "Instead of stepping out of bounds, he ducked his shoulder, and the guy crushed him."

The 235-pound McKeever delivered a blow that separated Staubach's shoulder and thrust Morton back into the starting lineup.

Morton struggled during the season, passing for 2,396 yards with 15 touchdowns and 21 interceptions. But with Calvin Hill becoming the first runner in franchise history to surpass the 1,000-yard mark and Walt Garrison adding 784 yards and seven touchdowns, the Cowboys still managed to score enough points to consistently win games.

It helped that the Doomsday Defense was playing at a high level. The Cowboys allowed just 240 points and finished first in the NFL against the run and seventh overall.

Staubach missed much of the season, but returned with about a month remaining. He played sparingly, throwing only 20 passes, as Morton guided the Cowboys into the playoffs with a 10-4 record that was good enough for second place in the NFC East.

But the quarterback drama continued into the postseason.

With 1:48 left in the third quarter of the NFC divisional playoff game against San Francisco, Dallas trailed 28-13. Landry benched Morton and inserted Staubach, who ultimately rallied Dallas to a victory with two touchdown passes in the final 1:30.

"Everything started rolling in the last quarter of that game, and Roger rallied us," Hill said. "Landry made a decision that Tuesday to start Roger in the NFC championship game. He brought both of them and told Roger that he was going to start. Billy Bob Harris, one of Craig's best friends, told me how crestfallen Craig was."

Staubach couldn't find the same magic against Washington, and the Redskins beat Dallas 26-3 in the NFC championship game.

About midway through the 1974 season, Lilly woke up one morning with a crick in his neck. It wouldn't go away, so one of the team doctors examined him.

"They said my vertebras were wearing down," Lilly said. "They shot me with novocaine before every game and every practice the rest of the year."

He played well, but his streak of 11 consecutive Pro Bowls ended as Dallas finished 8-6 and missed the playoffs.

"That was really a weird year," Roger Staubach said. "I was injured during the exhibition season, and we had a strike and then we started the season 1-4. But we managed to regroup and finish strong and almost got into the playoffs."

Coach Tom Landry spoke to Lilly about his future and ensured him that he wanted the 14-year veteran to return—even if he chose to do it as a player-coach.

Lilly pondered his options for a while and then told Landry of his decision.

"Coach, I can't do it. I have enough pride that I don't want to play at the level I was going to have to play," Lilly said. "I don't want to be out there just wearing that uniform and getting paid."

Soon after the season ended, Lilly drove out to the club's practice facility and soaked in the ambiance one last time. He sat at his locker and remembered conversations. He thought about all of the memories he shared with his various teammates through the years and how leaving them was going to be more difficult than leaving the game.

After he took his nameplate down, Lilly walked to the equipment room and asked equipment manager Buck Buchanan for some mementos.

"Buck put a uniform, shoulder pads, a helmet, some shoes, and two to three jerseys in a big bag," Lilly said. "Then I took all of the stuff out of my locker and put it in the bag.

"Buck put an arm around me and said, 'I know you'll be back.'

"I told him, 'Buck, I just can't play anymore. I'm hurt.'"

Then Lilly drove home.

"I cried all the way," he said. "I had to grieve. It wasn't just the football. It was leaving all of my teammates. I was leaving my family."

The year after Lilly retired, team president Tex Schramm made him the first player inducted into the Ring of Honor.

"I was shocked," said Lilly, who lives outside Austin in Sun City, Texas, with his wife, Ann. "I had noticed similar things at other stadiums but I never expected to be in the Ring of Honor. I just never even thought about something like that."

Now that he's retired Lilly has time to devote to a passion he discovered when he was given a camera in a goody bag at a college all-star game. There have been trips to Vermont to capture foliage and other trips around Texas in search of the perfect sunset.

When he's not creating art with his photos, Lilly and several other members of the Ring of Honor get together regularly to reminisce about the good old days and to participate in autograph sessions throughout the country.

Life is good these days for Lilly, and he's enjoying every minute of it.

THE BIRTH OF
AMERICA'S TEAM

CHAPTER 8

ROGER STAUBACH

The credit should go to Purcell High School football coach Jim McCarthy.

It's not just that he recognized Roger Staubach's talent and shifted him from cornerback to quarterback; he saw something else in the teenager.

He saw an ability to lead.

McCarthy noticed how the other students yielded to Staubach's authority, though he was soft-spoken. He figured that unique ability would serve him well on the football field, especially at quarterback, where he would be the epicenter of the offensive attack.

It didn't matter that Purcell used the T-formation and threw the ball only as a last resort. What mattered was that Staubach was a terrific athlete with a powerful arm who could throw it when necessary.

"Coach McCarthy said the other players listened to me," said Staubach, an only child, who grew up in a tight-knit, middle-class family in Cincinnati.

"I had played tight end and defensive back until he moved me to quarterback my senior year."

Staubach thrived at the position. From the start, he dazzled as a runner. He performed so well that he drew the attention of most schools in the Big Ten, including Ohio State and Michigan. Ohio State coach Woody Hayes, who coveted running quarterbacks, recruited him personally.

But Staubach wanted to throw the ball. Purdue and its wide-open passing offense would provide the best opportunity to showcase his arm. The military academies were also showing interest, especially the U.S. Naval Academy. Although he starred at an all-male Catholic school, Notre Dame wasn't interested—until it was too late. After he turned in a terrific performance in a postseason all-star game, Notre Dame offered a scholarship. Staubach turned it down.

Staubach initially signed a letter of intent with Purdue with the under-standing that he might choose to attend one of the military academies.

"My mom said if I was interested in the Naval Academy, I should spend some time at their prep school," Staubach said. "She liked the idea of me going to the Naval Academy."

At the time, all of the military academies had a relationship with New Mexico Military Institute in Roswell, New Mexico, so that's where he spent the year after high school. It was the best decision he ever made.

"It was like a redshirt year for me," he said. "It was a year to get acquainted with the military and academic requirements, and we had one of the best junior college teams in the country. We were 9-1, and our offense was pretty wide open."

Freshmen weren't allowed to play on the varsity, and as he entered his sophomore year Staubach was fifth on the depth chart following spring practice. Going into the season, he was third. A month into the season, he was starting.

"I got in at the end of the first quarter of our third game against Cornell, and we beat them 41-7. They were pretty good then, and I start-ed the rest of the year," Staubach said. "That gave us the momentum for a really good season in 1963."

It would be a season that ended with him winning the Heisman Trophy.

"It was a little uncomfortable because I had another year to play," Staubach said. "It's a prestigious award, but we had a great team that year. I don't think there's a player who's ever won it that was on a bad team except, maybe, Paul Hornung."

Since he had spent a year in junior college, Staubach was eligible to be drafted after the 1963 season. Dallas of the National Football League and Kansas City of the American Football League each drafted him. Both franchises expected him to spend another year at Navy. Staubach, picked in the 10th round, chose the Cowboys because he wanted to play in the more established NFL.

Five years later, he had an opportunity to do it.

Roger Staubach (12) hands off to Tony Dorsett. © *Vernon J. Biever Photo*

"I knew after a couple of years in the service that I wanted to play again," he said. "I missed the game."

It was supposed to be a rebuilding year. After all, the Cowboys had missed the playoffs for the first time since 1965, and they were trying to withstand the retirements of the players who made them a championship contender for a decade.

In a three-year period stars like defensive tackle Bob Lilly, linebacker Chuck Howley, safety Cornell Green, defensive end George Andrie, running back Walt Garrison, and cornerback Herb Adderley retired. Others, like middle linebacker Lee Roy Jordan, outside linebacker Dave Edwards, defensive tackle Jethro Pugh, and cornerback Mel Renfro, were near the end of their careers and no longer dominated on a weekly basis.

They needed an infusion of talent to bridge the gap between the stars of yesterday and future stars such as defensive ends Ed Jones and Harvey Martin, safeties Cliff Harris and Charlie Waters, and tight end Billy Joe DuPree.

And, of course, Staubach.

The Dirty Dozen did that. The Cowboys kept 12 of the 19 players they drafted in 1975, and several played key roles in a surprising season that wound up with Dallas becoming the first team to qualify for the playoffs as a wild card and still reach the Super Bowl.

First-round picks Randy White, the second player selected in the draft, and Thomas Henderson, the 18th player picked; third-round pick Bob Breunig; and seventh-round pick Mike Hegaman were supposed to provide the next group of athletic, play-making linebackers that had become a Cowboys staple.

Howley, Jordan, and Edwards had played so long together they could communicate without speaking.

"Sometimes, I could just tell the way Chuck was leaning that he was going to do something instinctive that the defense didn't call for him to do," Jordan said. "Then I'd have to leave my position and make sure his man was covered, but he usually made the play. He made a lot of plays no one else could because of his instincts."

The Cowboys attempted to rebuild their offensive line by drafting guard Burton Lawless in the second round, center Kyle Davis in the fifth round, and guard Herb Scott in the 13th round. Defensive end Pat Donovan, a fourth-round pick, moved to tackle.

"We did not think about the Super Bowl," Staubach said. "We overachieved that year."

Staubach was the catalyst.

In 1975 he started a season in Dallas without Craig Morton on the roster for the first time. He could relax and play football without worrying about when Landry might replace him. Before that season, the competition at quarterback had been tough on the entire team.

"There's not a better coach or human being than Tom Landry, but he felt confident that if you executed the plays you would win," Staubach said. "But there's emotion on the field in addition to the players and there's leadership. Having two quarterbacks won't work. The team was divided.

"Craig was really hurting in 1970, and I should've played. In 1971, Coach Landry chose me and that changed my life."

At the start of that year, Landry announced the Cowboys had two starters: Staubach and Morton.

Staubach was scheduled to start the opener, but a leg injury forced Morton into the lineup, and he led Dallas to a 49-37 win over Buffalo. Staubach started the next week against Philadelphia, but was knocked out of the game.

Morton replaced him and guided Dallas to a 42-7 win, earning the opportunity to start against Washington in week three. The Redskins won and Staubach started the next two games—a win over the Giants and a loss to New Orleans.

Then Landry decided to do something different.

"We were sitting in a meeting, and Coach Landry announced we're going to alternate plays," Staubach said. "Me and Craig started looking at each other wondering whether he had had a concussion."

The Cowboys totaled 418 yards of offense as Morton and Staubach alternated every play except during the final two minutes of each half, when Morton played exclusively. Morton completed 20 of 36 passes for 257 yards with three interceptions. Staubach was seven of 11 for 87 yards and an interception.

Dallas lost 23-19 to fall two games behind Washington in the NFC East race, prompting Landry to change his stance on the quarterbacks one more time. This time, he named Staubach the starter.

The Cowboys never lost again, winning 10 straight games and the first championship in franchise history.

"Craig was in really good shape and healthy, but we needed to go with one guy," Staubach said. "If it wasn't me, it would've been my last season. Part of my deal was impatience. I was 29. ... I didn't come to the NFL to sit on the bench."

The rest of the team was tiring of the quarterback merry-go-round, too.

"It got to a point where the players didn't care," said Frank Luksa, who has covered the team since its inception as a writer for the *Fort Worth Star-Telegram,* the *Dallas Times Herald,* and the *Dallas Morning News.* "Each player had his supporters, but it dragged on so long that the team just wanted Landry to pick a player."

Staubach started all 14 games in 1973 and in October 1974, the Cowboys dealt Morton to the New York Giants for the first-round pick that produced White.

Having started 14 games for the first time in his career in 1974, Staubach also knew how to pace himself to withstand the season. Now that he didn't have to look for Morton over his shoulder, his natural ability could take over games.

"That's when I really felt in command of the football team," he said. "It was a great year. It showed you can win if you get the right people working together."

A 1-4 start doomed the Cowboys in 1974; they started fast in 1975. Dallas won its first four games, but found itself 5-3 after a 34-31 loss to Kansas City. Then the Cowboys won five of their last six games to clinch a spot in the playoffs against Minnesota.

"They called us the Dirty Dozen, and we all grew beards," White said. "We were just playing football and having a good time, but the youth and energy we brought helped motivate some of the veteran guys."

GAME OF MY LIFE
By Roger Staubach

The Vikings felt they had the best team they ever had, and I think they took us for granted because we were big underdogs. Everybody thought we were going to get blown out.

But we felt good about ourselves because we had a lot of young, confident guys on the team, and that's why we played them tough. Bob Breunig was a good young player, Thomas Henderson was a great athlete, and Randy White was doing a good job, although they weren't quite sure what to do with him.

It was cold, but it wasn't windy. That was important. It can be five degrees, but if there's no wind, you can handle it. It was a decent day. It was 18 degrees with no wind so it was cold, but bearable.

Our defense played well because they had Fran Tarkenton and their offense was really good. We were up at halftime, and we knew if we stayed in the game, we had a chance to win it in the fourth quarter. Down deep we believed in each other, and we played really well to be in position to win the game late.

We moved the ball up and down the field the whole game, and our defense was playing well, but we were only up by a field goal. They went up 14-10, and we wanted to use the shotgun, but were having a little trouble with it because John Fitzgerald had hurt his elbow. It was the fourth quarter, and I was scrambling around trying to salvage plays off the shotgun, so they put Kyle Davis in there at the end of the game.

We were running well and throwing it OK, but Drew Pearson hadn't caught a pass. But on the last drive Drew played like he usually did. Our guys thought it was over and even Coach Landry, I think, thought it was over when I got sacked and it was fourth-and-17.

Then Drew made a play like he always did. He caught a pass for a first down. Once we got the first down on the corner pass, we didn't have any timeouts. I asked Drew what he could do, and he told me he was really tired. Plus, somebody had kicked him when he was out of bounds, so he needed some time.

I threw a pass to Preston Pearson and luckily he didn't catch it. If he had, we could've run one more play, but we wouldn't have had a chance to huddle. In the huddle, I talked to Drew about a "16 Route."

I told him to make it look like he was running an in route and then break it deep on Nate Wright. I told him I would look off free safety Paul Krause. I told everybody else to block. I looked off Krause and pump-faked, and when I came back to throw it, Drew was open, but the pass was underthrown.

Drew caught the ball on his hip and ran into the end zone. Krause got over a couple of steps late and started yelling at the referee that Drew had pushed off, but it didn't happen.

I got knocked down when I threw the ball. I saw an orange on the field and when I stood up I thought it was a flag. I was kind of stunned, but then I saw Drew in the end zone celebrating.

After the game, the press asked me about the play. I said I closed my eyes and said a Hail Mary. The next day some writer dubbed it the Hail Mary pass.

Sooner or later Staubach knew the Cowboys were going to win another championship. So did his teammates.

The Hail Mary had inspired his teammates. Again.

The first time Staubach had proven he played his best in big games occurred when he was named Most Valuable Player of Super Bowl VI. Then there was the 1972 divisional playoff game against San Francisco, when he came off the bench and rallied the Cowboys to two touchdowns in the last 1:30.

Now, he had led them to a miracle win over Minnesota and put them in position to upset Pittsburgh in Super Bowl X. Staubach inspired his teammates. As long as he was on the field and there was time on the clock, they believed he gave them a chance to win.

The score didn't matter. Neither did the situation.

"Roger knew how to take charge," said Rayfield Wright, a Hall of Fame tackle who played for Dallas from 1967 to 1980. "But he never really talked a lot. His leadership was based on performance."

He also had *it*—the charismatic trait some athletes possess that allows them to impose their will on a game and tilt it in their favor. Or make average players believe they're good enough to win a championship. It's the trait that allows them to always turn in their best performances when there's the most at stake. Kobe Bryant has *it*. Tom Brady has *it*. Derek Jeter has *it*.

Morton didn't.

He rarely played well in the playoffs. He threw three interceptions—two in the fourth quarter—in Super Bowl V. In six playoff starts, the Cowboys never scored more than three touchdowns with him at the helm.

"Morton has an excellent arm. He once split the web of Bob Hayes' palm between the thumb and forefinger because the ball had so much velocity on it," Luksa said. "But he didn't have, whatever *it* is, that allows some guys to make the big play. He was the eternal tease."

Staubach, perhaps buoyed by his military experience, never lacked confidence. He executed best when under the most pressure. He led the Cowboys to 23 come-from-behind victories, including 14 in the final two minutes.

"As a quarterback you have to convey the belief to your teammates. They have to have confidence that you can make it happen, and then players will get on the bandwagon because you can't do it by yourself," Staubach said. "I never was in a situation where I thought we were going to lose or quit. We got beat, and we did lose, but never quit.

"If you have that confidence, you get your share of comebacks. We tried to get in position to win, and if you do it enough, then you get that reputation."

Two years after losing Super Bowl X, Dallas drafted star running back Tony Dorsett, who gave the offense a big-play capability it had been lacking. Staubach and Dorsett teamed with Doomsday II to beat Denver 27-10 and give Landry his second world championship.

A year later, Pittsburgh ended the Cowboys' quest for consecutive titles with a 35-31 victory in one of the most exciting Super Bowls in history. In that three-year stretch, the Cowboys went 35-9 with three NFC East titles and two trips to the Super Bowl.

"That Hail Mary game," Staubach said, "and getting Dorsett were the real catalysts for the whole period."

It wasn't the kind of hit that made the crowd gasp—and that's what bothered Staubach.

Los Angeles middle linebacker Jack "Hacksaw" Reynolds had delivered a hard, clean blow—it wasn't particularly vicious—in the fourth quarter of the 1979 NFC divisional playoff game, and Staubach was woozy.

It wasn't like the hit he had received from L.C. Greenwood against Pittsburgh in October that had forced him out of the game.

He didn't really comprehend that he had just tossed a five-yard touchdown pass to tight end Jay Saldi with 12:16 left, which seemed destined to propel the Cowboys to the NFC championship game for the fourth time in five seasons.

Still, he went back on the field when Billy Waddy's 50-yard touchdown catch gave the Rams (9-7 in the regular season) a 21-19 lead with less than two minutes remaining. Staubach couldn't manufacture another miracle finish, and the Cowboys' season ended.

No one knew it would be Staubach's last game.

"We got the ball back after the Waddy play, but I wasn't myself at the end of the game," Staubach said. "With some of the concussions you have to come out because you have no choice. I could still function, but I didn't think I got hit that hard, but my head bounced off the ground. I was thinking they're coming more than they should and they're affecting my play."

After the season, Staubach visited two doctors to determine if there was any neurological damage. One suggested he retire; the other said he could continue playing. Neither doctor saw significant damage, but the physician who suggested retirement told Staubach that his reflexes had slowed and another concussion might lead to scar tissue on the brain, something many boxers have.

He spoke to Tex Schramm, who offered him a two-year contract worth about $750,000, which would've made him one of the game's highest-paid players. Landry told Staubach to take some time before making a decision.

His wife, Mary Ann, and Father Joseph Ryan, a close friend from the Navy, each advised him to retire. In March, Staubach announced his retirement.

"I had a good year, and I still could've played," said Staubach, who had 27 touchdown passes, 11 interceptions, and a passer rating of 92.3 in 1979. "I wanted to retire on my own terms. I didn't want someone saying I lost my skills and it was time to retire.

"I came to the Cowboys during the Meredith era when he was building Dallas into a winner with the Howleys, Jordans, Lillys, and Greens. I was part of the new era with Randy White, Tony Hill, Drew Pearson, and Tony Dorsett. I was the leader of that new group. I just wish I had had a few more years with them."

Staubach, the highest-rated passer in NFL history when he retired, was inducted into the Cowboys' Ring of Honor in 1983 and the Pro Football Hall of Fame in 1985.

When he walked away from the game, Staubach was already in the real estate business. That provided a competitive outlet and something to fill the hours that used to be crammed with football.

"I had a business I was building, so I stayed busy," Staubach said, "but I really missed it."

He now runs The Staubach Company, a multipronged real estate company that generated more than $300 million in revenues in 2004 and has offices worldwide.

"There is some really great competition out there that's as tough as playing the Redskins and Giants," Staubach said. "If you work hard, persevere, and do the right thing, there's a lot of business out there. It doesn't come easy.

"To be an athlete can help you get in the door, but you have to be able to deliver what you say you will."

CHAPTER 9

PRESTON PEARSON

Preston Pearson never had a classic football player's body. He has a basketball player's sinewy frame. He has long legs and arms that hang well below his waist. His hands are nearly twice the size of a normal man with fingers that you would expect to find on a pianist.

Maybe that's why Pearson never set out to make football a career—let alone play 14 seasons under three Hall of Fame coaches and alongside dozens of Hall of Fame players. Football chose him, not the other way around.

Pearson played football in high school, where he spent much of his time in his older brother Rufus' large shadow. Still, Pearson was a good player, but he was a better basketball player. And he understood athletics might help him escape Freeport, Illinois, a blue-collar town about 135 miles northwest of Chicago near the Wisconsin border.

Dreams died in Freeport. The mostly Irish and Italian city swallowed up its youth in the factories that formed the economic base for most residents. To support their six children, Pearson's mother worked in a toy factory, while his father toiled in a steel factory. Neither had more than a fifth-grade education.

The Pearsons lived on the east side of town. The railroad tracks ran behind their home, and the locomotives shook the small frame house seemingly every night.

"If you had any goals and dreams, you had to get out, especially black kids," Pearson said. "You just had to get out to get on with your life. If you were young and black in Freeport, you were only going to go so far. I knew wanted to catch the first thing smoking out of town."

Basketball gave him an opportunity to do that.

Pearson, a member of the same All-State team as basketball Hall of Famer Dan Issel, played well enough to earn several scholarship offers. None, though, appealed to Pearson, who had his heart set on attending the University of Illinois. He sent a handwritten letter to coach Harry Combs asking for a chance to play for the Fighting Illini.

Illinois responded with an offer for a half scholarship that covered only books and tuition. Pearson worked in the cafeteria and sold programs at football games to pay for his room and board.

"I can't tell you how hard it was to work, study, and try to play college basketball," Pearson said.

When his eligibility ended, Pearson couldn't figure out what to do with the rest of his life. Then fate intervened.

"There was a knock at the door. I looked through the peephole and saw a white dude," Pearson said. "I opened up the door and he told me that I had been drafted by the Baltimore Colts. He told me Don Shula wanted to talk to me, and he would wait for me."

Pearson found a pay phone and called the NFL's youngest head coach. The Colts offered him a $1,000 signing bonus and a $15,000 contract, though he would be paid only $7,500 if Baltimore placed him on the taxi squad, a version of the practice squad that teams use today.

"I had no job offers pending," said Pearson, "so I took it."

Pearson, signed as a defensive back and spent much of his first season on the practice squad learning the nuances of pro football.

In his second season, the Colts moved Pearson to running back because he was having so much success as a runner on the scout team.

He became one of the league's best kick returners, but wanted a larger role in the offense. Of course, with Lenny Moore in the backfield that wasn't going to happen. Baltimore traded him to Pittsburgh and coach Chuck Noll, who had been a position coach with the Colts, when they drafted Pearson.

Finally, Pearson thought he was going to get a chance to be a featured runner.

Pearson had a hunch the 1974 season was going to be a struggle.

Recent first-round pick Franco Harris' ability was forcing coach Chuck Noll to give him more and more playing time, and Pearson was the team's NFLPA representative. He sensed there was going to be a strike in 1974, and he knew he might catch the brunt of any retaliation as a union leader.

"I told Chuck in the off-season that we were about to go on strike, and my knees were shaking," Pearson said. "I was scared to death, because he could do anything he wanted to do to me."

Pearson lasted one more year with the Steelers. They cut him at the end of the preseason in 1975. On the day the Steelers announced their final cuts, a newspaper reporter phoned the nine-year veteran running back to get his thoughts on being waived.

"No one called me to tell me," Pearson said of the Steelers organization. "That surprised me, and it hurt me."

It hurt even more, when not one of the NFL's 26 teams deemed Pearson worthy of the $100 fee it would cost to claim him. Once he passed through waivers, the Cowboys Gil Brandt called and asked if he wanted to come to Dallas for a tryout.

Fullback Robert Newhouse, who had gained 501 yards in 1974, was the leading returning rusher, and Doug Denison was entering camp as the starting halfback. Clearly, Pearson could upgrade the position.

"We liked Preston when he was coming out of Illinois," Brandt said, "and I thought he would be a very good fit on our team because of his ability to run draws and screens, and be a third-down or long-yardage back. He turned out to be an even better player than we thought he would be."

Players who hadn't played college football didn't frighten the Cowboys as long as they were superior athletes. After all, it was a philosophy Brandt and Tex Schramm developed when they worked for the Los Angeles Rams.

They had signed K.C. Jones, a star basketball player at the University of San Francisco with Bill Russell, and he was going to make the team until he decided his future was brighter in the NBA. He joined the Celtics, became a star, and later coached the team.

Brandt and Schramm also had had success early in their tenure converting Cornell Green, a basketball star at Utah, into one of the top cornerbacks in franchise history.

"We got lucky with Cornell," Brandt said. "Had we not gotten lucky with him, we probably wouldn't have continued to go that route."

Before the Cowboys signed Pearson, they wanted to check his speed in the 40-yard dash. But they didn't want Pearson to race against a stopwatch. They wanted him to race their fastest player: linebacker Thomas Henderson.

Pearson took the lane closest to assistant coach Dan Reeves, who was blowing the whistle to signal the start of the race. Pearson figured that would give him a slight edge since Henderson would probably glance at Reeves when he blew the whistle—and that slight turning of the head would allow Pearson to win the race.

Pearson, who figured he was racing for his career, beat Henderson and earned a roster spot.

"At that time, we really didn't have a running back, so I thought he could help us," Newhouse said. "Once we started practicing, I was in shock because Preston could do things coming out of the backfield that I had never seen before. He could run routes, read defenses, and make adjustments. He had abilities that no one else on our team had."

Pearson, the player no one wanted, became one of the Cowboys' best performers, generating 1,251 yards. He finished second on the club in rushing (509 yards), fourth in receptions (27 for 351 yards), and led the team in kickoff returns (24.4 average on 16 returns) as the Cowboys became an unlikely wild-card team.

In 1974, Dallas had missed the playoffs for the first time in nine seasons, so expectations were tempered in 1975. But a fantastic rookie class—they labeled it "The Dirty Dozen"—led by defensive tackle Randy White, linebacker Thomas Henderson, and guards Burton Lawless and Herb Scott helped Dallas finish 10-4 and finish second in the NFC East.

The Cowboys won their final two games of the season—31-10 over Washington and 31-21 over the New York Jets—to clinch a wild-card berth. Then came a dramatic 17-14 win over Minnesota in a game dubbed The Hail Mary, propelling the Cowboys into the NFC championship game.

Pearson saved his best performance for that game.

He caught five passes for 123 yards, the eighth-best receiving performance in franchise history, and scored three touchdowns as Dallas advanced to the Super Bowl for the third time in six seasons.

GAME OF MY LIFE
By Preston Pearson

We were big-time underdogs to the Rams.

All week there was a lot of talk about the Hail Mary and how lucky we were to win the game. I had played well against the Vikings. It wasn't necessarily that I scored or had a lot of stats, but I did everything I was supposed to do. My timing was good. I hit the holes quickly, and I was in the right place at the right time.

We had a very nice week of practice heading into the Rams game, and maybe all of that attention we got because of the Hail Mary kept us focused. When you have a game like the Hail Mary, sometimes you can go in the other direction and lose focus, but I think we felt good about ourselves.

I had the kind of game that you dream about as a kid.

I scored my first touchdown on a screen pass that gave us a 7-0 lead. Coach Tom Landry loved having me in the game for screen passes, and we were good at it because we practiced it a lot and everyone understood how important it was to be an actor on the play.

I had to jump up a little to catch the pass. After I got it, I turned it up inside and it was blocked perfectly.

I scored my second touchdown on a diving catch, where I wasn't even the primary receiver. I believe Drew Pearson or Billy Joe DuPree was the primary receiver.

My job was to occupy anybody on the outside. Linebacker Ken Geddes had me one on one, and there ain't no way he could cover me. I think I actually put him out of the league. I don't think he played another game after the championship game. Geddes was one of those guys who would beat you up in the running game because he had a big long pad that he wore on his forearm and he used to just bang people with it.

Ken thought I was coming out to block him, but I kind of feinted, and he couldn't turn and run with me. Once I got even with him, I ran past him. For some reason, even though I wasn't the primary receiver, I knew Roger Staubach was going to throw that ball. I just knew it.

When I saw the ball coming, it seemed like it just stopped in midair. I could read commissioner Pete Rozelle's name on the side of the ball. I couldn't hear anything because I was completely focused on the ball. It was going to be a little long, and that was the only reason I had to dive.

But it was mine. I knew that.

When you're in that zone, you're completely focused. Things just slow down to the point where you could read what was on the side of the ball. I was in the zone that entire day. I caught five passes, three of them for touchdowns, for more than 100 yards.

Coach Landry should get all of the credit on the third touchdown that put us up 28-0. He set them up for the shovel pass.

The Rams had a pair of great defensive ends, but Rayfield Wright kicked Jack Youngblood's butt that day, and Ralph Neely was on the other side doing a good job against Fred Dryer. Youngblood and Dryer were up-the-field rushers, and Coach Landry made a perfect call.

Roger watched Dryer rush up the field just like Coach Landry said he would do and flipped me the ball. Herb Scott, the left guard, was pulling, and I had to make sure I was behind Herb because if Dryer didn't go up the field, Herb had to get him. The hole was so big I just waltzed through it. I think a guy got his hand on me at the 5, but couldn't bring me down.

It was a good feeling on the sideline. Although we were big-time underdogs, the feeling was that we could just kick their butt all day. And when we won, it meant we were headed to the Super Bowl. We were going to the Super Bowl.

I was sitting on the sideline near the end of the game, when it really hit me. I said to myself, "Boy, you done showed out. You scored three touchdowns, didn't make any mistakes mentally, and actually blocked who you were supposed to block."

The 1975 season didn't have a fairy-tale ending for Preston Pearson. Actually, it was more of a nightmare.

The player who played a starring role in the demolition of the Rams struggled against Pittsburgh because he couldn't handle his emotions.

Pearson wanted to show Pittsburgh coach Chuck Noll that he screwed up. He wanted to show his former teammates that he could still play. And he wanted to show the fans what they were missing.

Instead, he never found a rhythm.

"I was too geeked, and I rushed a few things. I didn't play too well," Pearson said. "To this day, if I had that game over, I would do a few things slower. You know, if you're not careful, you can hyperventilate in a game like that. I would've shut myself down, taken a few more deep breaths, and slowed myself down. I didn't play very well."

The Cowboys, a team with no expectations at the start of the season, played Pittsburgh and its collection of stars—Terry Bradshaw, Franco Harris, Lynn Swann, and "Mean Joe" Green—even for much of the game.

"The Cowboys were a fantastic team," Harris said. "They had some great talent on that team even though they were young, and we knew it was going to be a difficult game."

Dallas led 10-7 entering the fourth quarter, but couldn't make enough plays to hold off Pittsburgh. Receiver Lynn Swann caught a 64-yard touchdown pass with 3:02 left to give the Steelers a 21-10 lead. Swann, the game's Most Valuable Player, finished with four catches for 161 yards.

Staubach tossed a touchdown pass in the final minute, but it wasn't enough. Pittsburgh triumphed 21-17.

Preston Pearson breaks a tackle against the Vikings.
Photo by www.dallascowboysweekly.com

"We weren't supposed to be there because we were a wild-card team," Newhouse said. "It was my first Super Bowl—we had lost the championship game the year before—so I was happy to be there.

"We knew Pittsburgh had a solid ballclub, but we weren't intimidated by them. At the end of the game, I learned that it meant something to lose. It hurt."

He was hardly alone. The team-leading five catches for 53 yards and the 115 yards in total offense meant nothing to Pearson.

He wanted a ring badly because he had been on the Colts team that lost to Joe Namath and the New York Jets in Super Bowl III. Two years after the Colts had traded him, they beat Dallas in Super Bowl V.

The year before when Pittsburgh had released him, the Steelers ended the season with a Super Bowl title. Now, they had become the first team since Lombardi's Packers in 1967 and 1968 to win consecutive Super Bowls.

"It hurt twice as much because I didn't play well and we lost to Pittsburgh," Pearson said. "Years later, it doesn't hurt as much because if you compare that Steelers team to our team that wasn't supposed to be there, Pittsburgh was the better team. They were the Steel Curtain."

The work ethic came from hearing Preston Pearson's father leave for work each morning at 4 a.m., so he would have enough time to make the 22-mile drive to Roquefort for his shift.

Pearson grew up in a family where clothes were passed down from siblings and there was little extra money for luxuries. All of the children had assigned chores at home, and they were expected to be completed without being told.

"I got my work ethic from my parents. We didn't have a lot of money, but they always tried to give us everything they could," Pearson said. "When it snowed, I remember shoveling four or five driveways before school. A couple of ladies were so nice they paid me a little bit and gave me breakfast. I used the money to buy myself a desk, a bike, and some clothes."

Pearson took the same approach to life as an adult as he did as a youth.

Pearson's route-running ability and hands, and coach Tom Landry's creativity allowed Pearson's career to flourish long after most running backs had stopped trying to elude defenders and settled into life after football.

He was a backup in 1976 before regaining the starting job in 1977, Tony Dorsett's rookie season. A combination of Landry's conservative approach to playing rookies and Dorsett's poor practice habits kept the Heisman Trophy winner on the bench as the Cowboys won their first eight games.

After St. Louis ended the Cowboys' winning streak, Landry moved Dorsett into the starting lineup.

The timing angered Pearson for two reasons: He felt Landry was making him a scapegoat for the loss, and he wanted to return to Pittsburgh a starter.

Dorsett said the promotion gave him mixed emotions.

"I'm sure it kind of bothered him that he wasn't getting an opportunity to go back to Pittsburgh as a starter, so in a way I felt funny about it, but in another way I didn't," Dorsett said. "Preston probably won't even remember an incident that happened when I was a kid.

"Some of the Steelers came to our high school, and Preston looked at me and asked me what position I played. When I told him running back, he told me I was too small. As a kid, you don't forget those things, and it stuck with me because I was supposed to be too small, but I was taking his job."

Pearson overcame his disappointment and continued to be a valuable member of the Cowboys' offense. Using him almost exclusively in the shotgun formation, Pearson became one of the NFL's first third-down backs.

Landry used him on third downs and passing situations to limit Dorsett's plays and to keep him from blocking too many linebackers, who outweighed him by as many as 40 pounds. Pearson caught 26 passes for 333 yards and a touchdown in 1979, and wanted to play another season.

The Cowboys thought it was time to move on.

"I wasn't ready to go," said Pearson, "but Brandt called me and said, 'We can't afford the luxury of keeping you on the roster.'"

So Pearson embraced the business world and became an entrepreneur.

He's been involved in several different types of businesses, ranging from restaurants to real estate. He has hosted a radio show and shown the same type of tenacity in the world of business that he did on the football field.

Pearson currently owns a marketing firm that schedules appearances for pro athletes.

"It's something that I own and I enjoy," Pearson said, "and it gives me an opportunity to stay close to the game."

CHAPTER 10

TONY DORSETT

After every football game, the scrawny kid with the large brown eyes would peel off his uniform and walk home. He'd drag his uniform along the ground, staining it with grass and mud.

Tony Dorsett, you see, never really wanted to play football. He was too small, and he didn't want to get hurt, but each of his four older brothers played—so he did too.

Or at least he stood on the sidelines. Actually, he hid on the sideline, standing behind teammates and fidgeting on the end of the bench, hoping his coach's gaze would never find him. And when the game ended, he'd walk home and tell his parents about his performances.

"I would make up stories about how I played," Dorsett said.

Dorsett's exaggerated stories satisfied his parents and siblings for a few weeks. Then one of his brothers showed up to watch a game and threatened him if he didn't get on the field for a kickoff return.

"It was just my bad luck that the ball was kicked to me. My eyes got as big as silver dollars, and I took off like a little rabbit as soon as I got the ball," Dorsett said. "I ran about 75 yards for a touchdown, and it kind of got good for me after that."

So good that Dorsett evolved into one of the nation's best high school running backs. Coaches from as far west as California came to the government housing project where he lived in Aliquippa, Pennsylvania, about 30 miles northwest of Pittsburgh, to get his name on a national letter of intent.

Penn State infatuated him because of the way coach Joe Paterno had used Franco Harris and Lydell Mitchell, but he never sensed they felt the same about him. The day before Dorsett was supposed to announce his commitment, Paterno met with the teenager and his family.

It was too little too late. The next day, Dorsett committed to Pitt with the blessing of his mother, Myrtle Grace, a strong, independent woman who fought her son over the pecan pies that Pitt assistant Jackie Sherrill brought on recruiting trips.

But even star running backs can have trouble adjusting to college and living away from home for the first time.

"I was introverted, and it was hard for me to make friends. I said, 'I don't know if I'm going to stick this out. I'm going back to the 'Quip with my friends and in my surroundings where I was comfortable,'" Dorsett said. "'I think I'm coming home.' She said I was the only son who had a chance to go to school, and it would hurt me more than anything. She really wanted me to stay in school, and it got better."

Did it ever.

Dorsett gained 100 yards in his first game, a 7-7 tie against Georgia. He finished the season with 1,586 yards, the most ever by a college freshman. He rushed for 1,948 yards as a senior, giving 6,082 for his career and making him the all-time leading rusher in NCAA history, a record that lasted 22 years.

The team also improved under coach Johnny Majors each year. Pitt went 6-5-1, 7-4, 8-4, and 12-0 in 1976. Dorsett rushed for 202 yards in the 1977 Sugar Bowl to easily beat No. 4 Georgia 27-3.

That made Dorsett one of the draft's most coveted players. Tampa Bay and Seattle, the league's two new expansion teams that gave the NFL 28 teams, had the first two picks in the draft. Tampa Bay, coached by former Southern California coach John McKay, wanted Ricky Bell, the player McKay coached in college, which meant Dorsett was headed to Seattle.

"I really didn't want to go there because I didn't want to run behind an expansion offensive line," Dorsett said. "I put a lot of stuff out there about exploring my options in Canada to convince Seattle not to draft me, but I was never serious about that.

"I had seen [personnel director] Gil Brandt at a couple of off-season awards shows, and I just kind of mentioned that I didn't want to play for Seattle, and he told me that maybe something would work out for me."

That's because the Cowboys needed a running back to take their offense to another level. Dallas had been without a 1,000-yard rusher since 1973 when Calvin Hill, a No. 1 draft choice in 1969, had gained 1,142 yards in 1973. In fact, Dallas had had a different leading rusher each of the previous three seasons.

So president Tex Schramm, coach Tom Landry, and Brandt began discussing ways to acquire Dorsett. The Cowboys had always been creative when it came to getting impact players they had targeted in the draft through trades.

That approach had yielded defensive linemen Bob Lilly, Ed "Too Tall" Jones, and defensive tackle Randy White. Schramm pulled off another coup days before the 1977 draft by shipping the Cowboys' first-round pick (No. 24 overall) and three second-round choices to Seattle for the second pick in the draft.

"We had a really good team, but we needed a running back with some speed and breakaway ability," Brandt said. "[Doug] Denison and [Robert] Newhouse weren't those types of backs. We had a good quarterback and good receivers, and we needed that one ingredient—Tony Dorsett—to make our offense special."

The trade, though, was contingent on Tampa Bay taking Bell.

"I was so happy," Dorsett said. "I wanted to play for America's Team."

Life in the NFL, though, was nothing like Tony Dorsett anticipated. For the first time, he was coming off the bench.

"It was frustrating. Part of the reason is that I wasn't starting," said Dorsett, who injured his knee in training camp, hindering his progress. "Tony Hill and I were sitting on the sideline almost falling asleep because we were so bored and frustrated at not starting.

"Tom would put me in, and I'd have a big run and then he'd take me out. The fans and media were expecting these things on a regular basis, but I wasn't even a starter. It was a little unfair to me, but it was understandable with all of the hype that came with the Heisman Trophy and an undefeated senior season at Pitt that ended with a national championship."

Veteran Preston Pearson entered the season as the starter, but Dorsett had consistent playing time. It just wasn't as much as he liked.

Part of the reason is that Landry didn't like playing rookies because young players inevitably make mistakes that can cost teams games. He also thought Dorsett needed better practice habits. There were too many dropped passes and missed assignments for his liking.

Tony Dorsett carries the ball in Super Bowl XIII. © *Vernon J. Biever Photo*

Landry also wanted to protect Dorsett, who had gained 30 pounds since arriving at Pitt as a 155-pound freshman. Still, he was small by NFL standards, and Landry wanted to limit his carries and receptions to ensure his body withstood the rigors of a 14-game NFL season.

Even with limited opportunities, Dorsett's talent still flashed.

There was a 34-yard run against the New York Giants in week 2, and a 10-carry, 72-yard performance against Tampa Bay the following week.

"The first time I saw Tony on the field," Newhouse said, "the first thing that went through my mind is that he was faster than Bob Hayes. That was unbelievable."

As the Cowboys prepared for an important divisional game against St. Louis, Dorsett and the coaching staff, particularly running backs coach Dan Reeves, found themselves at odds. Reeves wanted Dorsett to run an off-tackle play the way it was designed against the Cardinals defense. Dorsett wanted to run where his eyes told him to go.

"On their defense there's no way it's going to cutback behind the center," Reeves said. "It will never in 100 years open up like that."

"I'm just running to what I see," Dorsett said.

The debate continued the rest of the week. On Sunday, Landry called the off-tackle play on first-and-10 from the Dallas 23. Dorsett broke two tackles and sprinted 77 yards for a touchdown, breaking Amos Bullocks' 15-year team record in the process for longest run (73 yards).

"Bam, I'm gone exactly the way they said it would never happen," Dorsett said. "I just have a big grin on my face when I get to the sideline, and I'm looking for Coach Reeves and he says, 'I know, I know. I said it would never happen in 100 years, but I guess it did.'"

Dorsett finished with 14 carries for 141 yards—only 12 yards shy of Calvin Hill's team record. Despite the big day, Reeves and the Cowboys continued to try to corral Dorsett's instincts, frustrating the rookie runner.

During one game, Dorsett blew up on the sideline when backup quarterback Steve Pelluer handed him a headset and told him that Reeves wanted to speak with him.

"You drafted me as a runner. Let me run," Dorsett shouted. "I'm tired of being a robot."

Finally, Landry concurred. The day after his blowup, Landry addressed the offense in a team meeting.

"I'll never forget it," Newhouse said. "Coach Landry said, 'Guys, usually the back has to adjust to our offense, but we're going to adjust to Dorsett and let him run to daylight.'

"I couldn't believe it. He changed the whole scheme and philosophy for one guy—Tony Dorsett—and it worked out perfectly. I realized Tony had special ability and if we carried out our assignments things would work out."

Although Dorsett appreciated Landry acquiescing to his talent, he didn't like being a backup, and it affected his attitude and his approach to practice.

"By the eighth or ninth week of the season, I had convinced myself I'm not going to be a starter so I had kind of written this season off," Dorsett said, "and I was determined to go to training camp the next year and win me a starting job. I was kind of nonchalant. I'd drop a pass in practice and say, 'It's no big deal. I'll catch it on Sunday.'"

The Cowboys won their first eight games before St. Louis beat Dallas 24-17. The following week, Landry called Dorsett into his office after practice for a 10-minute discussion.

"We expected you to be starting by now," Landry said.

"Coach, I expected to be a starter too," Dorsett replied.

Landry told Dorsett he wanted him to practice with more intensity and pay more attention to detail. Landry didn't want Dorsett making mental mistakes or dropping passes or playing with a laissez-faire attitude.

Then Landry told him, "If you do all of these things, you'll probably start Sunday."

Dorsett's replied, "Coach, I wish you had called me in and told me this a long time ago."

Dorsett gained 73 yards on 17 carries and scored on a 13-yard touchdown run off right tackle in the 28-13 loss to the Steelers. Two games later, he took the first step toward becoming a star in an important NFC East game against Philadelphia, which could clinch the club's second consecutive division title.

He gained a franchise-record 206 yards that included an 84-yard touchdown run in the fourth quarter. It was the longest run by a Cowboys player and set a franchise record for yards in a game that would last 16 years until Emmitt Smith, the NFL's all-time leading rusher, broke it with a 237-yard performance, ironically, against the Eagles on a rainy day in 1993.

"A lot of guys had wiggle, but Dorsett had raw speed," said Herman Edwards, a rookie cornerback with Philadelphia in 1977 and now the Kansas City Chiefs head coach. "He was fast—so fast—that you never got a big hit on him because you had to slow down and gather yourself, or he'd be gone and you'd have nothing."

Dorsett's performance left him with 865 yards and 11 touchdowns, tying Duane Thomas' franchise record, putting him in position to surpass the 1,000-yard mark.

"I never even thought about gaining 1,000 yards or winning Rookie of the Year or anything because I had pretty much written the season off," Dorsett said. "I was just glad to finally be in the starting lineup and contribute because there had been so much written that I was the final piece to the puzzle—but how can I be the final piece if I'm not on the field … I'm not Superman."

GAME OF MY LIFE
By Tony Dorsett

Before the game I was scared to death because I was late. I was starting, and I was late because I took the wrong route to the game. By the time I got to the stadium, they had already gone through pregame warmups and returned to the locker room.

I had to park on other side of the stadium because I went in the wrong way, so I ran across a bridge just to get into the stadium. Then I ran through stands—it was on the opposite end from our locker room—and people were yelling, "Hey, T.D." and wishing me good luck, but all I could think about was getting into the locker room.

When I finally got there, I was sweating bullets because I just knew Tom was going to fine me and bench me. But a calmness came over the coaches when I finally showed up. They didn't even yell at me, but I still excitedly tried to explain to them that I got caught in all this traffic and then I tried to take some shortcuts and got lost, but they told me to forget about it and put my uniform on.

Normally, I'd go through the game plan before the game. Some guys would be laughing and joking, but that's not how I liked to prepare for a game. I would find a corner, put my headphones on, and go through every play—how I would react if it didn't turn out the way it was supposed to.

It was important to do that because your mind will recall whatever you put in it. Some of the things I did on the football field were instinctive, but some were planned through visualization. I didn't have an opportunity to do that before this game, so I was just reacting to what I saw.

It turned out to be a great game for us and for me.

The Eagles had just hired Dick Vermeil to coach, and they were trying to change their losing culture, but they had some good players like middle linebacker Bill Bergey and defensive end Carl Hairston. Besides, everybody played their best game against the Dallas Cowboys because of the success we had experienced over the years.

I remember Billy Joe DuPree and Harvey Martin telling me about the NFC East before the season. They told me we'd probably beat Philadelphia and New York, but to buckle up my chinstrap because those games were going to be all-out wars. They said those teams would try to physically beat us up because they weren't quite as good.

We put in some special plays that week just for Philadelphia: "Eagle Special" that we ran from a split back formation and "Eagle Special 1" that we ran from the I-formation.

"Eagle Special" was a trap play where tight end Jay Saldi had the key block. He was in the slot, and he came in motion. The ball was snapped before he crossed the center so he could trap the nose tackle Art Thomas and I would dive in right behind that block.

I got a couple of long runs on that play, and it turned out to be the most productive game of my 12-year career.

I felt like I was in the zone that day. It was a feeling I had several times in my career. It was a feeling where you think whatever play they call was going to be successful. You got into a good groove. You got a feel for what the defense was doing and they couldn't stop you.

I had a long run early in the game that set up a field goal on "Eagle Special" and in the fourth quarter, I got another one that clinched the game.

I got good blocks from Jay, Pat Donovan, and Ralph Neely, and as I got into the secondary, somebody clipped me and I stumbled a little bit. But Drew Pearson blocked Herman Edwards—it seemed like Drew was always with me on those long runs—and I pretty much outran everybody else.

After the game Coach Landry kind of made a joke about the situation. He said, "We're not going to fine you, and maybe you should be late more often."

————————————————

After their two-game losing streak in the middle of the season, the Cowboys won their last four games to post a 12-2 record entering the playoffs.

Tony Dorsett was getting better every game.

He became the eighth rookie in NFL history to surpass the 1,000-yard mark in the regular-season finale, a 14-6 win over Denver, which tied Dallas for the NFL's best record at 12-2. Dorsett finished the season with 1,007 yards and 12 touchdowns, establishing a new rookie record for touchdowns.

He didn't slow down in the playoffs with 85 yards on 17 carries and touchdown runs of 7 and 23 yards in a 37-7 rout of Chicago. He added an 11-yard touchdown run in a methodical 23-6 win over Minnesota in the NFC championship game, sending the Cowboys to the Super Bowl against Denver. The Broncos were led by former Cowboys quarterback Craig Morton.

"The Super Bowl was the highlight of my career. I was setting myself up for failure because you can't help but go down after the year I had," Dorsett said with a chuckle. "My senior year in college we won the national championship and I won the Heisman Trophy, and here I was my rookie year going back to the same stadium playing for a world championship in the National Football League."

Denver, an original American Football League franchise, had never been any good. They didn't even break .500 until 1973, their 14th season of existence, when they finished 7-5-2. In 1977, they set a franchise record for victories with a powerful defense nicknamed "The Orange Crush."

None of that impressed Dallas.

"We had Doomsday II, and they were going to put a lot of pressure on Craig Morton," Dorsett said. "He wasn't a mobile guy and we had a fierce rush from our front four, so we were very confident that we were going to come out as world champions because our defense was going to give us the ball in position to score."

Dorsett gave Dallas a 7-0 lead with 10:31 left in the first quarter on a 3-yard run. The lead swelled to 13-0 before halftime. He left the game with a knee injury at the end of the third quarter after netting 66 yards on 15 carries.

"I was down on my stomach with my leg up relaxed and my knee was bent, and one of their lineman came smashing down on top of my leg. This whistle had already blown," Dorsett said. "I was off to a great start and I was thrilled to score the first touchdown, and then I got hurt in the second quarter because I was going to go well over 100 yards because it was really clicking."

Tony Dorsett has always had an entrepreneurial spirit. His father, who toiled in the steel mines of western Pennsylvania, provided the inspiration. West Dorsett always told his son to find a better way of life.

"I never wanted to be in the steel mills, but that was the thing to do when you got out of high school or summer break, or when you came of age, you went to work in the steel mills."

The image of his father emerging from the mills one day helped drive home the point. Covered in dirt and grime so thick, Dorsett couldn't recognize the man who pulled a set of keys from his pocket and handed them to his wide-eyed son.

"He would tell me, 'Son, you don't want to want to work here because you might not come out. If you do, you might be missing an eye or a finger. Anything can happen to you down here,'" Dorsett said. "'This is not a life you want.'"

Dorsett took his father's words to heart. He's been involved in several businesses since his career ended in 1987—some succeeded; others failed. But his standard of living has never changed.

"I'm so blessed and I'm so thankful and appreciative for all that I have. I have seen so many tragedies involving players in all sports where their finances and reputation is gone, and it robs them of their pride and self-esteem," Dorsett said. "I've been lucky. I've been in the right place at the right time to maintain my lifestyle even better than when I was playing.

"I'm happy and I'm very, very proud to have accomplished what I've accomplished. To not make that work for me would've been a real tragedy."

Today, Dorsett lives in a gated community in suburban Dallas with his wife and three young daughters. His son, Anthony, who played in the NFL for seven seasons is a frequent visitor.

Dorsett is busier now than he's ever been.

He works with fellow Ring of Honor members Mel Renfro and Rayfield Wright at First Team Lending, a Dallas-based mortgage company, and he is a spokesman for several local and national products that require him to make appearances all over the country.

"Being in Dallas and being one of those visible guys on America's Team, you should always be able to get by. People still recognize me all over the country and all over the world," Dorsett said. "Sometimes, I say it could be better because I'm not maximizing what I could do, but you only need so much to be happy. I'm very proud of who I am and what I am."

CHAPTER 11

DREW PEARSON

Football has always been important in South River, New Jersey—Exit 9 off the Jersey turnpike to the locals.

Tradition made it that way.

South River, nestled between New York City and Philadelphia, was the hometown of Alex Wojciechowicz, one of the famed seven blocks of granite who starred at Fordham. And South River High School usually had one of the state's best football teams.

There were also competitive teams in other Middlesex County towns such as East Brunswick and New Brunswick.

So Drew Pearson learned to love the game at an early age. After all, there wasn't much a kid could do on Saturday morning in South River besides gather up his buddies and pick a sport to play. Sometimes, the games took place on the fields at the high school or the elementary school. Other times, the kids gathered on the empty lot next to Joey Theismann's house.

"We were just a bunch of kids playing ball," said Theismann, who earned a Super Bowl ring as the Washington Redskins quarterback in 1982. "It didn't matter what religion, race, or color you were. It was so great sharing life with those guys because you met them in grammar school and they were your friends until you graduated from high school.

"When Drew and I were in school together, South River was Mayberry, RFD. It was an unbelievably eclectic town with a lot of characters and cultures because that's where a lot of our parents and grand-parents had settled when they came to America."

Samuel and Minnie Pearson ran a disciplined home where education was important and their children learned responsibility and accountability. Samuel Pearson dabbled in local politics and named his son after Drew Pearson, whose syndicated political column, "The Merry Go Round," was required reading for those interested in politics for decades.

"We said, 'Yes, sir' and 'No, sir.' We had manners at the dinner table, and we respected adults and authority," Pearson said. "My father whipped us. My mother whipped us. They both taught us about hard work."

Those lessons helped make Pearson a star on the football field. In three seasons, his team lost two games and tied another. As a sophomore, Pearson and Theismann, a senior quarterback, helped South River go 9-0.

"I always wanted Drew on my side. I don't know why anybody recruited me because Drew made all the plays," Theismann said. "We'd run the same route every game—a post from the left side off a play-action—and he'd catch the ball for a touchdown.

"He was a phenomenal athlete whether it was basketball, baseball, or football. Drew could do anything he wanted athletically."

Pearson said there was nothing better than being a star on the football team in South River.

"If you played football, you were a stud because it was such a big deal," Pearson said. "Football games on Saturday afternoons were big. The stands were packed and people flowed onto the sidelines.

"Every Saturday morning, I'd walk downtown to the Ben Franklin Five and Dime and get new shoelaces and new white socks for the game."

Theismann went to Notre Dame, where he became a star. Pearson spent his senior year deciding between Nebraska and Tulsa, which was going to let him play baseball, his favorite sport.

"I was a loner, and I just wanted to get away. I didn't want to go in-state," Pearson said. "When I called the coach and told him I was coming to Tulsa, he was surprised because he didn't expect it. I was supposed to be the quarterback, but I didn't want to play quarterback, I wanted to be a receiver.

"Nebraska went to Orange Bowls and Sugar Bowls. Our only claim to fame at Tulsa was my junior year when we beat Arkansas 21-20 when they were ranked in the top 10."

Pearson played quarterback for two seasons before switching to receiver and catching 55 passes his last two seasons.

"I knew I wasn't going to be a quarterback in the pros," Pearson said. "I had a good arm, but I wasn't a pro quarterback."

When he didn't get drafted, Pearson sifted through several free-agent offers. Green Bay and Pittsburgh offered more money, but he knew the Cowboys had a reputation for keeping free agents, so he signed with Dallas.

"We didn't know how Drew was going to turn out, but he had great work habits and he ran good routes even though he wasn't fast," Cowboys personnel director Gil Brandt said. "He had a lot of other offers, but he signed with us."

By the time his career ended, Pearson had become one of the finest players in franchise history.

––––––––––––

The way Drew Pearson saw it, Danny White wanted to establish his own identity. Pearson couldn't blame him for that since White had spent four years on the bench waiting for the opportunity that finally arrived after the 1979 season, when Roger Staubach retired.

But it meant Pearson didn't see as many passes directed his way as he did with Staubach at quarterback. After all, Staubach and Pearson shared a bond that White really couldn't have been expected to immediately establish.

In fact, it appeared White was building that chemistry with Tony Hill, the wide receiver opposite Pearson. Hill had caught more passes and gained more yards than Pearson in 1977 and 1978, but their statistics had always been comparable. In 1978, each went over the 1,000-yard mark.

In 1980, White's first year as the starter, Hill caught 60 passes for 1,055 yards and eight touchdowns, while Pearson grabbed 43 passes for 568 yards and three touchdowns.

"All season long, I struggled to find identity. Danny wanted to establish his own go-to guy, and Tony Hill caught a lot of balls and did a great job," Pearson said. "Danny didn't necessarily want me to be his go-to guy because I was Roger's guy. When Butch [Johnson] came in on third down, Danny would go to Butch a lot, but I accepted it because we were winning."

And because he had more on his mind than football.

His father, Samuel Pearson, was fighting a losing battle with lung cancer, and it took a toll on his son. It began in the summer, when Drew and his father made the weekly 30-minute drive to New York City for chemotherapy sessions.

"I was with him all summer and watched how drained and lifeless he was after the chemo sessions," Pearson said. "You keep those memories and visions in your head, and when you get smacked over the middle, it hurts, but it doesn't hurt as bad as what my dad was going through."

He used those memories as inspiration during the season. There were a lot of emotional phone calls home and lengthy conversations with God, but Samuel didn't get any better. Pearson found support in teammates like Hill, Harvey Martin, Tony Dorsett, and coach Tom Landry.

"I had been going back and forth all season long. It was a trying season for me because of all that," Pearson said. "After we played the Giants up there [in a 38-35 loss], Coach Landry let me stay over and come back on Wednesday."

Two weeks later, the Cowboys beat Washington 14-10. At halftime, the Cowboys informed Pearson that his father had died.

"I left the team after the game and was gone that whole week, and Coach Landry pissed me off because he started Butch since I hadn't practiced all week and he thought I was emotionally drained," Pearson said. "It was tough, but you have to be a pro, and the one thing my father would want me to do is play. We held off the funeral for an extra day so I could come back and play against Seattle [in a 51-7 victory].

"I played the game and flew right back to do the funeral the next day. That's what my father would've wanted. The rest of the season, it was like he was with me on the field, guiding me and letting me make those plays."

White proved to be more than a capable replacement for Staubach, passing for 3,287 yards with 28 touchdowns and 25 interceptions. The Cowboys scored 454 points—28.3 points per game—and ranked ninth in the NFL.

"One of the reasons Roger left is he knew the team was in good hands," Pearson said. "He felt Danny White was ready, and he knew we still had a lot of good players on offense and defense.

"The only question was how Danny was going to adjust as the starter. We had confidence in Danny because we had worked with him for a number of years and we knew he could do it. We always felt he was going to be a starting quarterback in the NFL.

"The only thing we were concerned about was whether he would try to do too much to fill Roger's shoes."

Cowboys personnel director Gil Brandt said there was some trepidation when White became the starter.

"You're always going to have some doubt until a person does it," Brandt said. "Roger was the best. It's hard to replace a guy like that."

The Cowboys never lost consecutive games and finished 12-4, tied with Philadelphia for first place in the NFC East. The Eagles won their first division title in 20 years on the fifth tiebreaker—points scored against division opponents—when Dallas failed to beat them by more than 25 points in the final game of the season at Texas Stadium.

Dallas won 35-27, but led 35-10 with more than 10 minutes left in the fourth quarter.

"Each year, Coach Landry used to give us two goals—a reasonable goal and an outstanding goal. The reasonable goal was to win the NFC East; the outstanding goal was to win the Super Bowl," Pearson said. "Any other year we would've won the East, but Dick Vermeil had Philadelphia playing better than it had in a long time.

"It was disappointing, but we said we'll take this route. We've done it before. In 1975, we were the first team to take the wild-card route to the Super Bowl. We figured we'd do it again."

GAME OF MY LIFE
By Drew Pearson

The Falcons didn't get to the playoffs much, but they had a great season with Steve Bartkowski at quarterback, Gerald Riggs at running back, and Alfred Jenkins at receiver. The whole state was in a frenzy because the Georgia Bulldogs had won the national championship with Herschel Walker, and they were going crazy.

Normally, you were lucky to get a full crowd when you played in Atlanta, but this time when we went out early for pregame warmups, the fans were going crazy. We knew it was going to be a tough game. In fact, the last thing Coach Landry said when we were getting ready to leave the locker room was, "It's wild out there. Let's see where we are when the dust settles."

When the dust settled, we were down 14-0, and if the Falcons had kept throwing the ball, they probably would've blown us out because we would've never recovered. They were throwing the ball and attacking our cornerbacks.

We had a lot of smart defensive backs like Dennis Thurman, Steve Wilson, and Charlie Waters, but they weren't fast, and the Falcons just kept taking shots deep. Instead of trying to pound the ball with Riggs like we expected, they were throwing it, and Bartkowski was hot. But once they jumped out to that lead, they just stopped attacking. It was like they were trying to shorten the game and get it over.

We were only down by 10 at halftime, and we felt like we had weathered the storm, but they were still controlling the game. But it changed with about four minutes left, when we started deviating a little bit from what Coach Landry had wanted us to do. Coach Landry was calling the plays, but Danny was changing them, making adjustments and changing some of the routes.

Danny felt real confident that he could do that successfully, and as long as we were successful, Coach Landry didn't have a problem with it. Danny hadn't gone to me a lot during the season, but at that point in the game he knew where to go with the ball.

I scored my first touchdown when Danny and I ad-libbed. Danny was scrambling around to his right, and I was in the right corner of the end zone when Danny pointed for me to shoot across to the other side of the end zone. I made a jab step like I was going, Danny pumped, and the defender took off.

I figured that if I saw him, then the defensive backs saw him, too. It was like being on the playground again. If I faked it, I figured I could get open. It was a good pass because he threw it hard, and I caught it with my hands in a crowd.

Tony Hill was the first to grab me and hug me. Then he started pointing to the Falcons fans, and you could tell they were getting nervous. A lot of the players who had contributed to our mystique were still on the team so we had confidence we could score again and win the game.

It was a hot and humid night, and I started cramping during the last two drives. When the trainers came to the huddle on the last drive, I was cramping bad, even though I was drinking Gatorade and water and stretching and trying to stay loose. One of the trainers told me to pinch my lip because it has nerve endings and pinching it should release some of the tension in my legs, and it actually worked. I pinched my lip that whole last drive, and it helped me get loose enough to make the plays.

On the winning touchdown, I came across the backfield from left to right, and because of my movement, the cornerback covering couldn't get set. I was hot on the blitz—so was Tony Hill—and when I saw the linebacker disappear, I knew it was a blitz and I figured Danny would throw it to Tony.

I ran a quick post, and when I broke it in and looked back, the ball was already in the air. That was the whole blessing to the play. The defensive back didn't expect the ball to come that quickly, so he couldn't react. If Danny had waited to throw, they would've knocked it away, but he anticipated my route and put a lot of air on the pass. When I came out of my break, it was right there. As soon as I caught it, the safety bumped me, but I held on. It was total elation and total satisfaction. As a kid, you dream about succeeding in those kinds of situations.

———————————

The Cowboys played Philadelphia for the third time on a frigid day at Veterans Stadium where the wind-chill registered 17 degrees below zero.

They didn't have much of a chance—and it had nothing to do with the "bad luck" blue jerseys.

Tied at 7-7 at halftime, Philadelphia turned a pair of turnovers into a 10-point lead en route to a 20-7 victory.

"Because of the weather and the state of their field, most of our pregame talk and adjustments were about what cleats and undergarments we were going to wear," Pearson said. "I think we lost a little focus early in the football game, and they did a number on us.

"They were more physical on us, and we couldn't get anything going offensively. It was a tough day. We thought we could win, but we knew we would have to overcome some big odds."

Dallas also lost in the NFC championship game each of the next two years.

"It's devastating when you get that close because you don't know if you're going to get there again because you don't want to blow those opportunities," he said. "A lot of us were getting toward the end of our careers, and we didn't know how many more times we could get there.

"I played in seven NFC championship games in 11 years and lost four of them. You're happy that you played in that many big games, but it's disappointing when you reflect on them. We played to win it all. Getting close wasn't enough for us."

Pearson's career ended in the spring of 1984, when he fell asleep at the wheel of his car and plowed into the back of an 18-wheeler parked on the side of the road. He suffered several injuries, including a lacerated liver. His younger brother, Carey, died.

"It was devastating because I wasn't about to retire. I was about to sign a new contract when the accident happened," Pearson said. "It was tough to give up, but my brother gave up his life, so I had to keep it in perspective.

"That's what made it OK for me. I didn't want it to end like that. But when you look at the whole picture—you're here and he's not—if that's what I have to give up, then OK."

Pearson worked for CBS for a year before attempting a comeback. He had passed a physical from his doctor, but the Cowboys wanted him to see one more specialist in Pittsburgh.

Drew Pearson carries the ball upfield against the San Francisco 49ers at Candlestick Park. *Andy Hayt/Getty Images*

"He said my liver was 99 percent OK. He wouldn't give me 100 percent," Pearson said. "He said even if I got hit on the liver and it started hemorrhaging, that it wouldn't be a life-and-death situation, but that wasn't enough for Coach Landry.

"Because of the type of receiver I was, he said it might cause some doubts in my mind if I wasn't 100 percent, and that might make me a different player. We discussed it for a long time over the phone, and I finally said, 'Coach, you're right. I wish I could do it. I want to do it, but if I can't do it the way I used to, then I don't want to.'"

That's when Landry asked Pearson to join the coaching staff. He left after a year.

Although he was moving on with his life, Pearson didn't always handle the grief well.

"The car wreck is with me every day. I was taking my younger brother to my brother Andre's house because it was late and I was going out of town all weekend," Pearson said. "Every time I drive past that patch of land, I feel it as I approach it and I really feel it when I go past the area where it all happened and I feel better when I get past it.

"It's something that will always be with me and something I don't try to forget. I try to use it. Sometimes, it provides the motivation for why I'm still here."

The death of his father, his brother, a sister, and his mother gradually made him withdraw further and further from the celebrity status he had known as one of the clutch performers in professional sports.

Pearson had always been a loner—even as a teenager—so he sought comfort in his own thoughts and emotions. He declined autograph shows and Cowboys functions. He skipped family reunions and rarely left his home.

"I would get dressed to go out and get to the place and go right back home because I didn't want to deal with people. It wore me down for years," Pearson said. "I went through some serious depression, although I didn't know that's what I was going through.

"I never had a chance to talk to anybody about it and let it out. Sometimes your high profile and your status and celebrity work against you as far as people being honest with you and talking to you—even your family. They don't want to upset you so they're not honest with you. My family wouldn't tell me how they felt, and that hurt. Are they mad? Is it OK? I just wanted to know."

A *Sports Illustrated* article on how Terry Bradshaw and Ricky Williams dealt with depression helped set Pearson free.

"I was going through a tough time until I read the article and I said, 'Man that sounds just like me,'" Pearson said. "I went to see a doctor, and he said I was suffering from depression—and the root of it was the car accident. I've been on medication ever since and things have been great."

When Drew Pearson's NFL career ended, he took the skills he had learned from observing one of the most successful organizations in sports and started his own business: Drew Pearson Marketing.

In 2005, Pearson's business grossed $50 million and sold 30 million hats.

"Drew Pearson Marketing is pretty much built on the same business model as the Dallas Cowboys, because the only business education I had was 11 years as a player and one year as a coach," Pearson said. "When I coached, I saw how they ran the business and why it was successful. I didn't know I was going to get into business, but I observed just in case it came in handy one day.

"When you look at the front office, Tex [Schramm], Tom [Landry], and Gil [Brandt] had three totally different personalities, but they worked well together because they brought expertise from three different areas to make the business work. It's not about getting along; it's about getting the right people.

"Coach Landry would get players—not always the big names—but people who would fit what we wanted to do. They were smart, disciplined, and had intangibles. When I started my business, I took the same approach."

The seed for Drew Pearson Marketing was planted when Pearson contacted Mike Russell and Ken Shead midway through the 1985 football season. Weary of the 18-hour days, he wanted more information on a hat-manufacturing venture they had pitched to him several times.

Less than a week after the season ended, Drew Pearson Marketing was born.

"It was their idea, and it was their business acumen that got it started because I didn't know a lot about business," Pearson said. "We made a lot of mistakes. A lot of times when you make the mistakes we made, it can cost you."

The turning point occurred in 1990, when the company was about to fold.

"We merged with another company and got a $500,000 infusion of capital because they did apparel and they needed hats to go with it," Pearson said. "That got us over the hump. We had loyalty and continuity on the Cowboys, and that gave us structure, and that's what we tried to do with our business, so when storms came, we could weather them and handle them."

Dave Briskie now runs the day-to-day operation. When he arrived, 90 percent of the company's revenues were tied up in pro sports. He wanted more diversity, and now the company has licensing agreements with companies such as Disney, Warner Brothers, and Lucas Films in addition to brands like Dr Pepper and Tide.

"I'm surprised and happy that it has turned out the way it has," Pearson said. "I'm indebted to the guys who started with me because I shudder to think what I would've done with my life after football if it hadn't turned out this way."

CHAPTER 12

RANDY WHITE

Guy White taught his son work ethic. Six days a week the former World War II Navy paratrooper left home before dawn and spent 14-hour days cutting and packaging meat as a butcher to provide for his family.

LaVerne White taught her son toughness. She believed in fighting through adversity—not giving in. "When things get tough, stick it out and push," LaVerne was fond of saying. In other words, try harder. And if that doesn't work, try even harder.

Randy White absorbed those lessons as a youth in Wilmington, Delaware, and they helped him develop into one of the best to ever play the game.

"The fear of embarrassing myself was the most important factor to me. I just never wanted to do that," White said. "When I was a kid, my dad said if you're gonna do something, do it right. If you're gonna do it half-assed, then don't do it at all. If you start something, you never quit.

"My mom is a tough gal. I've seen her have fist fights. She likes sports, and she expresses her opinions. You never wondered what she was thinking. She and my dad came from a small coal-mining town in Pennsylvania. They were regular people, but they were tough."

They instilled that trait in their son.

It's one of the reasons White loved football. He could take all of his frustrations out on the field. He could hit people as hard as he wanted, and there were no repercussions.

White, a 210-pound fullback and linebacker in high school, had three Division I scholarship offers in football. Arizona State wanted him, but that was too far from home. White was used to his parents attending every game, and he didn't want that to change. He had even become accustomed to his father's occasional outbursts at halftime.

"Sometimes, he'd meet me at the gate and say, 'They're kicking your ass,'" White said. "Other times, if I played good, he'd give me some money. It was kind of like an incentive-based contract."

Virginia Tech was interested, but White wasn't. Maryland seemed the best fit because it was only 90 minutes from Wilmington. First-year coach Jerry Claiborne didn't go out of his way to recruit White, but he needed players to rebuild a program that had one winning campaign in the past nine seasons.

"We don't know if you can play here or not, Randy," Claiborne told White and his father, "but we're going to give you a scholarship."

Committing to football meant White had to give up baseball.

The Philadelphia Phillies and Baltimore Orioles each wanted the hard-hitting first baseman, who had batted over .500 in each of his last three seasons, to concentrate on baseball. Each offered him a minor-league contract. The Phillies offered him $30,000 to sign.

"To me, that was all of the money in the world," White said, "but my father told them I wasn't going to play baseball because I was going to college to play football. That was the end of my organized baseball career."

As a youth, White collected football cards. He studied the information on the back of the cards to figure out if he was going to get big enough to play professional football.

That type of dedication helped make him a better player and Maryland a winner. In his last two seasons, Maryland went 16-8 and participated in its first bowl game since 1955. As a senior, the two-time All-American won the Outland Trophy and the Lombardi Trophy, signifying his place among college football's elite players.

Then he waited for the NFL draft.

All indications were the Baltimore Colts were going to take him with the first pick of the draft. Then the Colts traded their No. 1 pick to Atlanta, which selected quarterback Steve Bartkowski.

In October 1974, a year after Roger Staubach became Dallas' full-time starter, the Cowboys traded Craig Morton to the New York Giants for their top draft pick. The Giants finished the 1974 season 2-12, tied with the Colts for the worst record in the NFL, giving Dallas the second selection in the draft.

The Cowboys, who had missed the playoffs for the first time since 1965, needed a running back. But they passed on Jackson State's Walter Payton and selected White.

"The Baltimore Colts kept telling me they were going to take me No. 1, then they traded their pick to Atlanta and here I was going to Dallas," White said. "I didn't really care where I played. I was just excited I was going to have the opportunity to play professional football because it had been a dream of mine forever."

The Cowboys viewed him as a linebacker.

There was precedence. In the 1950s, when he was the Giants' defensive coordinator, Landry converted Sam Huff from a college defensive end into a Hall of Fame linebacker.

Landry figured he could do the same thing with White, who at 6 feet, 4 inches and 240 pounds was undersized to play defensive tackle in the NFL. Besides, White had 4.6-second speed in the 40-yard dash.

The Cowboys had Larry Cole, Bill Gregory, and Jethro Pugh at defensive tackle, so they were set. And they had Ed "Too Tall" Jones and Harvey Martin as defensive ends, so they didn't need help there, either.

Middle linebacker Lee Roy Jordan was in his mid-30s, and the Cowboys thought White would be his eventual replacement.

"When I played, you didn't ask nothing. You don't question—even if you don't like it, you don't say nothing. I just wanted to play football," White said. "It was frustrating for me at middle linebacker.

"Lee Roy Jordan coached me every day, and it just never was a natural position because in the Flex the middle linebacker had to make a lot of reads and play a lot of pass coverage. I was thinking rather than playing, and when you're thinking, you're always a beat off."

———————————————

Coach Tom Landry called Randy White into his office before the third preseason game in 1977 and admitted moving him to linebacker had been a failure.

He informed White that he was moving him to defensive tackle. Simultaneously, it seemed, joy and anxiety filled his body.

Those two years at middle linebacker, developed White into a more cerebral player. At middle linebacker, he was the quarterback of the defense. That meant he had to know every other defensive player's responsibility. Playing defensive tackle, he used that knowledge to his

Randy White (left) and Harvey Martin were named co-MVPs of Super Bowl XII. © *Vernon J. Biever Photo*

advantage because he knew when to improvise and be aggressive within the framework of the scheme and when to do it by the book.

Larry Cole and Bill Gregory shared the tackle position next to right defensive end Harvey Martin in 1975 and 1976. When White became the full-time starter in 1977, he and Martin became one of the game's most dominant tandems.

Martin, who had totaled 24 sacks the previous two seasons, set a franchise record with 23 sacks. White totaled 118 tackles and 13 sacks. The duo forced offensive coordinators to spend long hours adjusting their pass-protection schemes and devising ways to control White and Martin.

"It was like somebody took handcuffs off of me because I could go after the guy with the ball and I could rush the quarterback," he said. "It was a natural position, even though I was undersized because I made up for it by being quick and strong."

The Cowboys rode their defensive tandem to an 8-0 start, the best in franchise history. It helped that rookie running back Tony Dorsett, the 1976 Heisman Trophy winner, infused the offense's big-play capability.

"Doug Denison ran with the heart of a lion in 1976. He was strong and tough, but he just wasn't a dynamic running back," said Brad Sham, a member of the Cowboys' radio team for more than 25 years. "Adding Tony Dorsett to the 1977 Cowboys had the same effect as adding Charles Haley before the 1992 season: It gave the team exactly what it needed."

Dorsett's ability made quarterback Roger Staubach and receivers Tony Hill and Drew Pearson better, because stopping the rookie running back became the top priority for defensive coordinators. Using a safety near the line of scrimmage, a ploy defenses used to slow Dorsett, gave Staubach and his receivers more room to maneuver.

Although the Cowboys ranked fourth in the NFL in total offense in 1976, they scored only 34 touchdowns and 296 points. It represented their lowest point total since 1964, when they scored 250 points. They ranked 12th in the NFL in rushing (153.3 yards per game), their lowest ranking since the expansion season of 1960.

With Dorsett, Dallas scored 42 touchdowns and totaled 345 points. They led the NFL in total offense and ranked fourth in rushing and passing offense.

The defense was just as dominant.

The Cowboys led the NFL in total defense, allowing just 15.1 points per game as Landry and defensive coordinator Ernie Stautner guided a revamped unit.

Bob Breunig replaced middle linebacker Lee Roy Jordan, who had retired, and Thomas Henderson moved into Breunig's starting job at left outside linebacker. Aaron Kyle replaced Mel Renfro in the starting line-up at right cornerback.

But White's shift had the biggest impact.

"When they moved Randy next to Harvey, it was like they let the animal out of the cage," Sham said. "The things he did to other players just weren't fair. There was nobody like him."

Dallas finished the season 12-2, and its defense turned in one of the most dominating performances in Super Bowl history. White and Martin were named co–Most Valuable Players after forcing eight turnovers in a 27-10 victory over Denver. It's the only time that's ever happened.

The victory gave the NFC its first Super Bowl champion in six seasons, while Landry joined Vince Lombardi, Don Shula, and Chuck Noll as the only coaches to win two Super Bowls.

"I was happy for Coach Landry. We carried him off the field," White said. "I was a young player, but I wanted him to win because I knew what it felt like to lose a Super Bowl. Even though we were the second-best team in all of football in 1975, we felt like losers."

GAME OF MY LIFE

By Randy White

Every year Coach Landry gave us two goals: A reasonable goal and an outstanding goal. In 1977, our realistic goal was to get to the Super Bowl. Our outstanding goal was to win it.

In 1975, our outstanding goal was to get to the Super Bowl. But that was the first time in my three seasons that our goal was to win the Super Bowl.

Denver had a great defense—the Orange Crush—but we knew as a defensive line that if we could pressure their quarterback, Craig Morton, and disrupt his timing, we'd be successful. That was our goal and we were able to do that.

We ran a few stunts that day, but Harvey Martin and I pretty much beat them straight up. Hey, a lot of guys had great games that day—not just Harvey and me. Ed Jones had a great day. Randy Hughes had a great day, intercepting a couple of passes and recovering a couple of fumbles.

Randy intercepted the first pass on a play where Ed and I hit Morton almost at the same time. Morton had a hip injury, I think, and he wasn't very mobile. You could go after him with reckless abandon because he wasn't going to beat you by scrambling down the field.

That kind of played into our hands because we were a good pass-rushing team. And when the offense got us points—we were leading 13-0 at halftime—and they had to throw, then we really had some fun. I got a lot of satisfaction playing the run good, but there's nothing better than pinning your ears back and rushing the passer.

When you're a player, the game is a blur. You're going as hard as you can until the clock runs out. You're not thinking about the last play—at least that's how I was. I played hard until the last play of the game whether we were winning by 20 or losing by 20. The Super Bowl wasn't any different, because it was still a game.

I was so happy at the end of the game because I was going to get a Super Bowl ring. A world championship ring. I never thought about the money or the MVP or anything. The ring is the only thing I thought about. It was my birthday, and I was so happy.

Then Harvey came up and hugged me—that picture ended up on the cover of *Sports Illustrated*—and said we were the Most Valuable Players in this game. The next morning, *Good Morning America* wanted us to come on their show, but I didn't get up and go. Harvey did.

To win the world championship was special because it's something no one can ever take away from you.

———————————————

White played in three Super Bowls in his first four NFL seasons. He figured that was life as a member of the Dallas Cowboys, where winning and Super Bowl appearances were standard fare.

In his four seasons, the Cowboys went 45-13 in the regular season with three straight NFC East titles. Even when the Cowboys started the season 6-4, White never panicked. He figured the Cowboys would find their rhythm and win another Super Bowl.

He was right. Sort of.

After committing six turnovers in a 23-16 loss—they trailed 17-0 after the first quarter—on the road to Miami, the Cowboys regrouped.

They won their last six regular-season games by a combined score of 184-61 with four victories by at least 20 points and another by 18. White contributed 123 tackles and 16 sacks. It turned out to be the best year of his career.

And when the Cowboys trounced the New York Jets 30-7 on the road in the final game, Landry made his thoughts known in a postgame news conference.

"Yes," he said, "this team is capable of winning the Super Bowl."

Dallas beat Atlanta (27-20) and Los Angeles (28-0) in the NFC championship, earning the right to defend its championship against the hated Pittsburgh Steelers.

"I thought we could beat them, no doubt," White said. "But when the clock ran out, they had more points than we did."

Pittsburgh beat the Cowboys 35-31 in Super Bowl XIII. The game changed midway through the third quarter, when Lynn Swann made a leaping catch in the back of the end zone for a touchdown that pushed the Steelers' lead to 28-17.

On the ensuing kickoff, Pittsburgh used a squib kick, and White scooped it up and fumbled. Franco Harris burst up the middle 22 yards for a touchdown on the next play and an insurmountable 35-17 lead.

"We never lost any of those Super Bowls or championship games because the other team was better," said Hall of Fame tackle Rayfield Wright, who was on the team from 1967 to 1980. "We lost those games because we made mistakes or didn't execute."

White said the botched kickoff still bothers him. He was supposed to lateral the ball, but the high school fullback said he took so long to pick it up that he decided to run with it.

"I remember fumbling the kickoff against the Steelers. Those are the ones that haunt you," he said. "I don't remember a lot of the great plays I made or the big games we won. I remember the bad plays and the losses.

"Every year around the Super Bowl, I gotta watch me fumble the kickoff, and it still makes me mad. Or I gotta watch The Catch by Dwight Clark."

After losing the Super Bowl, Dallas played in the NFC championship game three of the next four seasons. But White never played in another Super Bowl.

"I thought we'd be back in the Super Bowl a number of times," he said. "But I never got back. We never went again."

A herniated disk in his back, involving two vertebras pressing against his spinal cord, forced White to contemplate retirement. He knew where the ball was going and where he was supposed to be, but his body could no longer carry him to those intersections on a consistent basis.

In 1988, playing primarily as a pass rusher, he totaled 16 tackles and 1.5 sacks. His medical condition worsened, causing numbness in his right arm and back.

"My last two years I was kind of banged up and I couldn't really play at the level that I had before," he said. "It was pretty frustrating because I couldn't make it happen on the field anymore."

All those years of being tutored by Stautner had convinced White that he wanted to coach. He spoke to Landry about his post-career plans, and they decided that he would be a player-coach in 1989 to fulfill the last year of his contract and shift into a full-time coaching career.

"He told me, 'Randy, you've got a job here as long as I do,'" White recalled. "A few weeks later, he was fired.

"I went and talked to Jimmy Johnson, and he had his own people and his own staff, and there wasn't a spot for me, so that's when I retired from football."

He did so with 1,104 tackles and 111 sacks. Only safety Darren Woodson and Jordan have more tackles. Only Martin has more sacks.

More importantly, he had earned the right to be compared to Hall of Fame defensive tackle Bob Lilly.

"I don't say either one was better, but by comparison, Lilly was more up and down," Stautner told *Sports Illustrated* in 1994.

"Why was that?" a reporter asked.

"Lilly was human," Stautner said.

Talk to just about any NFL player, and he'll tell you there's no adrenaline rush like running out of the tunnel on game day with 65,000 raucous fans cheering you.

White was no different.

The trick, though, is to find something besides football that brings that same type of enjoyment. Do that and the transition after retirement goes much smoother.

White has done it better than most, but it still took a couple of years for him to find inner peace.

He's part owner of a telecommunications business and owns a restaurant that bears his name in a Dallas suburb. He does promotional work for several companies and still finds time to provide some instruction on football.

He has visited the University of Maryland and shown some of their defensive linemen and linebackers the hand movements and techniques he used to record five pro seasons with at least 10 sacks.

"When I retired from football, I was looking for that edge," White said. "Your whole life you get up on Sunday morning [and] you got that edge … that adrenaline rush. All of a sudden it's gone, so what do you do? I tried bull-dogging steers and riding cutting horses.

"I'd do everything within reason that I could physically do to get that same adrenaline rush that you get on the field. Other than watching my daughter being born, I could never find a feeling like you get walking onto the football field where every emotion inside your body is alive."

White resides in Prosper, Texas, about 40 miles north of Dallas on a ranch with his daughter, Jordan. It's a peaceful, happy existence.

"I'm very fortunate," he said. "I have stayed busy doing different things since I have been retired, and I've had a good time."

CHAPTER 13

ED "TOO TALL" JONES

Jack Jones worked hard on a farm on the outskirts of Jackson, Tennessee, to support his wife, Abbie, and their eight children.

There was always so much to do—tend to the crops, feed the animals, repair equipment—that he rarely had free time. When he did, he used it to listen to boxing matches on the radio with his son, Ed.

Sonny Liston, nicknamed "The Bear," was Jack's guy.

"I remember when Ali fought Sonny Liston and how much it hurt my dad when he lost," said Ed "Too Tall" Jones. "My dad was from the South, and Sonny represented a dream for us. He let people go to work with their heads up. Ali was all mouth. No one knew if he had staying power or if he was just a guy who talked a lot.

"That was a time when a lot of fights weren't televised. So we listened to them on the radio, and I watched the expression on his face and how excited he'd get, and I just kind of fell in love with [the sport]."

Jack Jones wasn't the only father in Jackson with a fondness for boxing.

"When we got in trouble as kids in the country, the fathers would make a ring with fertilizer and tell us to get out there and fight," Ed Jones said. "They'd sit around with cigars and watch us and laugh. I guess the joy I saw on their faces from watching us box is where my love affair with boxing started."

When he wasn't boxing as a teenager, Jones starred in basketball, baseball, and track at East High School, which didn't have enough boys to field a football team.

Tragedy gave Jones an opportunity to play football.

"I had a basketball game one night, and all of us except my dad went to it," said Jones. "When we got home, the lights were on, the door was open, the kitchen table was knocked to the side, and my dad wasn't there. We knew something was wrong.

"One of the neighbors said, 'Your dad got sick, and the ambulance came and got him.' We walked into the emergency room past a lady who knew us, and she said, 'Your dad is gone.'"

The information didn't initially register.

"Gone where?" Jones asked the woman.

"Son, he's passed," she said, grabbing Jones and hugging him.

With no one to run the farm, Abbie Jones moved her family to the city, and Ed transferred to Merry High School, a traditional football power, for his senior year.

"My high school football coach was also my basketball coach, and he let me try out for the football team," Jones said. "But the only reason he let me try out was because my brother-in-law was one of the coaches."

James Mathews, nicknamed Big Red, always thought Ed would be a good football player because of his size and athleticism, but he didn't play him much.

"He didn't want me to get hurt, but I could tell from practicing that I liked it," Jones said. "In basketball, I couldn't do anything because I was always getting called for fouls; I was so much bigger than everyone else. In football, I could throw forearms and hit players and nothing happened. Football was fun."

Jones had scholarship offers to play basketball and baseball all over the country. There were no offers to play football, but Big Red kept telling him that that was where his long-term future lay. One Saturday afternoon, they made the two-hour drive to Nashville to watch Tennessee State star defensive end Claude Humphries play. Afterward, Big Red took Jones to meet Tennessee State coach John Merritt.

"Big Red told Coach Merritt that I was interested in playing football, and [the coach] almost swallowed his cigar," Jones said. "I was a confused kid. I wasn't sure what to do. I kind of left it up to my brother-in-law because my father had passed, so he was like a father to me.

"I was a country kid trying to make a decision on my future. I never asked him where I should go; I just decided to go wherever he thought I should go because he had my best interest at heart."

That turned out to be a good move.

An injury thrust Ed Jones into the lineup as a sophomore, and he played well. As a junior, he became a force, and as a senior, he was one of the top players in the nation.

Jones' ability as a basketball player put him on the Cowboys' radar. Gil Brandt, the team's personnel director, loved basketball players because they were superior athletes who could be taught the nuances of the game.

"His brother-in-law actually called us after his junior year and said, 'Ed has been in school four years, and you can draft him,'" Brandt said. "We didn't believe that was right, but he insisted he had a scrapbook with newspaper clippings to prove it, so Cornell Green [a scout] and I decided to meet him in Memphis and discuss the situation.

"He was right, so we went to the commissioner and asked if we could draft him, because no one knew, so we could use a late-round pick on him. But [Pete] Rozelle said he had to let everyone know his status before we could draft him. We didn't want to do that, so we just waited."

Actually, they traded Tody Smith and Billy Parks to Houston in hopes they would have an opportunity to draft Jones. Houston finished 1-13, giving Dallas the first overall selection in the draft for the first time.

Picking Jones was a no-brainer.

"Dallas was my No. 1 team," Jones said. "In Jackson, we either got St. Louis or Dallas on TV. Dallas was winning, and St. Louis wasn't. It was easy to root for Dallas."

Jones signed a five-year contract with the Cowboys and played well. But with a year left on his contract, he met with club president Tex Schramm and informed him he planned to pursue boxing when his contract expired.

"[Boxing] was my all-time favorite sport, and I was just waiting until I was secure enough financially that it didn't matter what happened," Jones said. "I didn't want to be 50, look back, and wish that I had pursued my lifelong dream."

After the 1978 season ended, Jones announced his retirement and became a professional boxer. He went 6-0 but returned to the NFL in 1980 a better player than before. He made the Pro Bowl for the first time in 1980. And again in 1981.

"If I hadn't boxed, there's no way I would've played 15 years in the NFL, because my head wasn't there," Jones said. "The game is too tough. If you're not focused on football, somebody will knock your head off."

A 13-point loss in the 1980 NFC championship game didn't dissuade Brandt from believing the Cowboys were a championship team.

Sure, Philadelphia had won 12 games and captured the NFC East on a tie-breaker in 1980, but New York, St. Louis, and Washington had each finished well below .500, each losing at least 10 games. Atlanta (12-4) and Los Angeles (11-5) were good teams, but the Cowboys didn't view either as a fearful opponent.

"I thought we were one or two plays away from winning another Super Bowl that year," Brandt said. "We thought our team was pretty good, but, if we had been a little better, we could have overcome some of the adversity we faced and won another championship."

Quarterback Danny White was entering his second season as a starter, and the Cowboys figured he would be significantly better than he was in 1980, when he passed for 3,287 yards with 28 touchdowns and 25 interceptions, because he was another year removed from Roger Staubach's shadow. Running back Tony Dorsett was also entering his prime, as was receiver Tony Hill. The core of the offensive line was entering its fifth season together, and the Cowboys had endured just one losing season since 1965. So it didn't matter to Brandt whether the secondary was unsettled and that two rookie free agents (Everson Walls and Michael Downs) were moving into the starting lineup and Dennis Thurman was making the difficult shift from safety to cornerback.

"We had some real macho guys like Butch Johnson and Tony Hill, and we just felt like we were supposed to win every Sunday," Downs said. "I remember hearing Charlie Waters making predictions about the season and how many games we were going to win and get into the playoffs.

"The year before, they went to the NFC championship. We just figured we were going to the Super Bowl."

The Cowboys reeled off four straight wins to start the season, including three victories over division opponents, followed by a disappointing 20-17 loss to St. Louis on a 37-yard field goal with 23 seconds left as the Cardinals won their second game of the season.

Then came a debacle in San Francisco.

The 49ers, two seasons removed from a 2-14 record, thumped the Cowboys, 45-14. And it really wasn't even *that* close. San Francisco outgained Dallas 440-192, and Dorsett managed just 21 yards on nine carries. Afterward, San Francisco coach Bill Walsh called it one of the franchise's most important victories in the modern era of football. Dallas coach Tom Landry said it was one of the worst performances he had seen from his team in years.

"All I could do was stand out there and watch. We played absolutely terrible," Landry told the *Dallas Morning News* after the game. "This game is as bad as any we've played since our early years."

Defensive lineman Ed "Too Tall" Jones smiles on the sideline during a game in 1981. *Diamond Images/Getty Images*

San Francisco grabbed an early 24-0 lead and coasted to victory, leaving the Cowboys two games behind the undefeated Eagles in the NFC East. San Francisco, which hadn't been to the playoffs since the early '70s, staked its claim as one of the NFC's contenders.

"I think they caught us on a bad day," Downs said. "I was surprised they beat us like that, because they hadn't been to the playoffs since John Brodie was the quarterback, and they hadn't been a force in the NFC for a long time.

"We were a confident team—maybe a little overconfident. Maybe we thought we were going to win some games just by showing up."

Dallas regrouped after the loss and put together a four-game winning streak, including a 17-14 victory over Philadelphia at Veterans Stadium that gave them a share of the lead in the NFC East. Six weeks later, the Cowboys proved their victory in Philadelphia was no fluke. The Cowboys rallied from a 10-0 deficit to beat the Eagles again, 21-10, and win the division.

They did it with defense. The defensive line of Jones, John Dutton, Randy White, and Harvey Martin made it difficult for the opposition to run the ball. And when teams were forced into passing situations, the defensive line put immense pressure on opposing quarterbacks. The Cowboys intercepted 37 passes—Walls led the team with 11, and Thurman added nine and held opponents to a 46.2-percent completion rate. They allowed just 17 touchdown passes.

"Ed was probably the most consistent guy we had," said Downs, "Harvey would lead the team in sacks, but he seldom made tackles at the line of scrimmage because he was always in the starting block, and Randy was always getting double-teamed.

"That put Ed in position to make a lot of plays, but for some reason he's a guy that people tended to overlook."

White wasn't one of them.

"He was a great player," White said. "He was one of the guys who helped me succeed just like Harvey did. In the Flex defense [a football innovation credited to Landry], everyone had to do their job for it to work."

The Cowboys played with little focus in the last game of the season, losing to the Giants, 13-10, in overtime, costing themselves any opportunity at home-field advantage throughout the playoffs.

Still, they felt confident entering the playoffs against Tampa Bay, which had finished its season 9-7.

"I didn't think anybody could beat us," Jones said. "That's the way all of us felt."

THE GAME OF MY LIFE
by Ed "Too Tall" Jones

I thought Doug Williams was going to develop into a very good quarterback. I had heard more about him than I actually knew about him myself, but the people telling me about him were players that I respected. A lot of people had told me there was a guy coming out of Grambling who was going to change things.

Harvey and I talked about playing against Doug because we all wanted to see one of us succeed at that position. But we had watched the film, and we knew there was no way their offensive linemen could block me, Harvey [Martin], Randy [White], and John Dutton. It was a bad matchup for them.

Still, I wanted Doug to succeed so badly because of what having a black quarterback meant to all of us, since a lot of people didn't think we could do it. Besides, I was already upset with the Raiders for what they had done to Eldridge Dickey. He had been a great quarterback at Tennessee State, and they made him a receiver. As much as I wanted Doug to play well, I knew Harvey and I had to do what we had to do.

We went into that game healthy and clicking, and we didn't think anybody could beat us. We thought we had the best team in football. I thought we had a better team than the teams Roger Staubach took to Super Bowl XII and Super Bowl XIII. We had a lot of young guys on those teams [such as Tony Dorsett], but now they had a couple years under their belts, and they were veterans.

Staubach had been retired for a couple of years, and we believed in Danny White. He was a smart quarterback, but he couldn't move around as well as Staubach, although he didn't have to, with the talent around him and the offensive line that we had.

Tampa Bay hadn't been in the league long, and they hadn't won a game in their first season, but [defensive line coach] Ernie Stautner, Coach Landry, and all of the coaches made sure we respected every opponent.

It was an attitude we had. You could tell all week that we were ready. It was in the air. It was in the locker room. Still, I was bubbling with confidence because I had studied film and I knew there was no way they could beat us. We had a lot of respect for Doug and the things he could do, but things were going to happen so quickly that he wasn't going to be able to do a whole lot.

And that's the way the game played out.

We dominated defensively from the start. We didn't give him a lot of time to throw; he had to run around quite a bit.

I hit him some times, and the way I fell wasn't the way I normally fell. One time I hit him and his legs were exposed. I could've really punished him if I had just let all of my weight fall on him. But I didn't do that. I tried to avoid putting all of that pressure and weight on him. We sacked him three or four times and hit a lot more than that. Every time I hit him or Harvey hit him, I was just praying he would get up.

Another time, I came so free that I could have put the crown of my Riddell helmet in his chest and hit him so hard that he would've never gotten up. If you ever see a replay of the game, you'll see that I hit him with my arms extended. I wanted to make sure he went down, but I didn't want to do any damage to him. So I kind of just threw myself at his body, and he went down.

After the game, we felt good about the win. Like I said, we were clicking on all cylinders, and I didn't think anybody was going to beat us. We were taping money up in the training room so, every time you went in, there was a little reminder of what we were going to get if we kept playing and won the Super Bowl.

There was no doubt in Jones' mind the Cowboys were going to the Super Bowl for the third time in five seasons. None. That's because San Francisco was 89 yards away from a game-winning touchdown, Doomsday II (as the Cowboys' defense was then known) was on the field, and only 4:54 remained on the clock. The Cowboys had given up yards liberally but had used six turnovers to keep San Francisco out of the end zone and take the lead.

A few months earlier, the 49ers had embarrassed the Cowboys, 45-14, at Candlestick Park. The Cowboys were exacting revenge.

Landry opted to go with a nickel defense, taking out the starting linebackers and putting linebacker Anthony Dickerson and defensive backs Ron Fellows and Benny Barnes into the game, figuring San Francisco would pass the ball.

Bill Walsh didn't panic. He decided to take a patient approach and attack methodically. The patient approach fit perfectly with the 49ers' West Coast offense, which was designed for the quarterback to make three- and five-step drops and get rid of the ball quickly before getting consumed by the pass rush. San Francisco executed its plan flawlessly.

"I will always say if we hadn't gone to that nickel defense, we [would've] beat the 49ers," Jones said. "They nickel-and-dimed us all the way down the field. It was the best execution I've ever seen by a team in those circumstances, and I've told Joe Montana that.

"I know what our coaches were thinking. They thought it was going to be bombs away, but that's not what they did."

Instead, the 49ers took their time. Three carries by Lenvil Elliot gained 31 yards, and a reverse by Freddie Solomon picked up 14. An off-side penalty against Bruce Thornton gave San Francisco another first down as San Francisco moved closer to the Dallas end zone.

With 58 seconds left, San Francisco faced a third-and-3 from the Dallas 6-yard line. In the huddle, between gasps for air, Jones told defensive tackle Larry Bethea that it was time to use the stunt they had discussed all week.

While preparing for San Francisco, Jones had noticed that right tackle Keith Fahnhorst would always take a couple of steps backward when setting up to pass block.

"I told Bethea that I found something that, we could pull if we ever needed to," Jones said. "I told him, 'Line up a little bit off the ball so the guard figures he can wait on you. Then I'm going to knife right at Fahnhorst, snatch him, grab your guard, and keep driving, and Montana will be there for you,' because [Montana] never rolled left when he felt pressure. He always rolled right. Always."

With the 49ers 6 yards from the end zone and a potential victory that would send them to their first Super Bowl, Jones leaned over to Bethea and called the stunt.

"I knifed in there and hit Fahnhorst so hard that it couldn't have worked out any better," he said. "I knocked him back, grabbed Bethea's guy, and drove so hard into the pocket that I saw Montana look at me and take off.

"I was so happy because I knew Bethea was going to be there to get him. All of a sudden, . . . I realize that he's running through the hole I made to get Montana."

Montana rolled right, avoided the pressure, and lobbed a pass between rookie cornerback Everson Walls and rookie safety Michael Downs that Dwight Clark leaped to grab in the back of the end zone for a touchdown that gave San Francisco a 28-27 lead.

"I called [Bethea] out on the sideline and asked what happened," Jones said. "Bethea said it was so wide-open that he thought he could get in there and sack him. He blew it. That right there is why I couldn't be a coach. I'd be fighting on the sideline.

"We're professionals. We're not college players, who might forget. It left a bitter taste in my mouth."

That's because Jones knew the Cowboys had blown an opportunity to play in a Super Bowl for the third time in five seasons. Jones had already looked at the teams in the AFC championship game—Cincinnati and San Diego—and had deduced that neither could beat Dallas or San Francisco. In his mind, the NFC champion would win the Super Bowl. And that's what happened as San Francisco beat the Bengals, 26-21.

"We respected the 49ers, and we knew it would be a tougher battle than Tampa Bay because we had all of the respect in the world for them because we had to be on top of our game to beat them," Jones said. "Their coaching staff was so good that if you let them stay close, they would beat you. That's what happened to us."

———————————

The routine was always the same in 1989.

Coach Jimmy Johnson would knock on the meeting room door for the defense twice before entering. Then he would introduce the newest member of the team.

"Tom Rafferty and I would look at each other sometimes and say, 'What is going on with this team?'" Jones said. "All the time I had been with the Cowboys, if you played well, you would end your career in Dallas. Well, that wasn't happening anymore.

"I liked Jimmy's approach because he demanded the best from everybody. One time, he made all of the secretaries and support staff watch practice to give us a little energy. Another time, we smelled something on the practice field, and he was cooking burgers. He was asking a lot from us, but he was giving us everything he had."

In 1989, 36 different players started games for the Cowboys. At 12 different positions, Johnson used at least two different starters. At center and left defensive end, Jones' position, he used three different starters.

Players often signed on Tuesday, the players' off day, and started on Sunday. Nothing worked, though, and Dallas lost its first eight games. When the season ended, Jones contemplated his future.

"My mom had died in November, and it seemed like it took forever for the end of the season to come," Jones said. "When it did, I said to myself, 'I've been in this game 15 years. I've got my legs. And when [the management] turns this team around, I'm not going to be here.'

"I went to talk to [defensive line] coach Butch Davis about my situation. I told him he needed to know who his horses were going to be and that I was going to retire even though I still had a year left on my contract."

Once he did, Jones took some time and decided to follow his passion for the entertainment business full time. He established Team Jones, a full-service talent-booking and promotion agency.

"All you have to do is tell me your budget and the type of music that you want," Jones said. "We take care of the rest. No event is too big or too small. We don't turn anything down. We'll do anything from events with 10,000 people to high school proms."

Jones, who has never been married, says the business keeps him busy. He spends several weeks a year on the road but loves his job because no two events are ever alike.

"I'm so glad I haven't gotten burned out," said Jones, who has lived in the same Carrollton, Texas, home for more than 20 years. "If I couldn't make a living doing this, I don't know what I'd be doing."

Actually, he'd probably be on the golf course, where he plays as much as possible.

"It's a great outlet to relax," he said. "During those four or five hours that I'm on the course, I don't have to think about anything but the next shot. When I played football, music was my escape. Now that I'm in the entertainment industry, golf is my release."

CHAPTER 14

EVERSON WALLS

Basketball, not football, was his first love. His idol was Willis Reed—not Jim Brown. Everson Walls loved everything about basketball. Its frenetic pace. Its graceful artistry. Its creativity.

There was just one problem: he couldn't master it. Ever.

"I thought I was going to be a basketball player," he said with a chuckle. "I just loved the game so much. I'm one of the few guys from Texas that looked forward to basketball season more than football season."

That explains one of the reasons that he didn't play competitive football until his senior season at Richardson Berkner High School.

Fortunately, Walls had an aptitude for football. Or maybe he picked it up by osmosis, since he lived in a section of North Dallas called Hamilton Park, which was about a mile from the Dallas Cowboys' practice facility. Walls spent many afternoons watching the Cowboys practice.

As a fifth-grader, Walls dominated the Spring Valley Athletic Association, scoring 18 touchdowns in six games.

"I was the baddest thing in the SVAA. I was the biggest kid in the league. The next year they passed a rule that you couldn't weigh more than 100 pounds and play in the backfield," he said. "The next year, we went from losing one game to winning one game, and I had to play tight end. Who's going to win throwing the ball at 10 or 11 years old?"

Walls didn't play football again until his final year in high school.

"I had gotten fired from two jobs at dinner houses, and I kept getting in trouble. I didn't even play sports as a junior in high school," Walls said. "Suddenly, the light bulb went off in my head. I got tired of worrying about my problems, and I wanted to start from scratch, so I went to Coach Holliday and said I wanted to try out for spring ball.

"I could look at the smile on his face, and I knew he was so happy. I was surprised by that. Every kid wants to be appreciated. When I saw that smile, I knew I was going to be appreciated and that's all I or any kid ever wanted."

Walls made his coach even happier with his performance; he intercepted 11 passes for the Rams.

Walls wanted to play in college, but there weren't a lot of offers pouring in for a kid who hadn't generated any attention or publicity entering his senior season.

The one thing Walls knew he wanted to do was play for a historically black institution like Morehouse College in Atlanta. Because his girlfriend was going to Grambling and his sister already was enrolled, Walls decided to check it out.

"I got depressed on the way there because my mom told me that Grambling was like East Texas, and that's not what I had in mind," he said. "I hated the country, but to know Grambling is to love it."

The Tigers gave Walls their last scholarship.

But success was hard to come by, initially. Walls didn't start until his senior year, although coach Eddie Robinson rotated him at each secondary spot during the last half of his junior season to make sure Walls got on the field. He intercepted four passes and recovered a fumble in that limited playing time, setting the stage for his senior season.

"I intercepted 11 passes as a senior, which led the nation and I was a [Division] I-AA All-American," Walls said. "I expected to get drafted in the third or fourth round. After the sixth round, I stopped watching the draft and went to class."

But Cowboys personnel director Gil Brandt had his eye on Walls. Brandt had personally seen Walls intercept three passes in a game against Boise State on the coldest day he'd ever seen—with the exception of the Ice Bowl in 1967 against Green Bay, where the temperature and wind chill dipped well below zero.

The Cowboys were one of the first teams to use computers in the scouting and evaluation of players. Their computer suggested Walls might be a good player.

"We put in the data, and the computer would tell us whether a smaller player or a slower player should get a higher grade in the evaluation process because he had great recognition skills or great hands," Brandt said. "People didn't draft him because he didn't have top speed, but he had a great understanding of how to play the game."

None of the NFL's 28 teams thought Everson Walls was worth a draft choice. Only Buffalo, New Orleans, and Dallas deemed him worthy of a free-agent invitation to training camp.

Walls had other ideas.

There was no doubt in his mind that he was going to make the roster. He knew the Cowboys had struggled at cornerback in 1980 with Bennie Barnes and Steve Wilson sharing the left cornerback position and Aaron Mitchell manning the right cornerback spot.

He signed with Dallas, in part, because he knew the Cowboys' cornerback situation provided him with an opportunity to make the team. Besides, Walls had led the nation with 11 interceptions at Grambling as a senior, and he fancied himself a playmaker.

That's why he packed six weeks' worth of clothes when he headed to the California Lutheran campus to battle 12 draft choices and more than 50 free agents during the six-week training camp for a coveted spot on the roster.

He also knew the Cowboys gave free agents a legitimate opportunity to make the team. Players such as receiver Drew Pearson and safety Cliff Harris, who were signed as free agents, had become star players. Walls figured the competition would be tough, but fair.

"Our philosophy is that we didn't want to sign a guy unless we thought he could make our team," Brandt said. "Everybody we signed had at least one trait that we thought would help our team if he made it."

Walls didn't disappoint.

In the preseason, Walls intercepted three passes and returned a blocked punt, forcing his way onto the roster. The hometown kid had made it.

"Every time you looked up he was on the field making a play. He wasn't the fastest or the quickest, but he made the play. If you weren't careful, he'd pick it off and run it the other way," said Robert Newhouse, a fullback from 1972 to 1983. 'Cubby' was a finesse guy. He didn't have good speed, but he had good recognition, and he had all of these tactics he used to knock receivers off stride or prevent them from getting their arms up.

"He was a technician, and he used everything within the rules and some things that weren't that he got away with."

Dwight Clark pulls in "The Catch" in front of Everson Walls at Candlestick Park during the 1981 NFC Championship Game.
Bruce Bennett Studios/Getty Images

Making the roster, though, was just the beginning. Four weeks into the season, coach Tom Landry benched Wilson and named Walls a starter.

Maybe the coach saw some of himself in Walls. As a defensive back with the New York Giants from 1950 to 1955, Landry intercepted 31 passes. Three times, Landry intercepted eight passes in a season. Like Walls, he relied on guile more than athleticism.

Opposing quarterbacks attacked Walls and completed passes, but never dented his confidence. Instead of questioning his talent or going into a funk when beaten, Walls simply plotted his revenge. He went after the ball as aggressively as the receivers did. When opportunity presented itself, Walls didn't drop the ball.

He ended the regular season with a league-leading 11 interceptions, which remains a franchise record. Detroit's Dick "Night Train" Lane established the NFL record for interceptions in a season with 14 during his rookie year of 1952. Walls also led the league in interceptions in 1983 (seven) and 1985 (nine) to become the only player in NFL history to lead the league in interceptions three times.

"A lot of defensive backs can't catch," Brandt said. "Everson had excellent hands. He didn't drop interceptions."

Walls entered the playoffs with confidence after his regular-season performance. It helped that Dallas beat Tampa Bay 38-0 in a divisional playoff game, holding his former college teammate, Doug Williams, to 187 yards passing. He completed just 10 of 29 passes with four interceptions.

Now the Cowboys were just one game away from the Super Bowl.

Walls turned in a terrific performance against San Francisco with two interceptions and a fumble recovery, but few remember that. The 1981 NFC championship game can be summed up in two words: "The Catch."

GAME OF MY LIFE
By Everson Walls

[San Francisco] beat us 45-14 in the regular season, but we felt strong going against them in the playoffs. We really did.

Being a finesse team, you set yourself up for a lot of whippings. When we first went down there, we had a lot of excuses especially about the field being messed up. It was the worst field I ever played on in my life. Period. But we let that crap get into our minds, and it was really over before it started.

And in the first game, it was the first time that I had ever seen the West Coast offense. They had their play-action going, they had wide-open formations, and if you weren't at the top of your game, you were going to get blown out. When we came back to play them in the play-offs, we said if we get longer cleats, we'll kick their butt.

That's the way we came out and played most of the game.

Their receivers were Freddie Solomon, Dwight Clark, and Mike Wilson, who were part of my rookie class with the Cowboys before he got cut. Although they were tough to handle one on one, we knew their system made them successful because it enhanced their abilities. The system called for short, quick-hitting passes that gave their receivers a chance to run after the catch.

I got my first interception of the game against Mike Wilson at our 1-yard line.

We were blitzing.

As a rookie I had to learn the Cowboys' philosophy about defense, and then I had to learn their offense's philosophy against our defense. I started to realize that once teams read blitz, they knew I was always in man to man. They wanted to create that situation, and I would invite that situation, but I would cut down their options. For example, if I lined up tight, they could only run a couple of different patterns.

San Francisco was at about the 35, so there was a good chance to go for the end zone because they were already in field-goal range. If they punted it, then they could pin us deep, so why not go for the touchdown.

It was a hot route. I dictated it by playing bump, so I was waiting for it. It was like a rebound situation. I forced him outside where the sideline was my friend, put my back to him, and went up Dennis Rodman-style to get the rebound.

My knee went down at the 1, so that's where we got the ball. That play really helped my confidence because I had given up a big pass on a sideline post to Dwight Clark to put them in that field position.

I got a fumble recovery in the third quarter.

I rarely got fumbles. I was always looking for them. It was one of those days. Harvey Martin ripped it from their running back, and there it was. I should've scooped it up and run, but I wanted to make sure I got my hands on the ball because the game was so important.

The last pick came near the end of the game.

With that pick, we were sitting so pretty. They tried an out-and-up with Freddie Solomon, but he didn't run a good out. I saw it coming. It was another jump ball, and I got it.

Although we had the lead and they had to go 89 yards for a touchdown, you knew they were capable of driving for a touchdown to win the game. Joe Montana was a good quarterback, and he already had a reputation for leading comebacks after what he did in the Cotton Bowl against Houston when he was at Notre Dame.

I also knew the Cowboys were notorious for making things hard on themselves. I grew up a Cowboys fan. I knew the history. We were always putting ourselves in trouble. We couldn't do anything without drama.

Bill Walsh, the 49ers coach, knew we were in man to man on half of the field with deep help from the safeties. If they saw us in the dime with seven defensive backs, they audibled to a run. If we put in more linebackers, he would call a pass play. We were at their mercy.

That's when we started yelling—"Somebody make a play!"—at each other in the huddle. Nothing worked. I got beat on a couple of crucial third-down plays. On one of them, I swear the ball went right through my hands. The sideline route hurt me more than The Catch. That could've stopped them.

The Catch came on another third down.

My back was to the play the whole time. Mike Downs was inside, and I was outside. I remember Montana dancing around, and when I finally looked the ball was too high. You find the ball, and it looks like it's gone—like he threw it away.

But it floated. It just floated. Dwight went up and got that bad boy. I didn't even have time to react.

I grew up in Dallas, so I knew we had a chance. That's the way I felt. That's the way we played all year. I never gave up hope. That wasn't in my nature. I had too much faith. There's always an opportunity to win a game.

A game of that magnitude always has a lot of ups and downs. I just knew how good our offense was. I knew we had a chance. When Danny White hit Drew Pearson over the middle, I thought it was six, but somebody barely pulled him down.

I was sitting on the bench near Rafael Septien, who made the Pro Bowl that year. All we had to do was get a little closer. The Hail Mary game was on my birthday, so I always believed.

The following season, the Cowboys lost the NFC championship on the road for a third consecutive year. But Walls had another terrific performance in a season tainted by a work stoppage.

The players went on strike after week 2 and didn't return until the middle of November. The league shortened the season from 16 games to nine, which might be the only reason Walls didn't break Lane's record for interceptions in a season. He led the league with seven interceptions, helping Dallas earn a spot in the Super Bowl tournament.

Dallas beat Green Bay and Tampa Bay in the first two rounds of the tournament before falling to Washington, a team it had beaten by 14 points in RFK Stadium three weeks after the season resumed.

Washington stomped the Cowboys 31-17 en route to their first Super Bowl championship. The loss also signaled the end of an era for Dallas. The Cowboys made the playoffs just twice more in the 1980s and didn't play in another NFC championship game until Troy Aikman, Emmitt Smith, and Michael Irvin led the Cowboys over San Francisco a decade later in 1992.

After intercepting 18 passes in his first 25 regular-season games, making two Pro Bowls, and being named All-Pro, Walls wanted to be paid like one of the NFL's best players. Dallas offered a five-year deal that averaged $250,000; Walls wanted a three-year deal that averaged about $330,000.

A day before the start of training camp in 1983, Walls sent commissioner Pete Rozelle and club president Tex Schramm a letter that read, "Effective today, I am retiring from the NFL."

"I wasn't really going to retire. They knew it. I was just trying to avoid the $1,000-a-day fine," Walls said.

A week later, Walls arrived in camp with a Lloyd's of London insurance policy that protected him against a career-ending injury. Later, he agreed to a unique five-year contract that included a $125,000 signing bonus and gave him the right to renegotiate after three seasons if he achieved a certain point total based on awards and honors like being named All-Pro, making the Pro Bowl, or leading the NFL in interceptions.

Walls played nine seasons with the Cowboys, but contentious negotiations often left him feeling underappreciated.

"It was a string of negotiations and broken promises. During negotiations certain promises were made that neither one of us—me or the organization—lived up to. I didn't trust them, and they were used to doing things a certain way.

"I grew up a Cowboys fan. I saw how they negotiated. I could see it coming from day one. Rayfield Wright always comes to mind. He played 13 years for the Cowboys, and they just gave him up—that hurt me. They had problems with Bob Hayes, and it was the '70s, and we were dealing with bussing. It was a part of being black in whatever city or situation you were in. You felt like if you were black that you were getting the short end of the stick. That's the way I grew up."

Family has always been important to Walls.

He credits his father for teaching him how to judge the ball and catch it at its highest point, one of the reasons he managed to intercept 52 passes in his career and lead the league in interceptions a record three times. He credits his mother and three sisters for keeping him grounded and teaching him how to treat women.

After all, Walls lived in the same home where his mother raised him for the first three years of his NFL career. It was near the Cowboys' practice field and living at home helped keep him focused on his NFL goals because he wasn't out partying all night.

Walls, nicknamed "Cubby" at birth because he had so much hair all over his body, met his wife when they were in elementary school. They dated for a while in high school and reconnected at Grambling.

Now, they live in North Dallas, a 20-minute drive from where they grew up in Hamilton Park.

They have a daughter, Charis, at Southern University and a son, Cameron, who just graduated from high school.

Walls owns a real estate development company and has dabbled as a local football analyst in Dallas. The bitterness that once engulfed him as a young man has faded.

He hasn't forgotten the past because it's forged the man he is today. A man Walls likes and respects.

CHAPTER 15

TONY HILL

The son always wanted to please the father. If that meant more practice, then so be it. If meant being criticized for a performance, then so be it. As long as he received his old man's approval, Tony Hill was happy.

That's because he knew Lee Roy Hill was pushing him to be the best athlete he could be—even when he didn't always want to be pushed.

"Other than God, my parents had the most influence on my life," Hill said. "Everything I did was for them. I didn't want to embarrass them. At the time, I didn't realize I was really doing things for myself.

"I just knew that I didn't want to embarrass them. That was my motivation. I played for their approval. Obviously, when they felt good, I felt good."

Lee Roy Hill, a former Navy man, worked at GTE. His wife, Bernice, worked for the Long Beach, California, post office. When Tony was two years old, his father introduced him to athletics. Soon after, he was pushing him to be the best.

"I'm a country boy from Alabama. I used to plow the fields two days a week with a cow because we didn't have a horse or a mule and go to school three days a week. I know how important hard work is to get where you want to go," Lee Roy Hill said. "Some people said I pushed, but I don't think so. I just taught him that if he wanted to be the best, he had to work for it.

"He had lot of ability as a young kid, and by the time he was seven, he was superior to most of the kids he met."

Lee Roy Hill's military background made him focus on details—the little things between being good and great. He believed most in practice. Perform in practice, especially under stress, and the games will be easier. He attended virtually every one of his son's practices. The sport didn't matter.

"Before every game we had to practice. Before the football games, I had to catch passes," Tony Hill said. "In basketball, I had to shoot before the games. In baseball, he'd pitch to me before the games. He was tough. If I screwed up, he let me know. If I played well, he let me know.

"There wasn't much I could say because my dad was such a good athlete, so I figured he knew what he was talking about. My dad was outrunning me until I was in the 12th grade. We used to get out in the street and run barefoot. Everyone in the neighborhood would be trying to outrun Mr. Hill, and nobody could do it."

So it shouldn't have been much of a surprise that Hill developed into one of the finest athletes to come through Long Beach.

He developed into a star at Long Beach Poly High School—no easy feat at a traditional powerhouse like Poly, which has sent more than 40 players to the NFL. At the start of the 2004 season, Poly had six players on opening-day NFL rosters. No other high school had more.

But he didn't get to showcase his skills until his senior year, in part because he started elementary school early, which meant he was only 14 in the 10th grade. At the time, he said, state rules prohibited students younger than 15 from playing varsity sports.

As a junior, he rode the bench behind a senior quarterback. When Hill's time to play as a senior arrived, he wanted to put on a show. And he did.

When he left, Hill had broken all of Gene Washington's records. That's the same Gene Washington who later starred at Stanford and with the San Francisco 49ers.

"At that point, I wanted to let them know they made a big mistake," Hill said. "I rushed for 1,000 and passed for 1,000."

Poly, 1-9 in Hill's junior year, went 10-0 with him at quarterback. In the process, he became one of the nation's most highly coveted players. Hill, 16 when he graduated from high school, wanted to stay in California and play quarterback, but there weren't as many options as he thought.

The University of Southern California was all about giving the ball to the halfback. They were also running the ball at UCLA, and California-Berkley had a pocket passer in Vince Ferragamo. Suddenly, Stanford moved into the picture.

"They told me I could play wide receiver and come in and play right away," Hill said, "and if I wanted to go back to quarterback, then I could. At that time they had Guy Benjamin at quarterback and he became an All-American. I figured if they threw the ball 50 times a game and I got a third of those, I would be all right."

It didn't turn out exactly as he planned.

The adjustments to college, socially and athletically, were difficult.

"I was hardly a valedictorian, and the demographics were totally different than Long Beach," Hill said. "I was there for football. I wish I could say something else, but my goal—long term and short term—was always to be a professional athlete."

The dream almost died when Hill tore his anterior cruciate ligament as a freshman in a game against Washington.

"That was the first time I saw my dad cry," he said. "I was ready to leave Stanford. My grades went down, and I didn't want to deal with it anymore, but I didn't want to embarrass my parents so I stayed. The rest is history."

The Cowboys drafted Hill with the first pick of the third round in the 1977 draft—Hill thought he was going in the first round—but he didn't make much of an impact behind Golden Richards. Besides, Roger Staubach had a lot of people he could throw the ball to, such as receivers Richards and Drew Pearson, tight end Billy Joe DuPree, and running backs Tony Dorsett and Preston Pearson.

Hill caught two passes for 21 yards.

"I was killing them in practice. I didn't lack confidence, and I don't think they liked that," Hill said. "It was difficult that first year because I wasn't used to sitting on the sideline. I didn't know how I was supposed to help if I didn't get the opportunities. That's when I started saying, 'Let Hill give you a thrill on the field.'"

He finally got an opportunity in 1978 when he beat out Butch Johnson and Richards for the starting job in training camp. He made the most of the opportunity, catching 46 passes for 823 yards and six touchdowns. A year later, he caught 60 for 1,062 yards and 10 touchdowns, and earned a trip to the Pro Bowl.

"They thought Tony was cocky when he first got there," Lee Roy Hill said. "But he was just doing what I taught him to do. He always believed he was the best."

———————————

The last time Danny White had stepped onto the field at RFK Stadium, just eight months earlier in the NFC championship game, it had been a disaster.

Wide receiver Tony Hill. *Diamond Images/Getty Images*

Washington defensive end Dexter Manley had delivered a vicious blow, when he blew around left tackle Pat Donovan for a blindside shot on White with less than a minute remaining in the first half. White suffered a concussion that forced him to miss the second half.

Dallas trailed 14-3 at the time. Enter Gary Hogeboom, who had signed a three-year deal in the off-season.

Hogeboom pulled Dallas within 21-17 in the second half, but two fourth-quarter interceptions eliminated any hope of yet another miracle comeback by America's Team.

"What made the rivalry great is that we were both very good," said Joe Theismann, a quarterback with the Redskins from 1974 to 1985. "There was hardly a time in the '70s or '80s you could look at the Cowboys–Redskins game and say it meant nothing.

"Somewhere down the line that game was going to determine a playoff position or a possible Super Bowl contender. Something was always at stake. No lead was ever safe. There was never a point total we could hit where I thought the game was out of reach, because there were too many great athletes on the field.

"It's not like it is today where there are half a dozen great athletes on the field. We had half a dozen on each team."

The Cowboys had lost three consecutive championship games, all on the road, and it had taken a toll on the team's psyche. They weren't sure what the future held because they couldn't get over the hump. In some ways, it was like the late '60s and early '70s all over again, when they were dubbed "next year's champions."

"This was probably the most frustrating game I can remember," middle linebacker Bob Breunig told the *Dallas Morning News* after the game. "It leaves you with an empty feeling. You have to think of where we go from here. What's next? I'm sure coach [Tom] Landry will put it into focus for us and set the goals." But this team was aging, and Landry couldn't be sure how much longer it could remain among the elite teams of the NFC.

They weren't about to get any sympathy from the Redskins, who had just captured their first championship since 1942, two years after their infamous 73-0 loss to the Chicago Bears. After a 0-5 start in 1981, coach Joe Gibbs' first season, the Redskins had won seven of their last nine games and carried momentum into the 1982 strike-shortened season.

They went 8-1 in the regular season and entered the NFL playoff tournament as the top seed. The strike wiped out nine games, so the NFL decided to use a special 16-team tournament to crown its champion. Each conference sent eight teams to the playoffs, and they were seeded No. 1 through No. 8 based on their regular-season record.

The Redskins won each of their four postseason games by at least 10 points, including a 27-10 victory over Miami in Super Bowl XVII.

That's why the 1983 regular-season opener was so important to the Cowboys. They needed to prove they could compete against Washington, and the league gave them a perfect opportunity by starting the season at RFK on *Monday Night Football.*

Hill made sure the Cowboys responded to the challenge with touchdown catches of 75 and 51 yards, respectively, on the first two possessions of the second half as Dallas rallied from a 23-3 deficit to win 31-30.

"I told them at halftime that it was just a matter of pride," Landry told reporters after the game. "We were down and hadn't done a thing, and the defense had been on the field two quarters. That's when you've got to draw from deep down. Our team showed it did have something.

"If Washington had won, it might have gotten a little cocky and thought it could beat the world."

GAME OF MY LIFE
By Tony Hill

Anytime we played the Washington Redskins, it was always a big game. It was a game we looked forward to because it wasn't like any of our rivalries with other teams like the Giants or Eagles. It was the only opponent where the fans sent us hate mail on a regular basis. We really got excited when we played them on *Monday Night Football.*

We would stay across the bay in Crystal City, Virginia, at a Marriott Hotel right in the business district. On the way to RFK we'd go through some neighborhoods, and they had graffiti on the building about how much they hated the Cowboys. All of that was great, because you knew if the fans were that intense, the Redskins were going to be ready to play.

When we got to the stadium, the fans would be talking big smack. Even the concession workers were talking smack. I thought it was great. That's what competition and rivalries are all about.

We played badly in the first half—really badly—and we were down 23-3 at halftime. In the first half, nothing clicked. The opportunities were there offensively, but we just weren't getting it done, but at least the opportunities were there.

Like when [Tony] Dorsett broke loose and we thought he was going to score, but Darrell Green could flat out fly. Tony could fly too, but Darrell had an angle on him and brought him down after 77 yards. We thought we might have a chance to score some points in the second half because the Redskins were the Redskins, and like most good teams they weren't going to change what they do. I thought they might add a few wrinkles, but overall we knew what they were going to do defensively.

We were pissed off and upset at halftime. The coaches were more upset than we were. They were on us at halftime. They called us a bunch of chumps.

They said, "How can you let the Redskins beat you like that?"

We knew we could still win the game, but they were talking smack and feeling good about themselves. I was upset because I wasn't getting the ball. It was typical wide receiver stuff. I got double-teamed a lot, but when they rolled coverage my way on certain defensive plays, we were going to audible to take advantage of that.

I told Danny White, "Hey, let's open it up because I can beat Vernon Dean on the post." Our goal was to come out and get something quick, hold them, and then get something quick again. Vernon Dean was covering on that first series of the second half, and he was getting cocky. I put a move to the outside, and Dean was sitting on the route, but he didn't have the speed to run with me once I turned it up. Danny threw it all the way to the other side of the field, so I caught it and just ran all the way in with it for a touchdown.

We stopped them and got the ball back just like we hoped we would. Washington was covering me bump and run, and I got a step on Anthony Washington, but he still had pretty good coverage on me. Danny threw the ball up, and I kind of had my left arm on him, so I threw my right arm out there, and the ball just stuck, and I took it on in for the touchdown. When I got in the end zone, I gave them the "wings of victory." I never slammed the ball. I never danced. I just threw the wings of victory on them and pointed to the crowd and said, "We're on our way."

The momentum had definitely changed. When I scored that first touchdown, you could see it in the eyes of our defensive players. They knew if they got us the ball back, we might be able to make something happen. When I scored that touchdown, it was 23-10—boom!—I scored again, and it was 23-17.

All of a sudden, they were nervous. They weren't talking smack. You could see it in their eyes. They knew we were coming back. We couldn't get on the field fast enough.

———————————

Los Angeles ended the Cowboys' 1983 season with an upset win at Texas Stadium in an NFC divisional playoff game.

Although the Cowboys finished the regular season 12-4, their flaws were starting to show. After starting the season 12-2, they lost their last two regular-season games in humbling fashion. Washington beat Dallas 31-10 at Texas Stadium and San Francisco beat them 42-17.

It was not the way any team wanted to enter the playoffs.

"We were aging to a degree—like a heavyweight fighter," Hill said. "You still think you can get the job done, but you don't have all of the skills that you used to."

Then came the loss to the Rams. It marked the Cowboys' first three-game losing streak since 1979 and only the second in the previous nine years.

Hill never experienced the joy of winning another playoff game.

The Cowboys went 9-7 in 1984 after losing their last two games of the season and missed the playoffs for the first time in a decade. They rebounded in 1985 and won the NFC East with a 10-6 record that many experts called the finest coaching job of Landry's career.

That team had players like Glen Titensor, Kurt Peterson, and Chris Schultz starting on the offensive line in a tough division that featured Bill Parcells' New York Giants and Gibbs' Redskins. Twice during the regular season the Cowboys were humiliated: 44-0 at home to Chicago and 50-24 at Cincinnati.

But they persevered.

Landry, who gave the team a reasonable goal and an outstanding goal each year before the start of the season, made winning the division the Cowboys' outstanding goal.

It was their first division title since 1981, an eternity for a team that dominated the 1970s and played in five Super Bowls.

But the Cowboys made another first-round playoff exit, when Los Angeles running back Eric Dickerson rushed for a playoff-record 248 yards in a 20-0 victory. No Cowboys team had ever been shut out in the playoffs or shut out twice in the same season.

"A lot of the veterans like Drew Pearson and Harvey Martin and Jethro Pugh and Bubba Cole who built this team were gone," Hill said. "You had a changing of the guard, and the dedication was a little different.

"I don't know if Coach Landry was used to the attitude of the guys in the '80s. Their motivation was different. The league was changing. It was about money. Guys weren't happy just being in the league; they wanted to get paid."

In 1986, one of the most impressive streaks in sports ended. The Cowboys went 7-9, ending their streak of 20 consecutive winning seasons—the third longest streak in professional sports. Only the New York Yankees (39 consecutive seasons from 1926 to 1964) of Major League

Baseball and the Montreal Canadiens (32 consecutive seasons from 1951 to 1982) of the National Hockey League had longer streaks.

"My whole career the only thing I was used to was winning," Hill said. "You come in and go to the Super Bowl and play in five straight NFC championship games … that has to be your attitude.

"You're just looking to go to the Super Bowl. Anything less than the NFC championship was unacceptable."

Hall of Fame defensive tackle Randy White said he didn't focus on the losing.

"The only thing I could control was how hard I played on every single play," he said. "Whether we were losing by 20 or winning by 20, I wanted to give the same effort every play and every game, because a lot of things go into winning football games."

In 1985, Hill led the Cowboys in receptions (74) and yards (1,113) and tied Dorsett for the team lead in touchdowns with seven— and played in his third Pro Bowl. The 10-year veteran was off to another strong start in 1986 in new offensive coordinator Paul Hackett's scheme, when the bottom fell out. After catching 33 passes for 545 yards in the first eight games, he caught only 16 for 225 in the final half of the season.

Hill blamed Hackett.

"Paul Hackett and I just didn't see eye to eye, but I wasn't the only one," Hill said. "I caught 16 passes in the last half of the season. It didn't take a Phi Beta Kappa to figure out what was going on. That was it with the Cowboys."

Hill averaged 15.7 yards on 49 catches in 1986 and scored three touchdowns. He signed a free-agent deal with San Francisco in the off-season, but it didn't feel right. At heart, he was a Cowboy.

"I had a good preseason, but the desire wasn't there, and it absolutely felt funny putting on a San Francisco uniform. It wasn't the same," he said. "I didn't even go work out after the 1986 season. I'm a Stanford graduate. It just didn't add up.

"I was coming off a Pro Bowl year, and all of a sudden I can't play anymore. Maybe I made a mistake by not preparing myself. I could've made it tough, but I made it easy for them."

———————————

Hill's numbers speak loudly.

He caught 479 passes. And gained 7,988 yards. And scored 51 touchdowns. There's more: Hill recorded 26 100-yard games and played in three Pro Bowls. Eight times his teams advanced to the playoffs.

But he rarely gets mentioned among the great receivers in franchise history like Pearson, Bob Hayes, and Michael Irvin.

"The stats that Drew and I have are Hall of Fame material," Hill said. "There easily could have been more Super Bowl-defining moments in my career, but Drew came in with Roger and I came in with Danny. The difference between Roger and Danny is night and day."

After his career ended, Hill let his entrepreneurial spirit take over.

He created a sports promotional company that sets up and handles appearances for players. He hosted a local radio show. He did color commentary on Arena Football League games, and he coached high school football at Lexington Academy, a small private school in Dallas.

It took a while, but Hill, who lives in suburban Dallas with his wife and children, finally found his niche as recreation service manager for the Allen Parks and Recreation Department the past four years.

The job provides an opportunity to work with kids and affect the lives of young people. An important part of his job is developing ideas and programs that get more people involved with the department.

"I can make a difference," he said. "That's the most important thing. I like being part of the community."

A New Era Begins

CHAPTER 16

PAUL PALMER

The youngster was nicknamed "Boo Boo"—and it had nothing to do with Yogi the Bear. It had everything to do with how much he loved football. He loved the game, played daily in the summer on the street between parked cars—so much that he wouldn't stop playing to go to the bathroom.

"I'd be having so much fun that I'd wait until it was too late," Palmer said with a chuckle, "and then I'd start sprinting home, and it was too late. Now, it's all about Yogi the Bear, but that's really where I got the nickname. When that happened, my great-grandmother would wear me out with a belt or a Hot Wheels track or whatever she could find."

The nickname stuck. Even today, only colleagues or strangers call him "Paul." For everyone else, it's "Boo Boo."

Palmer's passion for football as a youngster paid off. It provided an opportunity to attend college, where he became one of the best running backs in NCAA history. And it gave him a chance to make more money than he ever dreamed, when the Kansas City Chiefs drafted him in the first round of the 1987 draft.

Not bad for a kid who was raised, along with an older brother and sister by his great-grandmother, Francis Palmer, in Potomac, Maryland.

His mother, Vivian, lived in Massachusetts with four other brothers and a sister. His father, Paul, lived in the Washington DC area and visited often.

Housing projects and food stamps were part of his upbringing. Money wasn't plentiful, but there was always food on the table and enough money to get the things he needed to survive. Aunts, uncles and an assortment of father figures provided the rest.

"My mom and I have a great relationship. I think she was young, and she just couldn't do it," said Palmer, discussing why his great-grandmother raised him. "I'm just thankful someone in my family took care of me because a lot of people don't have family members that step up and take care of you."

Francis Palmer cared so much for Paul that she didn't want him to play organized football, fearing he would get hurt. So Palmer would leave his pads at a friend's house so she wouldn't know he was practicing.

Finally, though, he needed her signature on a permission slip to play. One of the coaches lobbied for him, and she finally relented.

The game came easy for him and he starred at Winston Churchill High School, where former NFL players Jeff Kemp and Brian Holloway had also played. Palmer, the first sophomore to ever try out for the varsity, made the team as a junior and senior.

"I took to football pretty quickly and pretty easily," Palmer said. "I was pretty good from the start."

He had more than 2,000 all-purpose yards, including more than 1,000 yards rushing as a senior, but he was about 5 feet 8 inches and 165 pounds with poor grades. That meant Shepard (West Virginia) College and Bloomsburg (Pennsylvania) State were his only options.

"Why would someone recruit a kid," said Palmer, "who was 5 foot nothing and 160 pounds with bad grades?"

Temple entered the picture because first-year coach Bruce Arians needed speed, and Palmer had plenty. The Owls were studying Travis Curtis, who eventually signed with West Virginia, when they became intrigued with Palmer.

"I ended up at Temple because I had no place else to go," Palmer said. "I didn't know anything about the school. I just knew it was Division I. On my visit, I realized Bill Cosby went there and Temple wore checkered pants."

A month into his freshman season, Palmer had moved from seventh string into the starting lineup. When his career ended, he was Temple's all-time leader in rushing (4,895 yards), 100-yard games (21), and rushing touchdowns (39). As a senior, he finished fifth in the Heisman Trophy voting.

Paul Palmer protects the ball in a game against the Dolphins.
Photo by www.dallascowboysweekly.com

"It was a nice ride. It was amazing. I had a lot of fun. They saved my life. Who knows what I'd been doing if I hadn't gone to Temple?" Palmer said. "I was fortunate. I don't know what they saw in me."

Kansas City needed a running back because star Joe Delaney had tragically drowned following the 1984 season, and Ethan Horton, a first-round pick in 1985, never panned out.

"Everybody knew they needed a running back," said *Kansas City Star* reporter Randy Covitz, who covered the team from 1986 to 2000. "[Coach] Frank Gansz even came out said, 'Palmer is our guy, if he's available.'

"The fact they drafted Christian Okoye in the second round gives you an idea of how big a hole they had at running back."

It was a throwaway comment fueled by frustration. But you don't joke about carrying a bomb on an airplane while you're in the security line, and you don't joke about fumbling when you're a running back.

That, however, is exactly what Palmer did. The brief conversation he had with Chiefs strength coach C.T. Hewgley essentially ruined his relationship with Kansas City and started his career on a downward spiral.

Palmer had reason to be frustrated after carrying the ball only 24 times for 155 yards and catching four passes for 27 yards during the 1987 season. Still, he was one of the league's premier kick returners with a 24.3-yard average and two touchdowns, so Palmer wanted the ball in his hands more often.

Christian Okoye derailed his plans.

The Chiefs viewed the 265-pound African—he was dubbed "The Nigerian Nightmare"—as a human wrecking ball that opposing defenses couldn't stop. They viewed Palmer as a change-of-pace runner, who was too small to carry the ball 20 times a game.

"Paul was extremely talented, but I'm not sure people really used him properly in the NFL," said Steve DeBerg, Kansas City's quarterback from 1988 to 1991, "He was very versatile, but he never seemed to have the success that I thought he was capable of having. It wasn't all his fault, but he just never seemed to fit."

The Chiefs built their offense around Okoye, a second-round pick from Azusa Pacific, who spent his youth playing soccer and competing as a sprinter and thrower in track. When the Chiefs drafted Okoye, he had played only three years of organized football.

"I was playing so well until the midpoint of the year, and I couldn't understand my playing time. There were times after midseason and I'd barely play, and my friends would call and say, 'Are you hurt?' And I'd say, 'No,'" Palmer said. "In KC they got caught up in the Christian Okoye story. It didn't matter what anybody else did. He was going to be the tailback."

Palmer dealt with the situation until late in the season, when a dispute over whether he was late to a team meeting in week 13 led him to utter the words that signaled the end of his career in Kansas City.

"I know I wasn't late. In fact, I was early because I was walking down the hall with Jack Del Rio and when I walked into the meeting room, Steve DeBerg was looking at film. After the meeting, I found out I was marked late, so I went to talk to the strength coach who made the list.

"I explained the situation to him and he said, 'You must have been late or I wouldn't have marked you late.'"

Then the conversation turned ugly.

"That's fine. That's OK," Palmer replied. "I'll deal with this crap for another few weeks. When the season is over, you guys won't be here anyway."

"What did you say?" Hewgley replied.

"When the season is over, you won't be here anyway," Palmer replied. "Maybe to make sure it happens, I'll lay the ball down a couple of times."

Then Palmer walked away. Naïvely, he didn't think much about his comments until coach Frank Gansz confronted him later that night.

"He kept saying, 'I want to know if you said it. I just need to know if you said it,'" Palmer said. "I told him, 'I said it, but I didn't mean it.'"

When that impromptu meeting ended, Palmer thought the situation had been defused. It wasn't. As he got dressed in the locker room prior to a game against Pittsburgh, he was informed that president and general manager Carl Peterson wanted to see him.

"I went to see him and he says, 'We're going to suspend you for a game for conduct detrimental to the team,'" Palmer remembered. "I didn't say anything. I just went back to my locker and got dressed."

Palmer left the stadium and watched the first quarter in an airport bar, while he waited for a flight back to Kansas City.

"I didn't start anymore, even though I was leading the team in rushing, receiving, and scoring and I was second in all-purpose yards behind Eric Dickerson," Palmer said. "Everything was going well. It was like being in college again. I was killing them.

"I finished the year second on the team in receiving, scoring, and rushing, but when Marty Schottenheimer came in, his mind was already made up. No matter what I did, it wasn't going to be enough."

Kansas City fired Gansz and his staff after the season and hired Schottenheimer, who had won in Cleveland with bruising runners like Ernest Byner and Kevin Mack. Okoye fit his scheme perfectly.

The Chiefs released Palmer during training camp prior to the 1989 season. He signed with Detroit, in part, because rookie Barry Sanders, the third player selected in the draft, was in the midst of a contract dispute.

"He never really had a shot when Marty was hired," Covitz said. "[Marty] decided Christian was his guy, and it's hard to argue with him since he led the league in rushing that year."

When Sanders signed, Palmer became the backup running back and returned kicks. The Lions even considered making him a full-time receiver.

But he found himself on the move again at the trade deadline in October. That's because Dallas had made a mega-deal with Minnesota— six players and six draft choices—which had acquired Herschel Walker.

"We thought we were going to be a pretty bad team," said Kevin Gogan, an offensive lineman from 1987 to 1993. "There wasn't a week that went by where we didn't have two or three new players in the starting lineup. At that point you're pretty much grabbing at straws."

As part of the deal, Dallas acquired running back Darrin Nelson, who refused to report to the Cowboys. Needing a runner, Dallas made a minor deal for Palmer.

He practiced Thursday and Friday and started on Sunday, ironically, against the Chiefs. A few minutes before kickoff, coach Jimmy Johnson told Palmer that he was starting.

"He didn't come back as any conquering hero, and it's not like he got a standing ovation or anything," said Covitz, "but you could tell the game was important to him. You could tell he wanted to do well."

Palmer fumbled his first carry, though the Cowboys recovered. A few plays later, he scored on a 63-yard touchdown run, the longest of his career.

The Cowboys lost 36-28, but Palmer felt good about the future.

GAME OF MY LIFE
By Paul Palmer

I grew up a Washington Redskins fan, and there was no team I hated more than the Dallas Cowboys, so I grew up hating these folks. But I also knew what the Dallas Cowboys stood for and the aura they had.

Once I was in Dallas, I thought it was a good fit for them and me. I was liking it, but I still couldn't believe I was playing for the damn Cowboys. I mean I've got family that even now says, "The only time I ever cheered for the Cowboys was when you played for them." I've got other relatives who admit they didn't cheer for me when I was with the Cowboys but justify it by saying they cheered for me every other time I stepped on the field.

Playing the Redskins was special. In my time with the Cowboys, that's the only time that was more exciting than the day I actually signed with Dallas because I was going home playing for the team I used to hate against the team I grew up loving and wanted to play for one day.

It was a Sunday night game, so everybody was watching. I bought a handful of tickets, and I had some family at the game. It was a warm, muggy night, and I could hear people from the stands yelling, "Boo Boo," and when I looked up, I felt bad because I couldn't remember everybody. People had made signs. One I remember said, "Boo Boo and ESPN are No. 1." It was everything you could ask for.

We were 0-11. No one expected us to win. I'm not sure we expected to win, either. But we were playing them tough from the start. Steve Walsh was starting at quarterback because Troy Aikman was hurt. The linemen blocked well. The defense played well, and we just came together that night. I guess that's what a rivalry will do. It was 3-3 at halftime, and we started believing that we could win because we were playing so well.

It was late in the third quarter, and we were in a third-down situation. We lined up in the shotgun, and I got the ball on a draw. It was a pretty good hole—not huge—but I remember hitting it and seeing nobody so I started going as fast as I could. When I passed the line of scrimmage, Wilbur Marshall was in front of me. I remember shaking him, but I stumbled. I never got my top speed again, so I was just trying to go as far as I could. I could feel two or three people converging on me. They all had good angles, and they all pretty much got me at the same time.

If I could've gotten my speed back up, then I would've outran them. I was mad at myself because I didn't score, but it was incredible to have a run like that. I scored on a 2-yard run over the top. It wasn't a great dive, but it got the job done and gave us a 10-3 lead. I grabbed the football and ran to where one of my cousins was sitting and gave her the football. She was jumping around and going crazy.

When the game was over, Jimmy Johnson was rushing us to the bus so we could get out of town. I'm not the fastest dresser in the world, so I don't remember having a chance to visit with my family after the game or talk to the local media. The script couldn't have been written better if I had done it myself. The long run. The touchdown. My friends. My family. The whole game was like an adrenaline rush.

I just kind of thought this is where I was supposed to be. I was proving to people that I could get it done. I just kept thinking playing in Dallas for these damn Cowboys and playing against the Redskins twice a year. It was exciting for me. I was happy to be on the Cowboys, and I had no idea it was going to be over as soon as it was.

———————

The Cowboys didn't win another game, finishing the season 1-15.

But Palmer did a good job in his role, leading the team with 446 yards rushing and a 4-yard average, though he never had another starring role. The Cowboys were improving but couldn't make plays in the fourth quarter to get a victory to consummate their effort.

"Paul was kind of shifty," Gogan said, "and he did a good job for us."

A 15-0 loss to the Giants in week 15 established a dubious record since it marked the third time the Cowboys had been shut out.

Still, Palmer felt good about his future. Even when he was informed less than three hours before the final regular-season game that he wasn't going to play, Palmer didn't think much of it. The Cowboys told him they wanted to take a look at rookie running back Curtis Stewart of Auburn, who had spent much of the season on the practice squad.

"I had just gotten my ankles taped. I was expecting to play, and Coach Johnson told me I wasn't going to dress for the game," Palmer said. "Curtis Stewart didn't even step on the field.

"If I gained more than 500 yards, I would've hit a bonus. I don't think they wanted to pay any extra money toward a 1-15 season, so that's probably why I didn't play. I watched the game and kept waiting for Curtis to step on the field, but Broderick [Sargent] and Darryl [Johnston] played running back. I watched in street clothes."

Although he didn't get a chance to earn a bonus by playing in the final game, Palmer wanted to remain with the Cowboys. That changed when the Cowboys didn't put him on their protected list as part of Plan B free agency. League rules allowed each team to protect 38 players; the others became unrestricted free agents and could sign with any team.

Remembering an impromptu conversation he had with defensive assistant Butch Davis the final week of the season, Palmer felt snubbed.

"Butch said, 'We're going to get it together and you're going to be a big part of it,'" Palmer said. "I agreed because I thought I was going to be a big part of what the Cowboys were going to do because I had done a good job in Dallas.

"In all honesty, being young I was like, 'I'm outta here, if this is the way they want to do it.' Later, someone inside the organization who I respect actually told me they probably left me unprotected because they didn't think anyone would sign me and they could've protected someone else and brought me back.

"If I was looking at it like a business or a businessman, I would've stayed because I was the leading rusher and the starting tailback. But the ballplayer in me allowed my feelings to get hurt. I should've stayed."

Four months later, the Cowboys drafted Emmitt Smith. Palmer wouldn't have been the starter in 1990, but maybe his skills as a receiver and returner would've allowed him to fill a valuable role with the Cowboys.

Instead, he signed with Cincinnati as a Plan B free agent and was released in training camp. He spent the next two years running the ball for Barcelona in the World League of American Football. When the Philadelphia Eagles released him in August 1991, Palmer decided to stop chasing the NFL dream.

"I was just a camper. I knew the speed of camp. I wasn't going to be intimidated, and they could use me if needed," Palmer said. "But I could see I was going to get cut because they were signing guys and cutting their replacements the same day. At the point, I was like, 'It has been a good ride.'

"I think I gave up on it too quickly. I felt like I deserved better opportunities than I was getting but I probably could've made better opportunities for myself. There's no doubt in my mind I could play in the NFL, but for whatever reason it was never being seen."

Paul Palmer didn't make a fortune playing football. Much of what Palmer did earn in his three-year NFL career, he lost through poor advice from corrupt agents.

After the Chiefs drafted him, Palmer said he paid taxes up front on the four-year deal he signed. Since he only played three seasons, he paid taxes on one year that he never played.

Palmer was also one of many players swindled out of hundreds of thousands of dollars by agents Norby Walters and Lloyd Bloom, who were indicted on charges of mail fraud and racketeering. The charges were in connection with their representation of student-athletes with whom they entered into agreements and loaned money to before the athletes' college eligibility expired.

"There's a chunk of money on taxes that's gone, and then my agents beat me out of few hundred thousand dollars," Palmer said, "so I've just been a normal guy working."

It has been an adjustment from being a superstar college athlete with a future as bright as the North Star, from a guy who signed autographs daily to an ordinary person working to support his children.

"You're dealing with people, and it's like, 'Don't you know who I am?' On the other hand, you feel like, 'Just let me do my job; don't let me be recognized,'" Palmer said. "You don't want to deal with people who say, 'Damn, aren't you Paul Palmer from Temple? What are doing now?' It's so strange."

Palmer has held a variety of jobs. He worked at NFL Films as a production assistant for several years. Then he worked at Temple as a color commentator on the football team's broadcasts.

He always wanted to coach and work with kids. Now, he's doing it at Haddon Heights (New Jersey) High School, where his daughter, Moet, played basketball and ran track before graduating in 2006.

He enjoys passing on the knowledge his coaches gave to him and relating stories about the time Reggie White apologized for tackling him too hard or William "The Refrigerator" Perry nearly broke his nose.

He enjoys trying to help out kids the way older people helped him by giving cleats to students or socks to those who didn't have any.

"This is fun," he said. "I'm having a good time."

CHAPTER 17

BILL
BATES

Even as a youngster, football consumed Bill Bates' thoughts—and it didn't matter whether he was awake.

He began sleepwalking in high school, and it reached an apex in his first training camp with the Cowboys at California Lutheran University in Thousand Oaks, California. Naturally, Bates hadn't informed his roommates, Mark Tuinei, Chris Schultz, and John Warren, that he occasionally had bouts with sleepwalking.

"John's bunk was right next to me, and there was a dresser," Bates said. "I woke up one day because I heard John yelling. I had knocked the dresser on top of him while I was sleeping. John was yelling, 'You've got to turn the page on this football stuff. You're hitting on the field, and now you're hitting me.'"

That wasn't the only time Warren, who played with Bates at the University of Tennessee, had to deal with his roommate's late-night activities.

"One time I jumped up and dove straight down on his bed trying to make a tackle," Bates said with a chuckle.

Even when he made the team, his wife found out that he didn't always leave his work at the office.

"I didn't tell Denise that I was a sleepwalker. That just didn't seem like the kind of thing you talk about," Bates said. "I had just made the team in my second year, and when she woke up one night, I was in the middle of the room with covers all around me in my football stance like I was talking to somebody.

"I guess the mental pictures and images in my mind never got turned off all the way, and somehow it affected me and made me sleepwalk."

Bates, though, makes no apologies for being obsessed with football. He loved the physical aspect of the game and the competitiveness. And he was good at it.

As a senior in Knoxville, Tennessee, Bates had scholarship offers from virtually every major football power in the nation. He visited Auburn, Ole Miss, Kentucky, and UCLA. In the end, it came down to UCLA and Tennessee.

"On the flight back I was writing down reasons to go to UT and UCLA. There were a lot of great reasons to go to UCLA, but [safety] Kenny Easley was going to be a junior and I wasn't going to play in front of him," Bates said. "There was going to be a better chance to play at Tennessee. Besides, if I didn't go to Tennessee, they might've burned down my house."

Bates also had plenty of ties to the Volunteers and their football tradition. He already knew the words to "Rocky Top." His father, who had served in the Navy and worked for Exxon, and his mother had attended Tennessee, and Bates had sold soft drinks and programs at Neyland Stadium as a youth.

It helped that coach Johnny Majors had won a national championship at the University of Pittsburgh in 1976. Bates started all but one game in four years at Tennessee, but he didn't have much fun his two seasons playing for the demanding Majors.

"I hated it because of Johnny. Now that it's behind me, I know a lot of the things he did as a coach helped me, but I wish he would've done it in a little different way," Bates said. "He made me tougher. Maybe I wasn't tough enough. Maybe that's how I became tough enough to withstand almost anything.

"I'm friends with him, and there are a lot of things about him that I respect, but during those first couple of years, I didn't like him much."

Although Bates was one of the top players in the Southeastern Conference, he didn't have the combination of height, weight, and speed that makes professional scouts and coaches drool. He moved slowly in a game that was being geared more and more toward speed.

The New Jersey Generals of the United States Football League drafted him; the NFL did not.

The next day, a scout from the Seattle Seahawks arrived at 7 a.m. with a contract. Two hours later, the Cowboys called offering him an opportunity to play for his favorite team. It was an easy decision until he arrived at training camp and saw how many other free agents and players he was competing against.

Defensive back Bill Bates looks on during a game against the Los Angeles Rams at Anaheim Stadium. *Ken Levine/Getty Images*

"If you didn't have scrimmages, he wouldn't have made the team," said Gil Brandt, Cowboys personnel director from 1960 to 1989, "because people would look at him and say he wasn't fast enough, but he worked hard and he stuck."

That was by design. Bates held on extra points, returned punts, and played on all of the coverage units. And in the first preseason game, he caught coach Tom Landry's eye, despite playing with a severe groin injury. During a film session the following day, Landry praised Bates.

"Coach Landry turns on the film and says to the team, 'I want you to watch this No. 40 run down here and make a tackle. This is the way you cover on kickoffs.'"

It was only the beginning.

Safety Bill Bates. Defensive end Jim Jeffcoat. Tackle Mark Tuinei. Punter Mike Saxon.

The quartet could have been the answer to a trivia question: "Who are the only players on the 1991 Cowboys who had ever been to the playoffs wearing a Cowboys uniform?"

Bates, though, had a feeling that streak was about to end. He had suffered through the 1-15 debacle in 1989, which was coach Jimmy Johnson's first year in Dallas. And he had seen the Cowboys forge a late-season, four-game winning streak that put them on the cusp of getting to the playoffs in 1990.

Instead, an injury to quarterback Troy Aikman forced backup Babe Laufenberg into the starting lineup, and the Cowboys lost their last two games. But they entered 1991 with hope, something they hadn't had since Tom Landry and his trademark fedora roamed the sideline.

"In 1989 and 1990 there was so much turnover. People were coming and going, but you could start to see and get a sense that things were going to be different," Bates said. "The organization was committed to getting the best athletes and players available. I knew it might cost me my job, but as a player it gives you hope.

"At the end of the 1990 season, we started having some continuity with the coaches and understanding the defensive system. Troy was getting more comfortable, and everything was coming together."

But it still took some time for the progress to manifest itself on the football field. After starting the season 5-2, the Cowboys lost three of four games and dipped to 6-5 after a 22-9 loss to the New York Giants.

Five games remained in the season, and undefeated Washington was the Cowboys' next opponent. It seemed like a strange time for Dallas to put a string of wins together, considering tight end Jay Novacek and guard Nate Newton missed the game—but that's what the team did.

The streak began when Aikman passed for 204 yards with a touchdown and an interception before leaving with a knee injury to propel Dallas to a 24-21 upset win over the Redskins.

"If you got a big old gorilla there, don't just go up and tap him on the shoulder," coach Jimmy Johnson said after the game. "I think it was Teddy Roosevelt who said, 'Don't ever hit lightly. Whether it's in a battle, a war, a fight—if you're going to hit, hit with all you've got.'

"I told the players Friday that's what we were going to do. We were going to be aggressive and go after them as hard as we can go in all three phases of the game. That's the only chance we had of beating a great football team."

Steve Beuerlein, acquired in August after Oakland released him, took over for Aikman and finished the Washington game. Then he helped the Cowboys reel off four more wins, including a 25-13 win at Philadelphia. The Eagles had beaten Dallas 24-0 earlier in the season and sacked Aikman 11 times.

Actually, Philadelphia had won eight straight against Dallas, including five games by two touchdowns or more. They did it with a physical defense that snuffed out the Cowboys' offense. Four times during that streak the Cowboys were held to one touchdown or less.

Kelvin Martin's 85-yard fourth-quarter punt return triggered a 25-13 victory that secured the Cowboys' first playoff berth since 1985.

"If we could beat them in Philadelphia then we felt like we had accomplished a great deal," Bates said. "They had been such a road block for us, and we had finally broken through. We had been working a long time to beat them."

The Cowboys knew they were going to have to start the playoffs on the road since Washington had won the NFC East with a 14-2 record, but they didn't care. After all, they had opened the season with a win in Cleveland's "Dog Pound." They had won at raucous RFK Stadium in Washington, and they had captured a playoff spot at Philadelphia's Veterans Stadium, where fans had once booed Santa Claus.

With Bates getting a sack, forcing a fumble, and finally intercepting a pass with 1:04 left in the game, the Cowboys beat Chicago and won their first playoff game since 1982.

"Winning up there catapulted us to the championships," said Kevin Gogan, an offensive lineman from 1987 to 1993. "We were so bad before then, but then the guys like Aikman and Emmitt [Smith] just kept getting better.

"I knew we were on the rise, but I didn't know we'd do it so fast, because the next year we were in the Super Bowl and we were still a pretty young team. We didn't have any idea what we were doing, so we bought into what Coach Johnson was saying and followed him."

GAME OF MY LIFE
By Bill Bates

I had only been in the playoffs twice, in 1983 and 1985, and both times we were unsuccessful. It was very exciting, but we were playing the Bears and they were good. They had Mike Ditka, and it was a daunting task. I don't remember a lot of people giving us much chance to win up there, but it was neat to still be playing when most teams were not. It was cold, and a lot of guys were worried about what the weather was going to be like, but it didn't bother me because I always liked playing in the cold. I didn't have any problem focusing.

Even though I was getting older and the team was getting better, I still played a lot. I was the middle linebacker in the nickel and the dime, and I was on all the special teams. I played enough that I still had to get IVs at halftime and after games when it was hot early in the season.

It was a little strange because Steve Beuerlein was going to be our quarterback because Troy Aikman was still getting back from his injury, but at that time Troy wasn't the great quarterback we know today. He was still proving himself. Steve always had an air of confidence as a player. He was a team guy, and he had a burning desire to be good. His confidence helped us believe we could win, and that was a major factor in the game.

I didn't blitz a whole lot, but we were being aggressive, and I got a sack on the first drive that forced a fumble. I don't remember much about that play except trying to dive on the ball, but Tony Hill got it.

I remember the interception a lot more clearly.

We were up on them, and the only way they could win the game was to score a touchdown, so it was a passing situation and we knew they were going to have to let Jim Harbaugh throw the ball all over the field.

I dropped back into coverage, and he tried to get a ball between the receiver and me, but he didn't, and I intercepted it. I remember catching the ball and hearing coach Dave Campo screaming, "Bates get on the ground! Get on the ground!" But I had the interception, and I wanted to run with it.

It was a great moment, knowing all of the hard work I put in over the years had paid off because I was in my ninth season and I didn't know if it was going to be my last year or what. Anytime you get an interception like that to seal a game, especially a playoff game, it's pretty huge. And that was a big turning point in our run of championships. We proved that we could beat a good football team—and do it on the road.

I knew Coach Ditka personally, and after the game I got to shake his hand, which has been a great memory for me. It was jubilation and excitement in the locker room after the game, but there were also sighs of relief. We were finally getting on a roll, and people were going to expect it from us, and we were going to expect it from ourselves.

As we got on the bus and headed to the airport, a strange thing happened. There were girls flashing their chests at us. I was like, "What in the world is going on? Is this what it's like when you start winning?"

The celebration from the Cowboys' victory over Chicago was short lived. They had to play Detroit, the NFC Central champions, who had enjoyed a bye. The Lions were undefeated in the Pontiac Silverdome and had beaten the Cowboys 34-10 in the regular season.

They also had running back Barry Sanders, one of the game's most electrifying players. He rushed for 1,548 yards and 16 touchdowns during the regular season, though Dallas had limited him to 55 yards on 21 carries with a scheme designed to eliminate him from the game.

"It felt like it was a short week to get ready to play Detroit, and they were good," Bates said. "Barry Sanders on the turf—holy moly—that was tough. I hit him one time, when he was being held up, and I just knew that I was going to end his career, but Barry had great vision and he saw me coming and absorbed the blow. It was like hitting a pillow.

"Emmitt was like that, too. You'd be running behind him and he'd feel you and make a quick move, so you couldn't hit him. [Tony] Dorsett was the same way. Their instincts were so quick and fast that you never got a clean blow."

Detroit, playing its first home playoff game since 1957, never gave Dallas a chance to win.

Journeyman quarterback Erik Kramer, playing the game of his life, completed 29 of 38 passes for 341 yards and three touchdowns as the Lions routed Dallas 38-6. They did it without much contribution from Sanders, who had just 14 yards on six carries after three quarters.

Trailing 14-3 in the second quarter, Johnson turned to Aikman in search of a spark. It was Aikman's first action since spraining his knee on November 24 against Washington. The Cowboys' six-game winning streak ended with a thud.

"It was a big downer, but the coaches probably took it worse than the players," Bates said. "We had really come a long way. Eric Kramer was just on fire that game. We were blitzing, and he was throwing the ball like he was Joe Montana. We knew we weren't good enough yet to beat them.

"But we felt like this was our time. We knew we were good, and we were going to be disappointed if we didn't make a big run for the championship. The confidence from Michael [Irvin] and those guys really started to build, and once you start believing you're good, it makes it harder for teams to beat you just like when you have some doubt, it makes it easier for you to lose."

The loss prompted Johnson and owner Jerry Jones to use the draft and trades to improve the secondary. The result: cornerbacks Kevin Smith (first round) and Clayton Holmes (third round) and safety Darren Woodson (second round) were drafted, and pass-rushing defensive end

Charles Haley and safety Thomas Everett were acquired in trades with San Francisco and Pittsburgh, respectively.

Johnson and Jones knew they couldn't win without playing better defense because first-year offensive coordinator Norv Turner had done wonders with the offense.

In 1990, the Cowboys ranked last in the NFL in offense with 27 touchdowns and 244 points. A year later, they ranked ninth in the NFL in offense with 37 touchdowns and 342 points.

"We realized that we were going in the right direction and that we were capable of having a good football team," said Joe Avezzano, special teams coach from 1990 to 2002. "The win over Chicago laid the foundation for the things we did the next few years."

Bill Bates didn't want to retire. Few players do.

As former coach Tom Landry once told Randy White, "If you're fortunate enough to stay around this game long enough, then it will humble you."

Jones and first-year coach Chan Gailey asked Bates to consider retiring in the off-season before the club's minicamps began, but he resisted the notion. He wanted a chance to prove he could make the team, and he needed one more season to set the franchise record for consecutive years of service.

But on the first day of training camp in 1998, an emotional Bates reluctantly accepted the Cowboys' offer to join the coaching staff.

"I want to play," Bates said at the time, reading from a statement. "To not play another year would be tough on me, no matter when it was. I think this is the right time. ...

"You did not hear a retirement speech. I will train and get ready to play, so if the opportunity [arises], I will be ready. But I'm not focusing on that. I'm focusing on helping this team win as a coach."

And with that, one of the finest special teams players in NFL history left the game. In 1983 and 1984, Bates was the NFL's Special Teams Player of the Year. In 1984, he became the first NFC player selected to the Pro Bowl as a special teams performer, and his play in that facet of the game is often credited with getting the NFL to add special teams players to the Pro Bowl roster.

"You can't be an overachiever for 15 years. That's a tag that was put on him, and it was a perfect storyline for Bill because he was an undrafted free agent," Avezzano said. "But if the average NFL career is three to four years and he stretched it out to 15 years, then it means he had a certain amount of physical ability and a mental capacity to withstand the competition that the team constantly brought in to beat him out."

Only Ed "Too Tall" Jones (224) played in more games with the Cowboys than Bates (207), who started just 45 games in his career—none during his last nine seasons.

"You tried to replace him a lot of times with a bigger, stronger, faster player, and you just couldn't do it," Avezzano said. "At some point, you just have to acknowledge that the combination of physical and mental attributes made Bill Bates a good player."

When Bill Parcells became the Cowboys' coach after three consecutive 5-11 seasons, Bates became one of several assistant coaches who was fired. He spent a year as Jacksonville's special teams coach before head coach Jack Del Rio, a former teammate, fired him.

"It made me realize how fortunate and blessed I was when I played," Bates said of being fired after one season in Jacksonville. "I don't have a bad taste about the NFL. You can work 24 hours a day, never sleep, and still get fired. It's about pleasing the owner and filling the seats.

"It's not easy to jump back into the real world after being in the NFL all that time, which is why I had been involved in other businesses as a player. When you're a player, you realize eventually that you have to be prepared for the day your career ends."

Bates was better prepared than most.

He remained in Jacksonville, Florida, with his wife, Denise, and their five children. He's an assistant coach at Nease High School and is working with Temperature Management Systems, a part of the Williams Sports Group, to develop a revolutionary shoulder pad that keeps a player's core body temperature cool during games.

"My journey in the NFL was the culmination of hard work, not listening to the doubters and overcoming the odds," Bates said. "It's all of the things people like to talk about, but don't like to write because it's not controversial."

CHAPTER 18

JIMMY JOHNSON

The plan was for Jimmy Johnson to be an industrial psychologist. He had his degree from the University of Arkansas, a wife and child to support, and had already started his master's program.

Then he received a call from Louisiana Tech's Jim MacKenzie.

Tech was desperate because defensive coordinator George Dougherty had suffered a heart attack, and they needed someone who knew how to coach the Arkansas Monster Slide defense. Doctors had told Dougherty that he could probably return to coaching after a year to improve his health, but that wasn't going to help Tech play in 1965. Besides, no established coach was going to take a job knowing he'd be replaced in a year when Dougherty returned.

"They were going to pay me $1,000 a month for three months, give me a car and an apartment," Johnson said. "For a college student with a young son and wife that was pretty good money."

And he could focus on his job because his wife, Linda Kay, was going to stay in Fayetteville and teach school and take care of Brent. When Johnson returned from Louisiana Tech, he'd have enough money to go to graduate school.

The plan was perfect except that it didn't account for Johnson falling in love with coaching.

"I stuck with it and never got out," he said. "I enjoyed it, and it was a big part of my life. I enjoyed interaction with players and the thrill of winning games, but I never thought I'd stay anywhere forever. I didn't have thoughts about the NFL because I kind of lived for today.

"For someone whose entire life is engulfed in football, there's no way to really describe the feeling that you have when you win a Super Bowl or national championship because of the time and effort that you put into it."

The job at Louisiana Tech began the Port Arthur, Texas, native's circuitous route to the NFL that took him to Picayune (Mississippi) High School, Wichita (Kansas) State, Iowa State, Oklahoma, Arkansas in 1973, and Pittsburgh before getting his first head coaching job at Oklahoma State in 1979.

"I never doubted Jimmy's ability to win with the Cowboys because I had seen it as an assistant coach at Iowa State in 1968," said Joe Avezzano, the Cowboys' special teams coach from 1990 to 2002. "I knew his background extremely well and [that of] the people he had learned from.

"I knew he was a quick thinker. I had been in the press box with him and had seen him analyze schemes and make adjustments quickly to help us win games. He also understood what problems were most important for us to address and solve and which we could put on the backburner."

Johnson, named Big 8 Coach of the Year in his first season at Oklahoma State, stayed four years before leaving for Miami. In five seasons with the Hurricanes, he had a 36-game winning streak and won a national title.

Then old friend Jerry Jones called with the opportunity of a lifetime. Jones was about to purchase the Dallas Cowboys for $142 million, and he wanted to know if his former college teammate at Arkansas wanted to coach the team.

"I [had] made my run at Miami. We had won a national championship and lost two regular-season games in four years, and I was kind of getting bored," Johnson said. "I was ready to do something else. It's not that it was monotonous, because I had fun and I enjoyed it.

"To this day, the most fun I ever had was at Miami. That's not to take anything away from my years with the Cowboys, but pro coaching is really more of a grind."

Johnson replaced a legend in Tom Landry, who was fired after 29 seasons and two Super Bowl championships.

Dallas went 3-13 in Landry's last season, giving Dallas the top pick in the 1989 draft. Jones and Johnson picked Troy Aikman, who was selected for the Hall of Fame in January 2006, five years after his career ended. At the end of Aikman's 12-year career, he had won three Super Bowls and more games in the 1990s than any other quarterback.

"Jimmy Johnson was a guy who was instrumental—not only in my success but in our team's success. We were a struggling team when I initially joined the Dallas Cowboys," Aikman said, "but he set a tempo and a tone for our organization that allowed us to win back-to-back world championship, and to a large extent he was responsible for us winning a third Super Bowl.

"I was Jerry Jones' first pick when he bought the Dallas Cowboys, and it has always meant a lot to me to be known as the first player chosen once Jerry took over the organization. The best thing any quarterback with aspirations of winning a world championship can have is an owner who is willing to spend money and do what it takes to win.

"There are a lot of owners in this league who talk about winning but don't necessarily do what it takes to win. There are a handful of guys who do it and do it very well—and Jerry Jones happens to be one of them. It was nice for me going to bed every night knowing we were doing everything we could to win football games."

None of that mattered much to fans in Jones' and Johnson's first year, when they started the season 0-8 and traded Herschel Walker, the only proven player on the team.

"We knew we were bad in 1989, and my offensive staff was mad at me because I traded away our only Pro Bowl player," Johnson said. "I released our leading receiver [Derrick Shepard] because he couldn't run—he ran a 4.8 40-yard dash—and I wouldn't allow our coaches to start Jesse Solomon or David Howard because I didn't want everyone falling in love with them because I might've had to cut them to get the draft picks.

"Every move we made in 1989 was to make us a better team in 1991 and 1992. Losing 15 games wasn't easy, but I knew we were going to win."

The Cowboys were ready to make a move in coach Jimmy Johnson's fourth season. Troy Aikman, Emmitt Smith, and Michael Irvin were entering their prime as players.

They understood how to prepare and withstand the rigors of the season. And how to manage the distractions that accompanied being a star in Dallas, where football rules and the Cowboys have carte blanche in the city when they're winning.

After going 11-5 in 1991 and winning a playoff game for the first time since 1983, Johnson took measures to correct the flaws in the sec-

Jimmy Johnson watches his team warm up before Super Bowl XXVII.
© *Vernon J. Biever Photo*

ondary that were exposed after Detroit trounced the Cowboys 38-6 in a
NFC Division playoff game.

Dallas drafted Texas A&M cornerback Kevin Smith with the 17th
pick in the first round and middle linebacker Robert Jones seven picks
later. The Cowboys added safety Darren Woodson in the second round
and cornerback Clayton Holmes in the third round, and traded for hard-
hitting safety Thomas Everett, who had spent his first five seasons with
Pittsburgh as a fourth-round draft choice from Baylor.

But the biggest addition was an August trade with San Francisco that
added mercurial pass-rusher Charles Haley to the roster for draft picks.
Haley was one of the game's best pass rushers, recording 64 sacks in six
seasons with San Francisco, including four seasons with at least 10 sacks.

But the 49ers had grown weary of his moodiness and his personality clashes with teammates that reached an apex when he urinated in linebacker Tim Harris' car.

"We had struggled with our pass defense the year before, so we felt like we needed to improve our coverage and our pass rush, and we did things to do that," Johnson said. "We were still one of the youngest teams in the NFL, but some of our key players had had a couple of years together. We had talent, we had fixed some of our problem areas, and we were ready to see how good we could be."

The season started with a convincing 23-10 victory on *Monday Night Football* over Washington, the defending Super Bowl champions, at Texas Stadium. In 1991, Washington lost two games by a total of five points. Emmitt Smith rushed for 139 yards, and the Haley-led defense sacked quarterback Mark Rypien twice and hit him with regularity.

That eliminated any doubt about the Cowboys' ability to compete in the NFC East, football's toughest division.

"We went from having a solid secondary to having a great secondary with the addition of [Kevin Smith], Woodson, and Everett," said James Washington, a safety with the Cowboys from 1990 to 1994. "We could match up with anyone."

Now that their defense was at a championship level, the Cowboys rolled to a 13-3 regular-season record and their first NFC East championship since 1985. The Cowboys won nine games by at least 10 points, including four by more than 20.

But Johnson proved hard to please.

He continually pressured the Cowboys to play to the level of their vast talent. A 20-17 loss to Washington in December produced a testy 60-second postgame news conference. Johnson had won a national title at Miami and knew the attention to detail it took to win a championship.

Backup running back Curvin Richards didn't—and it cost him an opportunity to be part of a championship team. A victory over Atlanta would have secured the NFC East title and meant the final regular-season game against Chicago would have no effect on the playoffs, although Smith was trying to win his second straight rushing title.

Smith had passed Pittsburgh's Barry Foster for the rushing title on a 31-yard run in the third quarter that gave Dallas a 10-0 lead. A fumble return for a touchdown by Russell Maryland pushed the lead to 17-0 with 10:59 left and sent most of the starters to the bench.

But Richards fumbled twice in 13 carries. Chris Zorich returned one of the fumbles 42 yards for a touchdown, forcing Johnson to reinsert Smith.

"I knew as soon as he had the second fumble that I was cutting him as soon as the game was over," Johnson said. "I had had enough of it, and it emphasized to the rest of the players—I don't care who you are—we're not going to put up with turnovers.

"It made no difference that we couldn't replace him on the roster or that he was going to get playoff money anyway. We couldn't have that kind of attitude and be successful in the playoffs. We didn't have another fumble all the way through the playoffs until [defensive tackle] Leon Lett's fumble in the Super Bowl."

GAME OF MY LIFE
By Jimmy Johnson

At that time, San Francisco was considered the best team in the NFL, and we knew we were going to have to play well to beat them at their place.

I had talked to our staff prior to the game, and we were going to lean heavily on having Emmitt run the football. At the same time, our approach was going to have to be a little bit different if we were going to be successful, because San Francisco had a great defensive football team and for the simple reason that we believed they were the best team in the NFL.

We thought we would start the game a little more wide open than we normally would and take some shots deep to Alvin Harper. Once we got into the flow of the game, if it was still tight, then we'd turn it over to Emmitt. But we weren't going to start the game running the football like they expected.

Aside from the talented players on their team, the other concern we had was the turf at Candlestick Park because they were accustomed to it and we had played on artificial turf most of the season. Their field is right there at sea level so it was usually damp, but that year it was extremely torn up so the league office replaced two-thirds of the field.

That concerned me, so the day before the game I went out with George Toma, the league's field specialist, to check out the field. I had never done that before, but it was a huge concern of ours before they installed the new sod. We walked across the entire field, and I charted where it was extremely slippery and where the turf was loose. George pointed out where the new sod had been installed because, surprisingly, the footing was better in those spots.

The next morning I had our trainer, Kevin O'Neill, call all of the coaches for a special meeting. I wanted to meet with all of them before we ate breakfast. I took a blackboard out and charted the entire field. Norv Turner had already finalized the offensive game plan; Dave Wannstedt was done with the defensive game plan; and Joe Avezzano was done with the special teams game plan, but I wanted to make sure they knew everything I had learned about the field.

I had them go through every single scenario on different parts of the field and mark down on their game-call charts where certain plays would be good and where they probably wouldn't. For example, there were certain areas on the field where we wouldn't run Emmitt on a sweep or wide play because he was going to have to make a hard cut and the footing was too poor for that. In that area of the field, we'd go with a lead draw or a counter play because the footing would be better in the middle of the field.

There were also certain areas where we didn't want to blitz because the footing was poor and we didn't want to take the risk and have a defender in man coverage slip down and give them a big play. And in the kicking game, the field was decent all the way across on one end. The other end, however, was especially slippery at the hash marks. When we returned kicks from that end, we would only use a middle return.

All of the time we spent talking about the field and charting it helped, because we really didn't have a problem with the footing all day. And on one of the biggest plays of the game, it gave us the confidence to call a pass play. We were leading 24-20, but San Francisco had just scored and they had the momentum.

A lot of people thought we would sit on it and try to run Emmitt, but I talked to Norv on the headset and told him that we had to throw the football because San Francisco was going to be stacked inside to stop Emmitt. Norv said we could throw the slant to Michael Irvin because it's a safe play, and we knew Michael would take a hit and still make the catch.

So I said, "Let's go ahead and do it."

Michael misunderstood the call. Michael thought we'd run a sideline comeback on the other side of the field so he switched positions with Alvin Harper. We rarely threw the ball on the slant to Alvin because sometimes he'd get those short arms, but he was great on takeoffs and other sideline routes. Even though Alvin would run slants from time to time, he was never the primary receiver when he did.

But the coverage dictated the slant was going to be open, and Troy was going to throw the ball where the coverage dictated, so he threw the slant to Alvin, the defensive back slipped down—we knew that was a slippery part of the field—and Alvin got a long gain that helped us score the touchdown that put the game out of reach.

We didn't approach the game like it was our first time in the NFC championship game, but we did approach it like we were the underdogs because on paper they were the better team and we were playing at their place. If we were going to be successful, we had to take some chances and make things happen. Our approach was to go against the percentages, which is what we did on the slant to Alvin. We were not going to be able to play it close to the vest and win that game. Of course, I didn't tell the team that, but I did tell them we had to start fast, and I told Emmitt not to get frustrated.

After the game, we were ecstatic because we knew if we won that game, we had a Super Bowl ring. We had seen Buffalo enough times to know they consistently turned the ball over. They were a talented team, but because of the turnovers, they couldn't play with us.

The Buffalo Bills never worried Jimmy Johnson.

It didn't matter to him that Buffalo had played in consecutive Super Bowls. Or that the Bills had one of the best offensive triumvirates—quarterback Jim Kelly, running back Thurman Thomas, and receiver Andre Reed—in the game.

Johnson simply didn't believe Buffalo could beat the Cowboys, and he shared that information with his team in the days before the game.

"Before we went to California, everyone had talked about how they went to two Super Bowls and how they were a veteran team and we were a young team," Johnson said. "Even though we might have been the more talented team on paper, they thought dealing with the media pressure would overwhelm us. I told the guys, 'It's all about what you put in your head.'"

In a team meeting, Johnson used a two-by-four piece of wood as an example to emphasize his point.

"Every one of you could walk from one end to the other, if I put this on the floor," Johnson said. "If I put it 15 feet up in the air, then your thought process would be about not falling instead of walking across it, and you'd fall because that's the seed planted in your mind.

"Think about what would happen if we played Buffalo on the practice field: We'd kick the hell out of them. It would be no contest. When you're preparing for this game, focus on the fact that nobody will be watching."

Johnson told his team they'd be taking a different tack than the game plan used against San Francisco. The Cowboys wanted to be aggressive and grab an early lead against a superior team in that game. Against Buffalo, they wanted to wait for Buffalo to make a mistake before pouncing.

"The night before the game, I told the players that if we didn't give them anything early, we'd take control of the game," Johnson said. "In fact, I told the players we were going to be a little conservative early because we knew they were going to give us the ball."

But it was Dallas that made a mistake early, allowing Buffalo to grab an early 7-0 lead when special teams star Steve Tasker blocked a punt to set up a touchdown. Johnson still wasn't worried, because he figured Buffalo couldn't stop their offense.

When they used safety Leonard Smith in run support, Troy Aikman looked for Michael Irvin and tight end Jay Novacek. When they played coverage with the safeties, Aikman gave the ball to Emmitt Smith. And as Johnson figured, the Cowboys' defense, ranked No. 1 in the NFL, provided some turnovers.

"We fell behind early," Johnson said, "but they started to turn the ball over, and we ran away with it."

Buffalo committed a Super Bowl–record nine turnovers—five fumbles and four interceptions—as Dallas raced to a 28-14 halftime lead when Irvin caught touchdown passes of 19 and 18 yards during an 18-second span in the final two minutes of the half.

At halftime, someone mentioned to Johnson that Buffalo had rallied from a 35-3 third-quarter deficit to defeat Houston 41-38 in one of the most thrilling come-from-behind wins in playoff history. All that did was make Johnson mad.

"I got pissed," Johnson said. "I said, 'We're not Houston.'"

Aikman passed for 273 yards and four touchdowns, and the Cowboys scored 21 points in the fourth quarter to rout Buffalo 52-17 and win their first world championship in 25 years.

"The first one was such a thrill. When I walked on the field before the game to meditate, it was such a great feeling, and when those jets flew over during the national anthem, I was ecstatic," Johnson said. "The second one we had to deal with a lot more expectations.

"I had more concerns about winning the second one because Troy suffered a concussion in the NFC championship game, and we only had a week to prepare, so he wasn't at the top of his game. There was absolutely no doubt we would win the first one."

———————————

Less than 24 hours after the Cowboys' second consecutive championship, Jimmy Johnson sat in a limousine with *Sports Illustrated* football writer Peter King.

"I told Peter King that I couldn't tell him I was coming back. He said three in a row would make me an automatic for the Hall of Fame, but I told him that it wasn't that big of a deal to me," Johnson said. "I had had somebody drive my car all the way down to the Florida Keys, where I had a home. I pretty much had made up my mind that I was going to move when the timing was right. I was happy we had won two in a row, but I was pretty set I wanted to move to Florida."

The decision was made easier a couple of months later, during the owners' meetings in Orlando when Johnson and several members of the coaching staff were sitting in a hotel restaurant table having a drink. Jerry Jones walked up and offered a toast that Johnson and several of his staff barely acknowledged, triggering several days of juicy, controversial he-said, he-said stories in the *Dallas Morning News* and the *Fort Worth Star-Telegram.*

It culminated with a joint news conference in which Jones and Johnson claimed they came to a mutual decision that Johnson would no longer coach the Cowboys. Jones gave his old college teammate a seven-figure check and a hug, and began his search for a successor that would end with Barry Switzer being named the third coach in franchise history.

Johnson relaxed in the Florida Keys—fishing and diving almost daily—drinking Heineken and checking the stock market on his computer. He was content to spend the rest of his life doing that, when Miami owner Wayne Huizenga phoned with a job offer.

"I didn't want to ever look back and say I should've given it one more shot," Johnson said. "I didn't want any regrets. I visited with Wayne and decided to give it a shot."

Miami was about $5 million over the NFL-mandated salary cap, which meant they couldn't keep key players such as linebacker Brian Cox, receiver Irving Fryar, defensive end Marco Coleman, and cornerback Troy Vincent.

The Dolphins went 8-8 in Johnson's first season. They improved each of the next two seasons, but Johnson couldn't get the team where he wanted. It was also becoming more difficult for Johnson to maintain his focus.

"After the third year, I told Wayne I was ready to retire," Johnson said. "Wayne told me to go to the Keys and don't come back until the start of the next season, but my contribution was as much in personnel as coaching. I told him I'd give it a full go for one more year. I was staying that last year to make it an easy transition. After the fourth year I [had] fulfilled my thirst for coaching."

Miami went 9-7 in Johnson's fourth season before suffering a humiliating 62-7 loss to Jacksonville in an AFC Division playoff game.

His record in Miami was 36-28 in the regular season and 1-3 in the playoffs. He couldn't recapture the magic he had in Dallas, and a large segment of fans despised him because of his failure to bring a championship to South Florida and because he pushed Hall of Fame quarterback Dan Marino into retirement.

He returned to the Florida Keys to live the Life of Reilly with his longtime girlfriend, Rhonda, and his beloved little dog, Buttercup, when FOX Sports called with a broadcasting opportunity. They wanted him to join hosts James Brown, Terry Bradshaw, and Howie Long.

It has been even better than he envisioned.

"It's better than what I thought. I went through the grind for a long period of time, and it was a great run. I enjoyed the coaching. I loved game day and dealing with players, but the way I approached it was a grind because I handled personnel. I enjoyed putting a team together and drafting more than coaching. When the season was over that was my busy time, getting ready for the draft.

"I love broadcasting. It fills my football thirst 20 weekends or so," Johnson said. "I love the lifestyle in the Keys. The only time I leave is to do the football show."

CHAPTER 19

TROY AIKMAN

The game always came easy for Troy Aikman—even at a young age. And it didn't matter whether it was baseball or football.

"Athletics and everything came real natural for me," Aikman said. "I was never not a starter. I thought about being a professional athlete from the time I was eight years old. I never thought it wouldn't happen."

So he pursued the dream as a youth in Cerritos, California, where he lived with his parents, Kenneth and Charlyn, and two older sisters until he was 12. Then the family moved to Henryetta, Oklahoma, a farming community about 50 miles south of Tulsa, where they lived on a 170-acre ranch. Suddenly, Aikman was responsible for taking care of livestock, including feeding slop to the pigs.

"It was complete culture shock," Aikman said. "I eventually made the adjustment pretty smoothly and made some great friends."

It helped that he was becoming a fine athlete.

From his father, he learned that discipline and hard work lead to success, whether it's on the practice field or taking care of a farm. From his mother, he learned to be sensitive to others who might not be as talented.

Aikman always preferred baseball, but football ruled in Oklahoma, and every eighth-grader wants to fit in, so Aikman went out for the team. By the time Aikman joined the varsity as a sophomore, he was establishing himself as a talented quarterback, though that wasn't going to be enough to lead Henryetta's football team to prominence. The Fighting Hens went 4-6 his sophomore season, 2-8 his junior year (actually making the playoffs), and 6-4 his senior season.

It marked only the fourth time in 25 years they had finished over .500.

At 6 feet, 4 inches and 200 pounds, he had prototype size and a powerful right arm that forced his teammates to stay late after practice so they could get used to his high-velocity passes.

He was a three-sport athlete at Henryetta, starring in football, basketball, and baseball. He played well enough in baseball for the New York Mets to consider drafting him. The night before the 1984 amateur baseball draft, a New York Mets scout reportedly told Aikman, a catcher/shortstop, that he would be taken in the third round if he was interested in signing a contract that included a $200,000 bonus.

Aikman passed.

Always pragmatic, he figured his future was in football. He was right. Coaches lined up from across the country to recruit the quarterback with the big arm. Oklahoma State coach Jimmy Johnson and then-assistant coach Larry Coker were recruiting Aikman hard. They needed him to help turn around the program at Oklahoma State.

He liked Tennessee and Missouri, but wanted to stay near Henryetta.

"I wasn't really prepared to go too far from home," he said. "Jimmy was spending a lot of time with me, and I told him I was coming."

And he would have, if he hadn't taken his final visit to the University of Oklahoma.

"They had Billy Sims and David Overstreet, and the environment and atmosphere were great," Aikman said. "There was a feeling of expectations and success there, and I felt like if I worked hard, I would have an opportunity to excel and we could win."

The news disappointed Johnson.

"I thought we had him," Johnson said. "I really liked him, and when he left Oklahoma, I tried to recruit him at Miami. I was glad to finally get him in Dallas."

Injuries allowed Aikman to enter the lineup as a freshman, and he started as a sophomore, leading OU to a 3-0 record and a matchup against Miami. He broke his leg when two members of the Hurricanes hit him at the same time.

"It just snapped," he said.

When OU returned to the wishbone in spring practice, Aikman decided to transfer. He settled on UCLA and sat out a year because of NCAA regulations. Over his final two seasons, he led the Bruins to a 20-

4 record and victories in the Aloha Bowl over Emmitt Smith's Florida Gators and in the Cotton Bowl over Jerry Jones' alma mater, Arkansas.

"I never really followed his career that closely at UCLA," Smith said, "but I had seen quite a few highlights, and I knew he could play the game."

In two seasons at UCLA, Aikman had 41 touchdowns and 17 interceptions, and became the first quarterback to lead the Bruins to consecutive 10-win seasons.

"Being No. 1 was important to me," Aikman said. "It meant a lot."

Aikman was the first player selected in the 1989 draft and signed a six-year deal worth $11 million with the Cowboys. It made him one of the highest-paid players in the game. That provided little solace, however, during his rookie year when he went 0-11 as a starter and missed five games with a finger injury.

"We went 3-1 in the preseason, and I thought it wasn't going to be much different than college," he said. "I got a false sense of confidence in the preseason. I didn't play great, and we lost a lot of close games in the last couple of minutes.

"It got to the point where I wondered what we had to do to get a win. That was the most frustrating part. That season really made me realize how hard it is to win games in the National Football League."

———————————

There was no doubt in Troy Aikman's mind the 1992 Cowboys were going to the playoffs. He was not alone.

"It was like a dream team," said Joe Brodsky, running backs coach from 1989 to 1997. "We had a lot of great players, and we had total confidence that we could play with anybody."

Coach Jimmy Johnson and owner Jerry Jones had upgraded the talent on defense in the off-season in the wake of a 38-6 loss to Detroit in the playoffs. They traded for star defensive end Charles Haley and safety Thomas Everett. They added cornerback Kevin Smith and safety Darren Woodson in the draft.

Aikman had full grasp of offensive coordinator Norv Turner's timing-based passing scheme, which had helped Dallas' offense go from 28th (27 touchdowns, 242 points, and 255 average yards per game) to ninth (37 touchdowns, 344 points, and 318.8 average yards per game) in his first season in 1991.

"We had a whole lot of issues in 1990, and it wasn't Troy," said Emmitt Smith, a running back with the Cowboys from 1990 to 2002. "Our No. 1 issue was our offensive coordinator [David Shula]. His offense was the most difficult scheme to understand that I had ever been around. It didn't have any rhyme or reason to it.

"When Norv Turner came, it gave us all an opportunity to flourish instead of spotlighting one guy. It was the ultimate team offense because it was so balanced. Troy, Michael, and myself could hurt you or [Jay] Novacek, Darryl Johnston, and [Alvin] Harper could hurt you.

"Anybody could hurt you, and Norv made sure everyone was involved in the offense. We didn't change much personnel from 1990 to 1991, but the system was so good it helped make the personnel better. It allowed our talent to shine individually and collectively."

The Cowboys offense was virtually unstoppable.

Smith set the franchise record for rushing with 1,713 yards, and Irvin had the second-highest receiving total in franchise history with 1,386. Aikman passed for 3,445 yards with 23 touchdowns, 14 interceptions, and a passer rating of 89.5.

Six times, Dallas scored more than 30 points, and six times they won games by more than 20 points, including two in the playoffs.

They started off 3-0, including important wins over NFC East rivals Washington and New York. Then came a showdown against undefeated Philadelphia on *Monday Night Football* at Veterans Stadium for first place.

It was a debacle.

Herschel Walker scored two touchdowns, the Cowboys committed four turnovers, and Philadelphia embarrassed Dallas 31-7.

"We'll play them again, and we think it will be a different story," defensive tackle Tony Casillas said after the game.

The Cowboys responded with consecutive wins over Seattle, Kansas City, and the Los Angeles Raiders, setting up another tussle with Philadelphia. Again, control of the NFC East was at stake.

Smith rushed for 163 yards, ending Philadelphia's streak of not allowing a 100-yard rusher at 53 games. Dallas never trailed in the 20-10 victory and took a two-game lead over Philadelphia and Washington in the division.

Next up, Detroit at the Pontiac Silverdome, where the Lions had beaten the Cowboys twice by an average of 28 points in 1991. This time, the venue didn't matter.

The defensive talent Dallas added in the off-season helped hold the Lions without a touchdown in a 37-3 victory that secured the NFL's best record.

"We weren't trying to build a team anymore," Aikman said. "Now, we were trying to go further in the playoffs than we did the year before.

Troy Aikman hands off at Super Bowl XXVII. He was the game's MVP.
© *Vernon J. Biever Photo*

We knew we were a good team, and we were young enough and naïve enough to enjoy the victories. Each win was special."

Dallas finished the regular season 13-3 and captured its first NFC East title since 1985. Then the Cowboys routed Philadelphia 34-10 and upset San Francisco 30-20 to make their first Super Bowl appearance in 14 seasons.

Aikman made the most of it.

He completed 22 of 30 passes for 273 yards and four touchdowns to earn the game's Most Valuable Player trophy and add his name to an exclusive group of quarterbacks taken with the first pick in the draft that won a Super Bowl.

GAME OF MY LIFE
By Troy Aikman

My first Super Bowl experience couldn't have been any better because we spent the week practicing at UCLA, so I was very familiar with my surroundings.

That was a good thing.

We were in the same locker room that I had used when I was in college, and I knew the city and how to get around. I even got to see some old friends on our day off. The game was at the Rose Bowl, and I knew exactly what to expect from the stadium, so I felt very comfortable.

That helped me.

I never had any anxiety or nervousness the week before the game. It literally didn't dawn on me that, "Wow, we're in the Super Bowl."

I had one of my best weeks of practice all season, but we were a young team, and the magnitude of the game got to us in the first quarter. We weren't doing too much offensively, and you got the feeling that the game was getting out of our control. If that happened, the game could get ugly real quick.

We had a third-and-16 on our third series, and Buffalo was already leading 7-0. Michael Irvin ran a square in and we got a first down. A couple of plays later, I hit Jay Novacek for a touchdown that tied the score at 7-7.

The play to Michael was the key because it relaxed us and let us know that we could have some success. It was the first play we had made all day. By the time the second quarter started, I had settled down and I could tell the guys felt good and relaxed.

I threw two touchdowns to Michael at the end of the first half, and I felt real confident coming out in the second half.

We got the kickoff and drove 77 yards down the field, took about seven minutes off the clock and kicked a field goal that gave us a 31-10 lead. After that, we never looked back.

When Buffalo scored at the end of the third quarter to get a little closer, and we punted, it gave them a chance to get back into the game. But they couldn't move the ball, and when we got it back, we decided to take a shot to Harper.

I threw a 45-yard touchdown pass to Harper, and I just knew the game was over. That was the only time in my career that I put my finger in the air to say we were No. 1. It's not something I thought about or contemplated, it just happened.

I knew that moment we had clinched the game. Buffalo quarterback Jim Kelly was hurt and that pushed the lead back to 21 after they had cut it to 14.

You can't ever recapture the feeling you have when you win a world championship for the first time—at least that's how it was for me. You dream about winning the Super Bowl, and it's great when it happens, but as soon as the game is over, expectations are changed forever.

The fans and the media want to know if you can win it again. No matter how many times you win it, it's never like the first time when every experience is new. But it's nice, and no one can ever take it away from you.

When you're taken in the first round as a quarterback, especially when you're the first player taken, your only purpose is to win a championship for the team that drafted you. So there's a real sense of fulfillment because you did what the franchise drafted you to do.

I always believed we'd win a Super Bowl in Dallas. That didn't mean it was going to happen, but when it did, it didn't really come as a surprise.

No one knew it at the time. How could they?

But a 24-21 victory over the Los Angeles Rams on November 18, 1990, triggered one of the greatest runs by a team in NFL history. And it occurred during a week in which Aikman and Emmitt Smith had complained about offensive coordinator David Shula's complicated and unproductive offense.

Aikman wanted the offense to be more wide open, and Smith just wanted the ball on a more consistent basis. Each got their wish. Aikman recorded the first 300-yard passing game of his career, and Smith totaled 171 yards in total offense.

"The offense we saw in the first half was the offense we're capable of playing," Michael Irvin said after the game. "We felt it all come together out there."

Did it ever.

Dallas went 75-24 in its next 99 games. In the process, the Cowboys made five playoff appearances, won four NFC East titles, played in four NFC championship games, and won a then-unprecedented three Super Bowl championships in four seasons.

Still, Aikman and his teammates were left unfulfilled. They were left to ponder what might have been.

That's because Jimmy Johnson left after the 1993 season, and Barry Switzer replaced him as the third head coach in franchise history. Dallas won a title in 1995 with Switzer, and they captured their fifth straight division championship in 1996.

Then the Cowboys began drifting into mediocrity.

"As good as it was for a long time, it was just as bad on the back end," Aikman said. "We did things that didn't give us a chance to compete. I can really appreciate how great it was for a stretch, but it still should have been even better, and that bothers me a little bit."

The draft was at the heart of the Cowboys' failure to continue their dynasty into the new millennium. The draft had provided the foundation for the Cowboys' championship run.

From 1988 to 1994, Dallas drafted 15 players who played in at least one Pro Bowl, though receiver Jimmy Smith (Jacksonville), free safety Brock Marion (Miami), and guard Ron Stone (New York Giants) did it for other teams. Aikman is in the Hall of Fame, and Smith, Irvin, and Larry Allen are eventually expected to join him.

From 1995 to 2001, Dallas drafted two Pro Bowl players—linebacker Dexter Coakley and left tackle Flozell Adams. Free agency also robbed the Cowboys of their depth and key starters like Larry Brown, Russell Maryland, and Ken Norton Jr. Dallas lost 38 free agents from 1992 to 1997, but the draft didn't replenish the roster.

"I knew we were in trouble when the rookies would show up at the mini-camps and they couldn't play," said Darren Woodson, a safety from 1992 to 2003. "If you can't play when we're wearing shorts, what are you going to do when we put the pads on?"

At the epicenter of the Cowboys' drafting woes was their decision to draft backups in 1995 because they had so much talent on the roster. It was an arrogant premise based on the theory that no rookies could make the starting lineup. The result: Dallas wasted three second-round picks on Sherman Williams, Kendall Watkins, and Shane Hannah, all of whom contributed virtually nothing to the franchise.

Dallas bottomed out at 6-10 in 1997, its first losing season since 1990, and Switzer was fired.

"It got ugly when Barry came in," said Joe Brodsky, running backs coach from 1989 to 1997. "There was a lot going on behind the scenes."

Chan Gailey replaced him after a lengthy search and guided the Cowboys to an 18-14 record in two seasons.

But the Cowboys lost in the first round of the playoffs each year, and Aikman didn't like Gailey's offensive philosophy. Owner Jerry Jones fired Gailey after the season and hired Dave Campo, the team's defensive coordinator since 1995.

Back and head injuries plagued Aikman's season, forcing him to miss five games. He was also subject to intense criticism from fans, who booed him at home in a week four loss to San Francisco. Dallas ended the season 5-11, one of the league's worst teams.

The Cowboys owed Aikman a $7 million roster bonus in March 2001, but waived him the day before it was due. Aikman considered playing for San Diego, but decided to retire.

"I was so frustrated between my back injury and hoping our situation would get better," Aikman said. "We just didn't have a chance to win.

"Everything we had done to be successful during the Super Bowl years we were no longer doing on a consistent basis. My disappointment was that we weren't giving ourselves a chance by doing the necessary things to be successful, and my productivity wasn't good either."

Sometimes, it feels like there aren't enough hours in the day for everything Aikman has to do. He wouldn't have it any other way.

He owns a car dealership, serves as a spokesman for several companies, and owns a NASCAR team with fellow Hall of Fame quarterback Roger Staubach. He's a shareholder at a major bank and is an investor in a video surveillance company.

And don't forget his primary job as the top NFL color commentator for FOX Sports.

"Life is pretty good," said Aikman, who lives in suburban Dallas with his wife, Rhonda, and their three children. "I'm probably busier now than when I played, but I'm not complaining. I'm very fortunate."

That's because he's doing what he loves.

He never figured himself as a broadcaster. Neither did many others. Aikman declined to show much of his personality during his playing career because he didn't think it served the greater good of the team. The quarterback, he believed, must always be even-keeled in public. He must show a certain calmness and confidence, even in the face of adversity.

Clearly, he knew the intricacies of the game.

When Aikman finished his career, he had passed for nearly 33,000 yards, 165 touchdowns, and 141 interceptions. More importantly, his 90 victories in the 1990s made him the winningest quarterback in any decade.

Brad Sham, the Cowboys' play-by-play radio voice for more than 20 years, needed a partner to do a series of games in NFL Europe. He suggested Aikman.

"I thought it would be a good opportunity to get a free vacation in Europe," Aikman said. "I had a good time."

Sham was shocked by his friend's performance.

"He was just terrific, and he didn't really even know what he was doing," Sham said. "He was better than he had a right to be."

Not long after he returned, FOX offered a job.

"[FOX president] Ed Goren called me and said, 'You're good at this,'" Aikman recalled. "That's the first time my thoughts turned to broadcasting. It has been great."

CHAPTER 20

DARREN WOODSON

Uncle Sam helped saved Darren Woodson from being just another Justice Department statistic.

Uncle Sam spent his life in and out of jail, but his sister, Freddie Luke, never gave up on him. She regularly made the 130-mile round trip to Florence State Prison, a maximum security facility.

"Sam was an intelligent person, but he didn't always use his intelligence for good," Luke said. "He never blamed anyone else for his predicament, but he knew he had done wrong, and when he got out, he vowed never to go back to prison—and he didn't. I think he gave my children an opportunity to see that prison was not a place they wanted to be."

Luke's youngest son, Darren Woodson, usually accompanied her.

"Prison ain't no good," Uncle Sam frequently told his nephew. "Don't end up in here."

The words impacted his nephew, who had seen how drugs and crime had ruined the lives of several relatives.

"I have uncles and family members raised in the pen," he said. "My uncle Sam played a big role in keeping me out of trouble. Just the fear of going in there was enough to make me avoid trouble."

That, however, wasn't always easy to do in Maryvale, a low-income section of Phoenix, Arizona, a few miles from downtown. It was the kind of place where gangs fought over city blocks and illegal drugs helped fund the neighborhood economy.

For Woodson, though, it was a place to call home. It's the place where he met his four best friends—Phillippi Sparks, Kevin Galbreath, Kevin Minniefield, and Keith Tucker—and for a child who was tired of moving to new homes, it represented stability. Woodson needed stability because his mother was trying to raise five kids with little help from his father, Arthur, who was a pretty good basketball player as a youngster.

Freddie Luke worked for more than 30 years at the Maricopa County Superior Court. Most years, she moonlighted to supplement her income.

"I rarely saw my mom from six in the morning to nine o'clock at night, she was working every day. Every damn day," Woodson said. "But she did a heck of a job, because all of us graduated from high school and two of us graduated from college."

Woodson's mother held her children accountable for their time and actions even when she wasn't at home.

"Sometimes I would call on my way from one job to another, and I had to make sure every one of them was in the house," Luke said. "If they didn't do the things they were supposed to do, then they couldn't do extra things on the weekend like going to parties."

On the rare occasions when those tactics didn't work, Luke held family meetings. Once, she showed the four children her paycheck and a list of the bills. Then she had them do the math. If they wanted her to work a second job to create more money for the household, then they had to be more responsible.

Like a lot of kids, sports helped save Woodson just like it did Galbreath, Minniefield, and Sparks. Woodson, Minniefield, and Sparks each played at Arizona State and in the NFL. Woodson saw football as a conduit to a better life. It was going to be the way he bought the fancy cars he saw the dealers driving and the way he purchased the mansions where the rich folks in Scottsdale lived.

Woodson starred at Maryvale and set a school record with six touchdowns along with 225 yards rushing in a win over Kofa High School in Yuma. The All-City linebacker and running back found himself with plenty of suitors, but his poor grades limited his options.

"He was always a good student up until his senior year in high school when the young ladies and the newspapers and the little fame he had at that time was taking over," Luke said. "When it finally dawned on him that he didn't do the best he could and it was catching up to him, he did a lot better, but it was still a little too late."

An Arizona State assistant told him about the importance of the SAT and improving his grades. Woodson needed two attempts to pass the SAT, but didn't score high enough to make up for his poor grades. That left him with two choices: attend a junior college or attend ASU as a Proposition 48 athlete.

Actually, it wasn't much of a choice.

Life in Maryvale was getting more complicated. Tucker, a member of the street gang Crips, was hanging with a rough crew, and his brother-in-law was a drug dealer. Woodson had family members dealing drugs and didn't want to get caught in the middle.

Instead of going to one of the local junior colleges, Woodson chose to pay his own way to Arizona State for a year until he could be placed on scholarship. Arizona State and its 49,000-member student body are only about 10 miles from Maryvale.

To Woodson, it seemed like a world away.

"It was time for me to go. I had to go. My boys were still in the neighborhood. Everybody wanted to party, and if I was going to be serious about furthering myself, I had to go to Arizona State," Woodson said. "It's only about 20 miles away, but it felt so far away."

The Cowboys had won consecutive Super Bowls and expected to win another, even though Jimmy Johnson was no longer the coach.

"There was no way we weren't going to win three in a row," Woodson said. "We had San Francisco's number, and they weren't going to beat us. We wanted home-field advantage, so we talked a lot about how [to] lock down home-field advantage."

Johnson and owner Jerry Jones had resurrected the Cowboys from one of the league's worst teams to one of its best with Johnson's demanding style and shrewd trades like dealing running back Herschel Walker and quarterback Steve Walsh to give Dallas enough selections to control the draft.

That led to the addition of players like Woodson, Emmitt Smith, Russell Maryland, Kevin Smith, Erik Williams, and Alvin Harper, who helped the Cowboys become the dominant team of the decade. Knowing the type of players Johnson wanted to execute his offensive and defensive schemes allowed Johnson and Jones to sign players like tight end Jay Novacek and safety James Washington, each of whom played significant roles in the Cowboys' three Super Bowl championships. Despite their on-field successes, Johnson and Jones bickered over a plethora of other things.

Their working relationship ended two months after their second Super Bowl victory and ushered in the Barry Switzer era. Switzer, who led Oklahoma to national championships in 1974, 1975, and 1985, compiled a 157-29-4 record (.837 winning percentage) and won 12 Big 8 Championships in 16 seasons with the Sooners.

But he had been away from the game since 1988, his last year at Oklahoma. Critics wondered whether he could adjust to pro football and the intensity it required. Supporters said Switzer was a motivator who would help the Cowboys relax after the pressure-cooker atmosphere Johnson preferred.

The plan was for Switzer to inspire the players, while his coaching staff indoctrinated him to the NFL. Jones, also the general manager, would provide the players. In the process, Jones felt sure the Cowboys could win Super Bowl XXIX.

San Francisco had other ideas.

"I gave the 49ers a swagger they didn't have," said Deion Sanders, the NFL's defensive player of the year in 1994 with San Francisco, who joined the Cowboys in 1995. "They were all uptight about the Cowboys, but I think they fed off the confidence that I had that we could control their offense enough to beat them in the playoffs. We knew we had to beat them if we were going to go to the Super Bowl."

Switzer started well. The Cowboys were 10-2 and had a three-game lead over second-place Philadelphia in the NFC East when they played the Eagles for the second time. The Cowboys had won three consecutive NFC East titles for the first time since 1976 to 1979, and another victory over Philadelphia would clinch a third straight division title.

The Cowboys, though, weren't obsessed with winning the NFC East title. They simply viewed it as the first step toward gaining home-field advantage throughout the playoffs, which was their ultimate goal, because that would ensure San Francisco would have to come through Texas Stadium to get to the Super Bowl.

But the first step toward achieving their goal was beating the struggling Eagles, who had lost three consecutive games by a combined score of 66-34. Four weeks earlier, Philadelphia had been tied for first place with Dallas, when they traveled to Texas Stadium and lost 24-13.

Now, the Eagles were a team in disarray.

Coach Rich Kotite was fielding daily questions concerning his job security, and Randall Cunningham, one of the league's best quarterbacks, was trying to avoid the first four-game losing streak of his career.

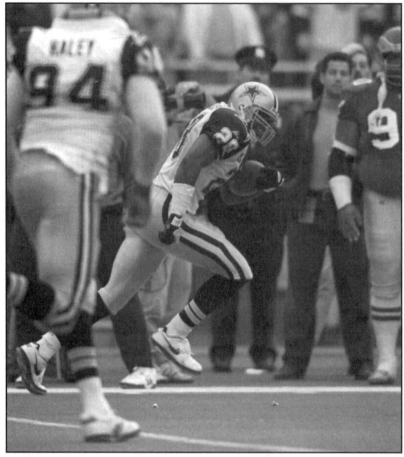

Darren Woodson intercepts a Randall Cunningham pass and races 95 yards for the game-clinching touchdown. *Doug Pensinger/Getty Images*

GAME OF MY LIFE
By Darren Woodson

We didn't give a damn what their record was, and they didn't care what our record was because we didn't like them and they didn't like us. We knew it was going to be a dogfight, especially in the Vet.

They didn't back down. In fact, they had the ball at our 8-yard line with a chance to go ahead after a long punt return put them in good field position. I was on the punt coverage team. I just remember being so tired at the start of that series.

The play before the interception, James Washington was in the huddle saying somebody had to make a play. That wasn't unusual, because we used to argue about who was going to make the big play every game. We used to bet on stuff like that during the game. Who was gonna make the tackle? Who was gonna make the big hit? Who was gonna make the big play? In my mind—I did this all the time—I was saying, "I'm that guy. I'm going to make a play." And I did.

I just made so many plays that year. It just seemed like everything fell into place for me. It felt easy. When I got older and I had less talent around me, it felt a lot harder to do the same things, because when you don't have pressure on the quarterback, you can't sit on routes.

It was third down, and they came out in a split backfield with Herschel Walker and James Joseph. They had run that play three or four times earlier in the game, and it had worked every time, but those times we had been in our base defense. This time we were in the nickel, which meant I was playing a linebacker spot.

Randall Cunningham basically wanted to look me off and throw the ball to Joseph in the flat. I remember dropping back and watching him try to look me off. James Joseph ran out in the flat, and Randall was trying to hold the ball, which would allow Joseph to get out in the flat a little further. There was a guy running a curl right behind me, and Randall was looking at that guy.

I was really just trying to hold my spot, because I knew he was going to throw it to Joseph. I could just feel it. Sometimes, you get a feeling like that, so I can't explain it. I just knew that he was going to throw it there. Randall had a hell of an arm, and he tried to get it out there.

I peeked at Joseph, and when I peeked back, I just took off and broke on the ball. It happened so fast that I didn't think about catching the ball. I just did it. I remember Joseph standing there. I was sort of surprised Randall threw it, but I broke on it so fast that it even surprised me a little bit.

I had enough energy to get past Randall because I saw him coming out of the corner of my eye. I gave him an ugly move—a couple of stutter steps—and then I took a peek to see where Joseph was, but he was nowhere to be seen. I knew an offensive lineman wasn't going to catch me.

Chad Hennings, a defensive lineman, ran the whole way with me. I don't remember him at all. But I do remember running down the sideline—no one was near me—and out of the corner of my eye I could see one of their coaches who was holding a clipboard, slamming it down as I ran past their sideline. The only thing I thought about was, "Don't get caught from behind." When I got to the end zone, I was spent.

After the game, I had to get an X-ray on my shoulder. Trainer Jim Maurer and I walked into Philadelphia's locker room, because that was the only place you could get X-rays. When I walked in there, their players just stared at me. I mean we had just beaten them; our teams hated each other, and I had returned an interception 95 yards for a touchdown. It was like I had showed up to rub it in.

Their coach, Rich Kotite, had just finished talking to the team, and he told everyone to grab someone's hand for the team prayer. Someone grabbed my hand, and I did the team prayer with them. It was the weirdest thing and most uncomfortable thing that ever happened to me. I think that was the most memorable part of that game even more than the interception and the touchdown.

———————————

After beating the Eagles, Dallas lost the next week to Cleveland 19-14, virtually ending the chance to secure home-field advantage in the playoffs, because they had already lost to San Francisco 21-14 in the regular season. That meant for the second time in three seasons they were going to have to go through the loose sod and sloppy turf that was Candlestick Park to advance to the Super Bowl.

Dallas opened the playoffs with a 35-9 win over Green Bay, its fifth consecutive win over the Packers in just four seasons. It was a pyrrhic victory.

While making a tackle, Woodson felt a twinge in his back. It didn't improve during the week despite hours of electrical stimulus, whirlpool, and massages that kept him from practicing. Woodson wanted to play but wasn't sure how he was going to be able to perform against Steve Young and Jerry Rice, who keyed one of the NFL's best passing attacks. Young set an NFL record that season with a rating of 112.8, while Rice had 1,499 yards receiving and 13 touchdowns.

Woodson's skills were even more important against San Francisco because of his ability to cover the slot and tight end Brent Jones, and still be a factor against the run.

The pain was so intense that Woodson didn't know how effective he was going to be as he went through pregame warmups. A few minutes before kickoff as the teams left the field and prepared for pregame introductions, Woodson walked into the training room, lay on a table, and received a shot.

"You talking about some pain? That area was tender, and he had to move the needle around for about 30 seconds to find the nerve, so he can numb it. That's why it hurt so much," Woodson said. "I was half the player I was that game because I just couldn't run."

San Francisco used three turnovers in the first seven minutes to build a 21-0 lead and end the Cowboys' two-year reign as champion.

"That was our best team, and we didn't even make it to the Super Bowl," Washington said. "Our offense had a little history of starting slow in the playoffs, and the defense would keep things close until they exploded. Against San Francisco that didn't happen.

"I don't care how good you are, you can't give a team like San Francisco 21 points in the first quarter and expect to come back and win. We almost did it, but they beat us."

Two weeks later, San Francisco disposed of San Diego 49-24 to become the first team to win five Super Bowls—Dallas and Pittsburgh have since matched that feat—as Woodson prepared to have surgery to repair a herniated disk in his back.

A decade later, the same injury forced him to retire.

———————————

Woodson, the Cowboys' all-time leading tackler, spent the spring of 2004 preparing himself for life after football. With his age and salary-cap number increasing each year, Woodson knew it was time to focus on life after football.

He had dabbled in several areas, but decided to give television a try after enough people told him that the industry always had room for a handsome, articulate former player, especially one with three Super Bowl rings.

So he traveled abroad for a few weeks to do color commentary on NFL Europe games. When his two-week commitment ended, Woodson returned home on a lengthy trans-Atlantic flight.

The next day, he was at the club's Valley Ranch training complex making up the workouts that he had missed. Coach Bill Parcells demands that his players complete a minimum of 40 workouts—four per week—during the club's 10-week off-season conditioning program.

Woodson was in the midst of doing sets of 50 repetitions on the leg press with 315 pounds, when he felt a twinge in his back.

"I wasn't all the way down on the bench, and I got to talking to somebody and I kinda felt a sting when I got off the leg press," Woodson said. "But it wasn't that big of a deal because I finished my workout. A couple of days later I tried to get out of my car and I knew something was wrong with my back."

Still, Woodson ignored the pain for a while as he increased his stretching program and had some massages. When the pain lingered, the 12-year veteran knew something was wrong.

"A week before camp I was running," he said, "and all of a sudden it started feeling like someone shot me in the back."

Woodson needed surgery to repair the same type of hernia he suffered in 1994, but he didn't think the surgery was a big deal because the first time had kept him off the field for only a couple of months. This surgery, though, was more complicated.

"I had scar tissue that had grown around that area and the nerve was damaged," he said. "They had to scrape some scar tissue off, and Dr. [Andrew] Dossett said the nerve was beet red. He said it was one of the reddest nerves he'd ever seen."

Dr. Dossett said he wasn't sure Woodson would be able to play again. Woodson spent much of the season on the physically unable to perform list before announcing his retirement a week before the end of the regular season. The job offers—ESPN, FOX, and the NFL Network—poured in, and Woodson settled on ESPN.

"I just figured that if I wanted to learn the business that ESPN was the best place to be," Woodson said, "because I knew they would give me all of the fundamentals I needed to be as successful as I was on the football field."

CHAPTER 21

EMMITT SMITH

Emmitt James Smith II didn't want his namesake—the boy who would eventually claim one of the most hallowed records in professional sports—playing football as a youngster. He didn't give a reason. He didn't have to.

The Pensacola, Florida, bus driver worked long hours and didn't say much except when he was talking on his CB radio to strangers as far away as Seattle.

"I have no idea why he didn't want me to play," Emmitt Smith said, "but it wasn't like we were going to have a family conversation about it. I just remember my mom saying my father didn't want us to play ball."

It's not that the elder Smith didn't like football or have a passion for the game. He had been a high school running back and played safety for a semi-pro team while Smith was in high school.

"He used to watch us on Fridays and play his games on Saturday," Smith said. "It was interesting because Dad wanted to show his skills, too. He had good speed and wanted to show us that we got these skills from somewhere."

When Emmitt turned eight, his mom, Mary Smith, decided to sign him up at the local Salvation Army league and let him play. He quickly made an impact.

On his first carry, Smith scored a 70-yard touchdown. It proved to be a harbinger.

When Smith's 15-year career ended in 2004, he had scored 175 touchdowns—164 rushing—and gained 18,355 yards to finish his career as the National Football League's all-time leading rusher.

It sounds funny, but a lot of his success can be linked to that first carry on an August day in 1977, because it gave him an aura of self-confidence and self-esteem that helped propel him to heights no one but Smith dreamed he could achieve.

After all, this is the man who set a goal as a rookie to become the NFL's all-time leading rusher before his career ended.

"As a child you already feel invincible," Smith said, "but when you know you can do something, it's such a confidence boost that you feel like there's nothing you can't accomplish."

He maintained the same attitude at Escambia High School, playing on the varsity as a freshman. The incumbent starter was moved to fullback so Smith could be the featured back. He gained 115 yards and scored two touchdowns in his first game against Pensacola Catholic.

When his high school career ended, Smith joined Ohio's Carlos Snow and California's Leonard Russell as the top three running backs in the nation. The order depended on the bias of the recruiting service touting them.

As he developed into a star running back at Escambia, the recruiting letters began filling his mailbox—and he was just a sophomore. The boy who had always assumed he'd be a bus driver like his father or work manual labor like his grandfather began having aspirations that would take him away from Pensacola.

"We had the fair and the beaches. We had concerts. We had high school games. We had the Navy base," Smith said. "Pensacola was cool, but it was also all I'd ever known."

Smith gained 8,804 yards and scored 106 touchdowns at Escambia, making him one of the most coveted recruits in the nation. Smith narrowed his list to Florida, Florida State, Miami, and Auburn before pragmatically eliminating them.

Florida State coach Bobby Bowden liked a backfield by committee, and Miami threw the ball too much. He loved Auburn, but Florida provided the best opportunity to play right away.

"Being the state university, we hoped we had an inside track, but I don't think we did," said former Florida coach Galen Hall. "It was a very tough recruiting process because he was the No. 1 player in the nation and we felt we needed to have him.

"He kept saying he wasn't sure where he was going, so I was definitely nervous the night before. I just hoped that we had done enough to get the job done."

He did. Smith picked between Florida and Auburn, though ultimately it wasn't that difficult.

"I considered going to Auburn, but my mama told me I wasn't going to Alabama," Smith said. "That was fine because my family was a big fan of the Gators. My high school was the Gators, and we wore orange and blue, so it made sense."

The same type of success Smith had in high school continued at Florida, where he rushed for 109 yards and two touchdowns in his first start—a 52-0 win against Tulsa—in week 2.

"Emmitt was a little upset we didn't start him in the first game [a 31-4 loss to Miami]," said Hall, "I felt [we should] ease him into [the] game because of all the things expected of him. In his own mind, he probably didn't understand, but everything worked out."

Smith left after three seasons, in part, because Steve Spurrier and his sophisticated passing game were going to replace coach Hall's run-oriented scheme.

"I didn't leave because of Spurrier, but he would've been the fourth offensive coordinator I [had] had," Smith said. "I never felt comfortable about staying."

Besides, Smith figured he'd be a high draft choice with the New York Jets, Tampa Bay, and Seattle all with selections among the first 10 picks and each in need of a running back. The Jets chose Penn State runner Blair Thomas, while Seattle and Tampa Bay chose defensive players.

Suddenly, Smith's decision not to have a draft-day party looked pretty good.

"When that thing got past the first 10 picks, I thought maybe I made the wrong decision," Smith said. "Green Bay was up and Pittsburgh was coming up, when my phone started ringing and my agent told me the Cowboys were looking to move up and get me."

Before the swap with Pittsburgh was completed, Johnson wanted to discuss the move with scout Walt Yaworski and running backs coach Joe Brodsky one last time.

"Jimmy must've had us in his office 25 times," Brodsky said. "I kept telling Jimmy that [Emmitt] can't run fast and he's small, but every time you put a football in his hands, he's as good as anyone in the nation. I had tried to recruit him when I was at Miami, so I knew the kid.

"He was a tough, hard-nosed runner and every time he moved to a higher level there wasn't any drop in his production. From the time he was an 80-pound tailback, he was prolific."

Dallas eventually made a deal with Pittsburgh to acquire the 17th pick in the first round, which they used to take Smith.

"I got a call from Jimmy. He said, 'How would you like to be a Dallas Cowboy?'"

"I said, 'Coach, I would love to be a Dallas Cowboy.'"

Like a lot of Pensacola natives, Smith grew up watching Roger Staubach and Tony Dorsett win games for America's Team. Now, he was about to become fraternity brothers with them.

"I was a big Cowboys fan as a kid," Smith said. "We saw the Cowboys and Saints on TV in Pensacola. Roger Staubach played on one of the fields at the base, and I played there as a little-bitty boy. The Cowboys were my team."

―――――――――――

Emmitt Smith wanted to be the highest-paid running back in the NFL. It was really that simple. After all, he had all of the hardware a player could accumulate in his first three seasons in the NFL.

He had won consecutive rushing titles and been the first player of the Jerry Jones era to be named to the Pro Bowl. He had earned All-Pro honors, been named Rookie of the Year and helped the Cowboys win the Super Bowl, rushing for more than 100 yards and a touchdown in the Cowboys' 52-17 triumph.

Now, he wanted to be paid like the best running back in the league.

"The stage was now set. There shouldn't be any reason why we're arguing over money. They should've said, 'Mr. Smith, your stats, your credentials, and your hardware all suggest you should be paid the highest or somewhere close to it,'" Smith said. "When that didn't happen, I said, 'I'm not going to play for this. This is not right.'

"I did what they asked me to do, so I didn't understand why we were arguing."

So a high-stakes game of chicken began. It lasted through the club's mini-camps and through training camp. Surely, Smith figured, the Cowboys and his agents, Richard Howell and Pat Dye, would get a deal worked out. As a restricted free agent, Smith assumed someone would covet his services, even though Dallas tendered him a contract that required any team that signed him to give Dallas first- and third-round draft choices.

Miami, a contender, needed a running back to team with Dan Marino. Surely, they would offer him a deal.

They didn't.

"The thing that left me dumbfounded is that no one signed me to a tender," Smith said. "Think about it. My personal opinion is that it was some type of collusion. I was expecting something from somebody."

Talks continued during training camp, but the Cowboys broke training camp without getting Smith's signature on a contract.

Then came the annual Kickoff Luncheon, where the team is introduced to several thousand fans at a fundraiser designed to help Happy Hills Farm in Granbury, about 90 minutes west of the club's Valley Ranch training complex. The farm has helped thousands of troubled youth turn their lives around since Ed Shipman founded it in 1975.

Smith let his lease lapse at his apartment and returned to Florida. He enrolled at Florida and was prepared to start attending classes. Still, Smith figured he would join the team a few days before the season-opener on *Monday Night Football* against archrival Washington.

When Friday came, Smith realized that he was going to spend the start of the 1993 season in Florida, sleeping at his mother's house and watching his teammates play on television. An unscientific poll taken by the *Dallas Morning News* revealed that most fans believed Jones was right and Smith wrong in their contract dispute.

"I think the Cowboys tried to play on my weakness because they knew I loved my teammates and I didn't want to let them down," Smith said, "so I had to show them some strength.

"I really expected to come in on Thursday, get one day of practice on Friday, and play the game. So [when that didn't happen,] I prepared to watch them at my mother's house and be disappointed. Whether I was with the team or not, I was supporting the team. I wanted them to win because I didn't want to come back to a losing situation. I watched the game, shaking my head and thinking how ridiculous this situation was."

Coach Jimmy Johnson said he let the situation mushroom and affect the team because he kept assuming Smith would return in time for the start of the season.

"It was my fault. Normally I'm a pretty optimistic person, and I knew the relationship I had with Emmitt," Johnson said. "Up until the last minute I thought Emmitt was going to show up. When he didn't, we were in disarray. It was frustrating because it was my blind thinking that he was going to show up. I was mad at myself because I didn't have the team handle it better.

"We didn't play well against Washington. Every article, every question, every conversation was about Emmitt. If I had handled it better we would've played better. When he wasn't there for the first game—being hard-headed—I thought he'd show up for the second game."

Derrick Lassic, a fourth-round draft choice from Alabama, started at running back against Washington. He gained 75 yards on 16 carries, but the Redskins overwhelmed Dallas 35-16 at Texas Stadium. Smith figured the loss would be enough to spur the sides to make a deal.

Running back Emmitt Smith advances the ball during a playoff game against the Green Bay Packers at Texas Stadium. *Al Bello/Getty Images*

It didn't.

Smith didn't want to spend another weekend at home waiting for the phone to ring, so he decided to go watch his brother, Emory, a running back for Clemson, play against Florida State in Tallahassee. In Dallas that week, the coaching staff tried to convince the players Smith was replaceable.

"We were in an offensive line meeting watching film with our offensive line coach, Hudson Houck, and Emmitt is just tearing it up," offensive lineman Kevin Gogan said, "and he's trying to convince us that our backup, whoever it was that week, is going to be just as good. We were like, 'Forget that, Coach.'"

On Sunday, Buffalo beat the Cowboys 13-10, when Troy Aikman threw an interception in the end zone in the waning seconds. Lassic managed 52 yards on 19 carries with a fumble. During the third quarter, the crowd chanted, "We want Emmitt."

Afterward, Charles Haley slammed his helmet into a locker room wall, leaving a gaping hole.

"Had I not created that scenario, Charles might not have been as frustrated," Johnson said. "It would've been better if I hadn't talked about it as much, because my frustration filtered through."

After the game, a cranky Johnson addressed the media.

"We've got a very frustrated, very frustrated group of players," Johnson said in the *Dallas Morning News.* "We've only played two games, but it seems like we've played a bunch. We're fighting a lot of things right now. We're fighting more than the game itself."

Later that night, Smith's phone rang. His agents told him to expect a deal to be completed quickly. He thought the same thing, especially after he saw the highlights and heard the comments of Johnson and Haley for himself.

"None of my teammates [was] mad at me. They were all happy," Smith said. "Now we could do what we expected to do."

Smith, who gained 45 yards on eight carries, didn't start his first game, a 17-10 win over Arizona. Two games later, he recorded his first 100-yard game of the season with 25 carries for 104 yards in a win over Indianapolis. Two games after that, Smith established his career high—237 yards—and broke Tony Dorsett's franchise records on a rainy night at Veterans Stadium in Philadelphia.

With Smith in the lineup, the Cowboys won 11 of their next 13 games, setting up a showdown with the New York Giants in the last game of the regular season to determine the NFC East champion and the NFL's rushing champion.

GAME OF MY LIFE
By Emmitt Smith

There were so many things at stake that day: home-field advantage throughout the playoffs, a bye until the divisional playoffs, and the rushing title. I wasn't going to let anybody take that from me after all I had been through.

It was late in the second quarter and we were ahead when I went off right tackle. I had a gigantic hole. I didn't know if I was going to make it to the end zone, but I knew I had a long run. When the defensive back grabbed me, I hit the turf—it was so hard—with my shoulder.

Right away, I knew my shoulder wasn't right. I didn't know if I could come back. All I knew is that my shoulder was jacked up. I couldn't believe it. I don't think there was any way the Cowboys' training staff was going to take me out of that game even if I wanted to come out—not that I wanted out. It's like I didn't have a choice.

They took me into the locker room, X-rayed it, and gave me some Vicodin to ease the pain, but it didn't really help. The trainers put a kneepad on my shoulder and taped it down. I could barely move my arm. I had no range of motion.

Our trainer, Kevin O'Neill, said, "You may feel some pain."

I said, "I know."

A lot of folks wouldn't have gone through what I went through. When I went back out there, I knew I was going to be in pain, but I had to strap it up and go. When I looked at my teammates' faces in the huddle, it was like the stadium got real quiet, and I felt calm. I tuned out everything around me except my teammates.

You know how they say your life flashes before you. Well, my life didn't flash before me, but different people that I've encountered throughout my whole career did. I went all of the way back to when I was a child playing in the park with my cousins.

I remembered getting knocked down one day, and I remember crying and my cousin saying, "You can't play the game if you can't play with pain." That resonated in my head the whole second half. That's all I could think about.

At one point in the second half, I'll never forget the look on Nate Newton's face. It was like he was afraid. So did Mark Tuinei. I was standing on the left side of the huddle, so those were the faces I saw. I didn't have to say anything because they looked at my face and they understood what I was going through.

Tears were running down my face because I was in pain.

Michael Irvin was leaning over, whispering in my ear, "Hang in there. Hang in there."

Troy asked me if I was all right. Nobody else said anything. The three of us were the only ones speaking.

The Giants tied the score at the end of the game, and we had to go into overtime. They kept calling my number, and I wasn't going to tell them to stop. I wasn't going to let my teammates or my coaches or the organization down.

Somehow, I made it through. While we were setting up for the field goal, I was thinking to myself we better not miss it. Eddie Murray hit that field goal, and I was so glad it was over. I couldn't really even truly enjoy the moment. I was just so happy it was over.

Ironically, that was the beginning of one of the worst moments for me. During the game my adrenaline was flowing so much that combined with the Vicodin a lot of the pain was neutralized. That's how I made it through the game. Afterward there was no amount of medicine they could give me to put me to sleep. It was one of the worst plane rides after a game that I have ever had.

Emmitt Smith rushed for 168 yards on 32 carries and caught 10 passes for 61 yards against the Giants. He became the fourth player to win three consecutive rushing titles, joining Earl Campbell, Jim Brown, and Steve Van Buren. Of his 229 yards, Smith gained 78 yards on 17 touches after his shoulder injury.

Beating the Giants gave the Cowboys a much-needed bye week to give his first-degree shoulder separation time to heal. Before the Cowboys' divisional game against Green Bay, O'Neill suggested Smith take a pain-killing shot in his shoulder.

He refused. Smith doesn't like needles. Besides, he wanted to make sure he felt every twinge in his shoulder in case he did more damage.

"I wanted to feel the pain," he said. "If I tore it up or something went wrong, I wanted to know it."

Against the Packers, Smith carried 13 times for 60 yards before line-backer Bryce Paup knocked him out of the game with a direct hit on his shoulder in the third quarter. Before the NFC championship game, Smith took a pain-killing shot.

"They shot it up and it felt so good," Smith said. "I went out there and did my thing."

He gained 88 yards and caught seven passes for 85 yards, including a touchdown as the Cowboys routed San Francisco 38-21 to reach the Super Bowl for the second consecutive season. Again, Smith took a shot before the game. In the most important game in which a professional football player can participate, Smith didn't want his shoulder to become an issue.

"I wasn't going to play in the Pro Bowl, so let's shoot it one more time and close it out," Smith said. "I wanted to be right, and this was the biggest game. It's why you play the game."

None of it mattered, though, without a championship. This time, Johnson wasn't as confident in Dallas' ability to beat Buffalo.

That's because there was only one week between the championship game and the Super Bowl, which didn't give quarterback Troy Aikman much time to recover from the concussion he suffered against San Francisco, and the Bills' no-huddle offense was as potent as it had ever been.

"I thought we were the best team in the league," Johnson said. "We had won it before, so there was such confidence on the team that we were the best team, but we were not as prepared as we were the year before."

It showed in the first-half performance of each team. Buffalo led 13-6, and Smith had carried the ball just nine times for 41 yards. Smith spoke with offensive coordinator Norv Turner at halftime about getting more opportunities. So did Johnson, who instructed Turner to turn the game over to Smith.

"Normally, I didn't get up in front of the offense, but I told them we were going to pound it," Johnson said. "We're going to run our counter play, see if we could hammer them, and get back in the ballgame."

On the third play of the third quarter, safety James Washington recovered a fumble and weaved through the Bills to score the game-tying touchdown on a 46-yard return. After the Cowboys forced a punt, Turner gave Smith the opportunities he wanted on Dallas' first possession of the second half.

Smith carried the ball seven times for 61 yards on an eight-play, 64-yard touchdown drive that gave the Cowboys the lead for good 20-13 on Smith's 15-yard run with 8:42 left in the third quarter.

"That was a statement," Smith said of the drive. "That was our way of saying let's get this thing under control. That was really satisfying. It put an exclamation point on the season. It proved I was worth the money and more. I was MVP of the league and the Super Bowl."

From the time Emmitt Smith became a professional football player, he was planning for the day his career ended.

That was one of the reasons it was so important that he kept his promise to his mother and earned his degree from Florida. Four rushing titles and three Super Bowl rings later, he did.

He saved his money and launched different businesses. He didn't even build his dream home until he had enough money saved from his off-the-field endorsements and ventures to finance the project.

Smith dabbled in real estate, buying a few properties with the $1 million signing bonus he received as a rookie. He wanted to be more aggressive, but didn't want to risk the bulk of his money at that time. But the more he researched, studied, and planned his future, the more convinced he became that real estate was the best way to become a mogul.

In 2005 after his illustrious 15-year career ended with Smith as the NFL's all-time leading rusher, he partnered with one of the Cowboys legends: Roger Staubach, who runs a multimillion-dollar company that handles all aspects of real estate. Smith joined a branch of the company that allows him to initiate and develop his own projects.

"When I looked at what Roger was doing, it made all of the sense in the world," Smith said. "They know how to deal with Roger, so they would know how to deal with me and how to protect me and it gives me instant credibility, and the more I learn the more I can spread my wings. There are no limits."

Smith, though, didn't want to get completely away from the game that has provided him with more wealth than he dreamed possible as a kid in the Florida panhandle. Many of his former teammates—Troy Aikman, Michael Irvin, Darryl Johnston, and Darren Woodson—had all gotten involved in broadcasting either as color commentators or studio analysts.

But Smith didn't want to be away from home too often because he wanted to be an active participant in the lives of his wife, Patricia, and their four children. When the NFL Network offered him a position that would require him to be in Los Angeles only one day a week, he jumped at the opportunity.

"It keeps me involved with the game," Smith said, "and it's fun to express my opinion as a former player and an analyst. It doesn't mean I'm always right or everyone has to agree with me, but it's fun to talk about the game."

CHAPTER 22

JAMES WASHINGTON

James Washington is one of the lucky ones—and he knows it. He makes no apologies for it and doesn't spend his days wondering how he survived a childhood that has doomed so many others.

Instead, he counts his blessings. Each of them. Eddie and Annie Alexander, Washington's maternal grandparents, saved his life and gave him a future.

"My father left when I was two, and the state took me away from my mom when I was four," Washington said. "I was with the state for a little while, and then my grandparents stepped in and raised me.

"These are the people who stepped up for me and gave me much love because that's all they had. I never went without the love. We were broke, but they gave me everything I needed—not what I wanted but what I needed. They said here's a house and don't go to jail. That was their way of giving me direction."

They also provided discipline. Eddie Alexander, nicknamed "Cobra," was described by his grandson as a hardworking man who was five by five—5 feet tall and 5 feet wide—who struck fear in his grandson with nothing more than a look.

"He's the only person I've ever been scared of," Washington said. "I saw him shoot my uncle in the foot and then whip his ass. My uncle came to the house one day hollering at my grandmother, and my grandfather told him not to ever disrespect his mother like that.

"After he threatened to beat up my grandfather, they went outside to the front yard and my grandfather shot him in both feet, beat him up, and then took him to the hospital. That's why he never had any trouble out of me."

That didn't mean Washington didn't find trouble at times. Growing up poor in south central Los Angeles, trouble beckoned every day. Once Washington found himself at a police station trying to avoid having charges filed against him. Athletics gave him a way out.

"The only reason I started playing football in the 11th grade is that I had gotten into some trouble," he said. "I was a street guy. Everybody knows that, but because I was scared of my grandfather, I always brought home good grades.

"When I got into trouble, they looked at my transcript and I had a 3.4 [grade-point] average and they couldn't figure it out. Henry Washington, my head coach at Jordan High School, took me under his wing. He wasn't my father, but he treated me like he was. His impact made me who I am today."

Henry Washington said he saw a talented, intelligent youngster who needed a break. He also saw a kid who needed discipline, if he was going to succeed in life.

"He was talented as hell and wild as hell, too," Washington said. "I became a father figure to him, and he responded real well. There were some conversations about being a good person and doing his very best in class and where his talent could take him if he did all of those things.

"James was pretty much on his own. He was doing whatever he wanted to do. It's not good to be young and have that much freedom."

The coach has spent much of his life trying to help kids achieve their dreams. Admittedly, he never knows which ones will take his words to heart and live by them. But he and James shared a last name and the same dark complexion.

They weren't father and son. It just appeared that way.

"Maybe it was the extra time I put in with him," Washington said. "I took him everywhere I went, and we had the same last name, so he couldn't act a fool."

Henry Washington also shaped the adolescent's football career by teaching James to play defensive back in addition to receiver. He figured that would give James more opportunities to play.

"James had all of the skills to be an awesome player. I could see that right away," Washington said. "Everybody wants to catch the football because they think they want to get away from that contact. You find very few that can backpedal and then come up and knock the hell out of you."

James starred at Jordan and drew attention from nearly all of the Pac-10 schools before settling on UCLA, in part, because of the school's colors. In James Washington's neighborhood, the Crips street gang had a higher profile than the rival Bloods. The Crips wore blue; the Bloods wore red.

At UCLA, Washington learned the position from Don Rogers and Kenny Easley, two of the best in school history. Each became a first-round pick, and Washington was on the same track until he tore a knee ligament as a junior.

He tore the same ligament as a senior, ending his season and dropping him into the fifth round of the NFL draft, where the hometown Los Angeles Rams selected him.

"He wasn't a starter with the Rams, so he didn't get a lot of publicity," Henry Washington said. "He would've lost his mind if he had been a starter in Los Angeles."

James Washington understood the business of the NFL. When the Cowboys took Darren Woodson with the 37th pick in the 1992 draft and traded for veteran safety Thomas Everett, Washington knew his days were numbered.

But that didn't bother him.

Competition never bothers a playmaker, because his self-confidence creates a mind-set that he is able to play at a high level. With so many playmakers on the Cowboys in the 1990s, practices were especially tough as each one tried to stand out above the others. The fact coach Jimmy Johnson only played his best players raised the stakes that much higher.

So Washington, acquired as a Plan B free agent in 1990 from Los Angeles, ended up on the bench—sort of—in 1993, a year after he started 16 games for a Super Bowl champion.

"That's what happens when you groom a kid like Darren Woodson to come in and take a position. If I would've started eight games, they would've had to pay me a whole bunch of money," Washington said. "I wouldn't start the game, but the next series I'd be in there. I had just as many plays as [Thomas] Everett and Woodson, and I was the leading tackler among nonstarters."

Washington also knew his attitude played a role in keeping him off of the field. Coach Jimmy Johnson wasn't inclined to put pressure on owner Jerry Jones to keep a player that he couldn't really control.

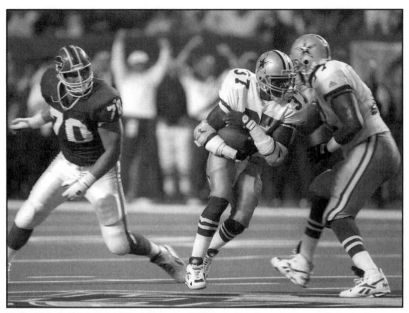

Defensive back James Washington (37) runs back an interception during Super Bowl XXVIII against the Buffalo Bills at the Georgia Dome in Atlanta.
Rick Stewart/Getty Images

Washington didn't mince words with teammates, coaches, or reporters. If he saw an injustice—real or perceived—he talked about it.

"I wasn't the kind of guy who got along with everybody. I beat to my own drum. I'm gonna say what I wanna say. I was a walking sound byte," Washington said. "Everything I thought, I said to the media, and if I didn't like you, I let you know.

"I caused a lot of controversy, but Jimmy kept me around because I made a lot of plays. Jimmy [and I] did not get along, but he always told me as long as you make plays, you're all right with me. I had fights on the field, off the field, and during games.

"That's not what Jimmy wanted to happen, and he'd pull me aside and say, 'JDub,' I love you and I love your energy, but as soon as you stop making plays, your ass is outta here."

Washington didn't like coming off the bench, but he respected Woodson and Everett, so he accepted the situation.

"I knew I could play, but the game is about adversity and dealing with it. Woodson was the best athlete I ever played with, so relinquishing the strong safety spot to him was just part of the business,"

Washington said. "Everett was a hard-working guy who understood what Jimmy wanted, and he didn't make any waves, which is what the Cowboys wanted.

"The secondary was loaded that year, but every time I stepped on the field, people knew where I was because I was still one of the hardest-hitting defensive backs on the team and in the league. If they had said they were going to replace me with Brock Marion, then I would have had a problem because he was a rookie and not the Pro Bowl player he became later in his career."

Woodson appreciated Washington's approach. Woodson said Washington taught him to be a cerebral player.

"He helped me out probably more than anybody," Woodson said. "I was a guy who played a whole bunch of positions, and he settled me down early on by taking on more responsibility and allowing me to find a comfort zone, so I could become a better player."

With running back Emmitt Smith missing two games during a contract dispute, Dallas started the season 0-2. Smith rejoined the team and the Cowboys won 12 of the last 14 games and entered the playoffs on a five-game winning streak.

A franchise-record 11 Cowboys—eight on offense and three on defense—went to the Pro Bowl, including Washington. Dallas was tied for 10th in the NFL in defense after finishing first in 1992, but it allowed 14 fewer points.

Wins over Green Bay and San Francisco propelled Dallas into the Super Bowl for the second consecutive year.

"We went into the game confident because we firmly believed we were going to win, which I'm sure every team does," said Joe Avezzano, special team coach from 1990 to 2002. "But we got our persona from people like [Charles] Haley, Michael [Irvin], and Troy [Aikman].

"They made everybody confident and they practiced so hard that it raised everybody's intensity level. We never got complacent, even though we knew somebody would have to play awfully well to beat us."

The Cowboys expected outstanding performances from their stars. What set them apart was the ability of players like receiver Alvin Harper, defensive tackle Jimmie Jones, cornerback Kevin Smith, and Washington to turn in stellar performances in the most important games.

Washington had 11 tackles, a forced fumble, an interception, and a 46-yard fumble return for a touchdown. That touchdown, coming on the third play of the second half, changed the entire complexion of the game and sent Dallas to its second consecutive championship.

"When I had a chance to shine," he said, "I shined brighter than any star in the sky."

GAME OF MY LIFE
By James Washington

We had a two-week layoff, but all I know is Jimmy Johnson came to me and said, "We are putting our best players on the field for the biggest game, and you're gonna start." Jimmy said he'd been looking at the matchup with the Bills' offense. They were gonna put me on the field and give me an opportunity to make plays.

They wanted me on the field because Buffalo used three wide receivers so much that we were going to start the game in our nickel defense, which meant Darren Woodson was going to move to linebacker and I was going to play free safety, my natural position. Everybody thinks I was a strong safety because of the way I hit, but I played strong safety most of the time because I was always filling in for somebody.

At free safety, I was going to have to make the calls and the checks and ensure everybody was lined up in the right spot, but Jimmy trusted me, and he knew I was going to give it my all. I looked at the week as an opportunity to showcase my talent so I could get to the next level.

I knew everybody would be watching the Super Bowl, especially coaches. If I had the best game of my life, then I could ask to be traded and there would be a market for me. I could tell owner Jerry Jones and Jimmy that if you don't want me to be here and you don't want to play me, then trade me.

I studied a lot of film—no more than usual because I always studied a lot—but I was so in tune with what they were doing that you would've thought I was on their team. I caused the first turnover on a shovel pass. I was there before Thurman Thomas even got the pass. I was even there before the linebackers, who were supposed to make the tackle.

I had studied so much film and I was picking up so many keys—the fullback, the tackle, Thurman—that it led me to the ball all day.

The film study helped me get an interception, too. In Super Bowl XXVII, Andre Reed had just killed us on drag routes. I had already knocked Andre out of the game on a deep slant route, and Don Beebe was the only deep threat they had in the game.

It was the end of the third quarter and Buffalo had a third-and-six, so I was talking to the coaches and I told secondary coach Dave Campo what defense we should be in based on what I had seen them do in similar situations on film. I told Campo that if they line up in this certain formation, they're going to run something between the tackle box, and Beebe is the only one I could see who they would trust.

So Campo told me to make an automatic call if they came out in that formation. They did, I made the check, and it happened just like I dreamed it and saw it on film. After the interception, I blew a kiss to my baby boy, Richard, who was sitting next to MC Hammer. I knew where they were sitting, and I was feeling so good that I had to send my baby boy some love.

Even though I had the first interception of the game in Super Bowl XXVII, we set the NFL record with nine turnovers, so that interception didn't really matter. I didn't have a very good game in Super Bowl XXVII, and that was the reason why I lost my position. Jimmy wanted playmakers.

I made up my mind that if I got the opportunity to play in Super Bowl XXVIII, I was going to make everybody remember me. That's one of the reasons I went back and watched all of that film of Andre Reed from Super Bowl XXVII.

I was talking to Michael Irvin and Ken Norton in the training room before the game. I told them, "You know this is my game. This is my opportunity." Ken had already played enough to get out of his contract, but I hadn't, so I was a little mad about that. I was definitely walking around with an attitude.

I made the mistake of giving Emmitt the ball at the Buffalo 34 instead of running the interception back for a touchdown. You don't give a guy like Emmitt that kind of opportunity, because he was one of the best players in the game and he was going to get the MVP after he scored a touchdown on that drive.

I wasn't really thinking about the MVP until Michael Irvin ran up to me in the fourth quarter and said, "'JDub,' congratulations on the MVP."

When they announced that Emmitt had won it, I got a little sad. I thought maybe they would at least split it because I had had such a good game. I had some big hits that changed the tempo of the game early, and I wasn't even a guy who started.

A few weeks after the Super Bowl, James Washington met with Johnson to make his position clear: He wasn't going to be happy as a backup again.

"I went to Jimmy and told him that I was still young and I think he should trade me or Thomas Everett because I only have so many years left in my body because of the way I played and ran into people," Washington said. "I told him I needed to get to an organization that was going to use me while I was at the peak of my career."

Johnson, though, was considering whether he was going to continue coaching the Cowboys. He had more on his mind than Washington's happiness.

"We probably would've won three or four Super Bowls if Jimmy and Jerry could've found a way to work together," said Joe Brodsky, a running backs coach with the Cowboys from 1989 to 1997. "I was surprised Jimmy couldn't cut Jerry any slack. I know Jerry was different from most owners, but if I had spent $142 million to buy something, I would've wanted a say in how things were being run."

Jones and his new coach, Barry Switzer, opted to trade Everett.

Washington, a full-time starter again, turned in a terrific season at his natural position of free safety. He tied Woodson for the team lead with five interceptions and recorded more than 100 tackles as Dallas led the NFL in total defense for the second time in three seasons.

"He had a knack for making game-changing plays in the biggest games, whether it was the playoffs or a big game like San Francisco in the regular season," Woodson said. "He brought a nastiness to our defense because he was such a physical player."

The Cowboys also led the league in pass defense, but San Francisco ended their dreams of becoming the first team to win a third consecutive Super Bowl with a 38-28 victory.

Washington, knowing he was near the end of his career, sought a big payday as a free agent. He found it in Washington, where former Cowboys offensive coordinator Norv Turner had become the head coach in 1994.

He played just one season, intercepting two passes in 12 games before retiring.

"I was pretty much done when I left Dallas. My body was aching from playing on that turf for five years and leaving it all out there on the field," Washington said. "People really don't realize the wear and tear that puts on your body. I was done.

"Sometimes, you just have to know when it's enough. When I came in the league, they told me I was just going to be able to play two years on my bad knee, but I played eight seasons, played in four NFC championship games, and won two Super Bowls."

When you play on a team with loquacious stars like Michael Irvin, Nate Newton, and Emmitt Smith, it can be hard to have a forum.

James Washington decided to fix that problem by getting a radio show. He teamed with Newton on a weekly show and had a blast.

"There were so many superstars on that team, and I always wanted to be heard, so I figured having my own radio show where I could be heard—whether it was good or bad—was a good idea," Washington said. "You can get overshadowed with the guys we had on our team."

Washington continued working in radio when he joined the Redskins, doing a few things with the team to stay sharp. After his career ended, Washington wasn't sure exactly what he wanted to do so he returned to UCLA and earned a master's degree in education.

"He wasn't going to be a pro football player forever," Henry Washington said. "It was great that he continued to educate himself."

Education had always been important to Washington, who graduated from high school early and earned his bachelor's degree from UCLA before the Rams drafted him.

His grandmother had a fourth-grade education. His grandfather had a sixth-grade education. Washington learned early that education was a valuable asset that he could never lose.

"They can take all of the jewelry. They can take all of the cars and even the house. They can even take all of your money," Washington said, "but if you're educated, you will always know how to make it back. I figured I would never be poor like I was when I was young. I figured the only way I could keep all of my money was to educate myself.

"I've always wanted to work with kids, and I thought that if I was going to preach education to them and motivate them, then I had to prove that it was important whether you're an athlete or not. A lot of people talk about things, but I'm a doer. I wanted to show them how important education was to me."

After earning his degree, Washington worked for ESPN Radio before leaving for FOX Sports radio.

"It was a little too stale for me at ESPN because they wouldn't let me get out of bounds," Washington said. "Then I found a home with FOX radio and they accepted my personality and what I was all about. It has been a wonderful partnership."

And it has given him an opportunity to be a better father and husband, because his schedule affords him time to spend quality hours with his wife, Dana, and their children, Shanel, Richard, Ryan, and Kinsley.

Washington didn't have his biological father in his life, and it has affected the way he has approached fatherhood.

"I know there have been times when I haven't been the best husband, but I have fought for my marriage," Washington said, "because I love my kids more than anything on Earth, and I know it's better for my kids to have two parents in the household—not one."

CHAPTER 23

GEORGE TEAGUE

His first idol was Edson Arantes do Nascimento, the Brazilian soccer deity also known as Pelé. That's whom George Teague wanted to emulate.

After all, he had the footwork and the speed and the deft scoring touch around the net. And growing up as a military brat on U.S. Air Force bases in Germany until he was 13, Teague didn't see any reason why he couldn't or shouldn't be a soccer star.

That all changed when James Teague, a civil engineer in the USAF, moved the family to Montgomery, Alabama, just before his son's freshman year at Jefferson Davis High School. Soccer was an afterthought in Montgomery, where the biggest decision every boy had to make was whether he wanted to grow up and wear Alabama's crimson uniform or Auburn's blue and orange.

Initially, Teague had other ideas.

"I was not going to play football. I was going to be a soccer player," he said. "I played on a bunch of German teams, and I was usually the only American. I was a very good soccer player. On the surface, I didn't think I would fit [in football] because [other players] were too big. The other tailbacks were 195 pounds, and the linebackers were 240. I told my mama I was going to play soccer."

Dorothy Teague didn't want to hear it.

"You ain't playing soccer," she said. "You're going to play football. You're good at it, and that's where you're going to make it."

Giving up soccer wasn't the only adjustment Teague had to make in Montgomery. He had lived most of his life on military bases in the United States, Japan, and Germany, isolating him from many of the racial issues facing blacks. Although it had been nearly 25 years since President Lyndon B. Johnson signed the Civil Rights Act of 1964, designed to protect blacks from discrimination, by the time the Teagues moved to Montgomery, all of the wounds from that tumultuous period had not healed.

That's because Montgomery was one of the epicenters of the Civil Rights Movement. It was home to Martin Luther King Jr., the pastor of the Dexter Avenue Baptist Church. King led the Montgomery bus boycott in 1955 that began when Rosa Parks refused to give her seat to a white man in compliance with the Jim Crow laws. The boycott last 381 days and ended with a U.S. Supreme Court decision outlawing racial segregation on intrastate buses.

"Although my roots had always been in Alabama because my parents were from Alabama, I hadn't been in an environment where there was so much racial tension or division until I moved there," Teague said.

"That was the first time I encountered racism. The word *boy* was used a lot. You could see the rebel flag. The KKK was prominent. There were just always reminders."

Living in a city with racial tension and attending a high school named after the president of the Confederate States of America taught Teague the importance of tolerance.

"I lived in an all-black neighborhood, but I probably had more white friends than anybody," he said. "I got talked about, but I kept on going because I wanted something better and something different out of life. I was strong enough to shrug stuff off."

It helped that he was a good football player.

Teague started his final two seasons, and the letters from college recruiters started pouring in during his senior season. He narrowed his choices to Alabama, Auburn, Georgia Tech, and Vanderbilt. The final two: Alabama and Georgia Tech.

"Georgia Tech had a bad team. It was in Atlanta, which was great, and they had an excellent engineering program, but Alabama was always on TV," he said.

So he went to Alabama. The Crimson Tide won the 1992 national championship with a perfect season. In the process, Teague secured his spot in Alabama lore with a play that will be talked about in barbershops all over the state long after his grandchildren have grandchildren.

Trailing 7-0, the University of Miami's Lamar Thomas caught a pass, broke a tackle, and seemed headed to a game-tying touchdown, but

Teague chased him down from behind and stole the ball, thwarting the score, changing the game's momentum, and earning a place in history.

"It was my fault because I was out of position," Teague said of Thomas' catch. "I was really trying to take a play off. Once I saw Thomas catch the ball, I panicked. I really wasn't trying to grab the ball. I knew once I caught him, I was going to try to strip it.

"I clubbed at the ball, but instead of going down it popped up in my face, and I grabbed it. I didn't think it was that big of a play—I was excited and I took my helmet off—but it never really hit that it was the kind of play I was going to be hearing about for years."

Later, Teague returned an interception for a touchdown in the game.

When the season ended, Teague figured he would be a third- or fourth-round pick in the NFL draft. But his memorable Sugar Bowl play combined with strong performances in the Japan Bowl (where he returned an interception for a touchdown) and the Senior Bowl boosted his stock.

Green Bay picked him with the 29th selection of the first round.

"Two picks before it was their time to make a choice, Green Bay called," Teague said. "Ron Wolf said if I was still available at 29, they were going to pick me. All I could say was, 'Man, I can't believe it.'"

America's Team had become America's Bad Boys. The Cowboys were known as much for their prowess off of the field as on the field.

That can happen in Texas where football is the most important thing in the state, and spring football is the second most important. Texas is a place where fans study high school recruiting sites like Wall Street brokers monitor the NASDAQ.

The Cowboys were the first franchise to capture three titles in four seasons, and they enjoyed all of the excesses that accompanied fame and success on the football. But their off-the-field lifestyles were starting to affect the football team.

The NFL suspended Pro Bowl receiver Michael Irvin for the first five games of the 1996 season after he pleaded no contest to felony cocaine possession.

"It was a very difficult year," said Rich Dalrymple, the public relations director since 1990. "You know you're going to face some adversity, but you're expecting injuries, not off-the-field issues. When those issues occur, rarely do they come in the loss of a key player and leader at the start of the season.

"We had to deal with the loss of a high-profile player during training camp and for the first five games of the season, and some players just got tired of dealing with it because it put everyone in an awkward position."

Defensive end Shante Carver, a former first-round pick, and defensive tackle Leon Lett also received suspensions for violating the league's substance abuse policy. From 1992 to 1996, the Cowboys had more players suspended for violating the substance abuse policy than any other NFL team.

"It was a distraction for us. Michael has admitted he caused a lot of the problems with our downfall," said Darren Woodson, a safety from 1992 to 2003. "Here was a guy who was instrumental with what we did on the field, and people looked up to him to make plays and do the right things.

"We were on top of the world after winning the Super Bowl and got the bubble burst in the off-season. We had a lot of dissension, and it affected us as a family, but that wasn't the sole reason we didn't play well in 1996. We just weren't as good of a team, and with all of the distractions didn't always play hard."

Dallas started the 1996 season 2-3, the first time it had a losing record after five games since the 1990 season, but each time the Cowboys seemed ready to buckle under the strain of their off-field issues, however, they would turn in a performance that showed their potential.

At 1-3, they beat Philadelphia on the road. They beat Jimmy Johnson's Dolphins on the road. They beat Green Bay on *Monday Night Football.* And they kept New England, the NFL's highest scoring team, out of the end zone in a 12-6 victory. The win over the Patriots gave Dallas its fifth consecutive NFC East title.

Coach Barry Switzer opted to rest most of his starters for the Cowboys' final regular-season game and the last game at RFK stadium, and the Redskins won easily 37-10.

Although Dallas was 10-6 and trying to match Pittsburgh as the only franchise to win consecutive Super Bowls twice, the Cowboys' fan base was unimpressed. It appeared the playoff game against Minnesota might be blacked out locally because it wasn't a sellout 72 hours before kickoff. The NFL, however, gave the Cowboys an extra day because of the Christmas holiday to sell out the game.

Teague, traded by Green Bay and released by Atlanta in the span of a month, had joined Dallas the day before the Cowboys' final preseason game.

"I knew I was going to be out of there at the end of December," he said. "All I wanted to know was where's my locker, where are my shoes, and who am I playing with. I didn't get involved with anybody. I didn't really feel like I was part of that team.

"I didn't have any enthusiasm the whole year. I can remember knocking down a fourth-down pass against New England—it was a huge play—and I remember not really realizing that I had made a huge play. I didn't have that drive."

Teague started for the final six games after Brock Marion broke his shoulder blade. He finished the season with 70 tackles and four interceptions. Nothing really mattered, though.

"I was just playing. I was back on the field, and I had a job. My innocence was gone, and I wasn't having fun. It took me about four years to start having fun again."

GAME OF MY LIFE
By George Teague

I knew how big the game was. At that point, I was probably motivated more by a playoff check than anything, although I felt like this was a very good shot for me to start on the road to the Super Bowl. I felt like I had missed out on the gradual steps we took in Green Bay and the growth we had to get to the Super Bowl. I felt like if we beat the Vikings, we would have a showdown between the Cowboys and the Packers. We needed to make that happen because I wanted revenge.

I had one of my best seasons. Maybe it was my anger, or I felt like I had stuff to prove. I do know the scheme was good for me, especially with the corners we had. With Kevin Smith and Deion Sanders, I had the freedom to go make plays. It was lovely.

Against Minnesota, Cris Carter was going to be the key. I knew I was going to have the opportunity to make some plays in the passing game that were going to have an impact, especially the way we were playing our corners. I knew somewhere in that game I was going to have the chance to make some plays.

In the scheme we played, teams always tried to use a lot of crossing routes to match their receivers against our linebackers, but I had the freedom to chase that guy and jump the route. Quarterbacks didn't expect the safety to come get the ball.

The first turnover was almost identical to the play I made at Alabama. Roger Harper, the other safety, took a bad angle on Amp Lee after he caught the ball on a short little ro ute out of the backfield, and all of a sudden nobody was there. The only thing to do was to try to go

George Teague intercepts the ball during a playoff game against the
Minnesota Vikings at Texas Stadium. *Brian Bahr/Getty Images*

get him. I kicked it into high gear—I have a never-give-up attitude—and took a good angle to go get him.

I don't know why—it must have been a blessing—but he switched hands right before he crossed the goal line. I don't know if anyone remembers that. He had it in one hand, and he switched hands. It was just perfect for me. As soon as he switched hands, he stuck it right where I could get it. I just punched it out. I didn't try to grab him. It was just boom! I hit it, and it just flew out of the back of the end zone!

He thought he had a touchdown, and I really didn't know. I was waiting for the ref to make a call. The refs were kind of looking around like what happened, then they signaled touchback. It was wild on the sideline. Anytime you get Michael Irvin and those guys running out on the field for a defensive play, it's a big deal.

I forced a fumble on the Vikings' next series. I stripped Leroy Hoard on the first play, and Emmitt Smith scored a touchdown on the next play.

The next time the Vikings had the ball, I intercepted a pass and returned it 29 yards for a touchdown. It was a dumb play by Brad Johnson. I knew the route. He threw across the field and across his body. He thought he had Cris Carter, but I was watching Cris the whole way. He should've thrown it somewhere else.

I was having so much fun, dude. I hadn't had that much fun in a long time. That was actually a fun football game. I wanted to do more because that was the most fun I'd ever had—maybe in my whole career. I walked in the media room after the game and saw all of the reporters, and the only thing I could think was, "This is so weird."

After the game I hung out with my family. That was my ritual after a game. I'd get with the family, go eat, go home, and watch *SportsCenter*.

Carolina, a precocious two-year-old franchise, ended the Cowboys' controversy-plagued season a week later with a 26-17 victory.

Michael Irvin left with an injury on the second play of the game and didn't return. When Carolina knocked Deion Sanders out of the game in the second half, they snuffed out what little life the defending Super Bowl champions had.

"It was devastating," Teague said. "I knew we were going to play Green Bay if we won that game. It was hard. I knew we had the talent, but we couldn't get it done."

Actually, the loss represented the end of an era for the Cowboys that included three championships in four seasons, an unprecedented feat until New England accomplished the same feat from 2001 to 2004.

The Cowboys have made the playoffs just three times since the 1996 season; they have not won a playoff game since Teague's virtuoso performance ignited a 40-15 win over Minnesota. They had more coaches (four) in the past nine seasons than the franchise had in its first 37 seasons, and there have been just two winning seasons and one NFC East title.

Teague's performance as a starter and in the playoffs wasn't good enough to warrant a lucrative new deal for Teague, who became a free agent at the end of the season. Dallas offered him only a one-year deal. He eventually signed with Miami.

"I didn't really expect to be back," Teague said. "Other teams were offering three- and five-year deals, so they weren't really in the picture. The reason they brought me in was because both of their safeties—Roger Harper and Charlie Williams—were hurt, so I wasn't really part of their plan."

George Teague has never been happier.

Ever.

He's the head football coach and athletic director at Harvest Christian Academy, a small, private kindergarten-through-12-grade school in Wautaga, Texas, about 30 miles west of downtown Dallas. He works in a cluttered office a few feet from the gymnasium.

These days, he's dealing with budget issues and equipment inventory and even cheerleader tryouts as he tries to build a dynamic athletic department. It's not what he had planned after his nine-year NFL career ended after the 2000 season. Teague and his wife, Consuela, have always had an entrepreneurial spirit. They've dabbled in several businesses, and even opened a lingerie shop—Jada's Place—named after their daughter. Their oldest child, James Teague II, is one of the reasons Teague is now a football coach and administrator.

Teague accompanied his son, who has attended Harvest Academy for years, to a basketball game in December 2003 to see a high-profile team from Alabama.

"It was a father-and-son deal," Teague said. "Coach [Ray] DeBord hit me right on the spot—I never really ever talked to him, and I didn't hardly even know him. He said, 'Our head coach is resigning and God laid it on my heart to ask you if you want to be our football coach. Don't say anything. Go home and pray about it. I'm not going to ask anybody about the job. I'm not going to offer it to anybody else. Just go home and pray about it for six weeks and come back and tell me if you want to do it.'"

Teague had always promised himself that he wasn't going to be a high school coach because he didn't want to deal with all of the issues, primarily parents, that go with high school football. But he wanted to coach, which is why he interned at Cleveland on coach Butch Davis' staff and why he considered being a graduate assistant at Alabama on coach Mike Price's staff.

"My purpose here is bigger than just coaching," he said. "I'm a lot more spiritual, and I feel like I can help these kids and have an impact on their lives. I wake up early, and I stay up late and I'm not tired, even though I'm dealing with a lot of issues and problems. I feel excited every day.

"I know this is where God wants me to be. I can't always say that I always felt that in my heart. All the money and fame that I've had in my life, I've never been happier than I am right now. I'm in the right place doing the right thing."

CHAPTER 24

LARRY BROWN

L arry Brown always felt underappreciated as an athlete. Maybe it was the slender frame and high cheekbones that made him look more like a model than a football player. Or maybe it was his soft-spoken nature and sensitivity to criticism. Or maybe it's that his high school and college teams always seemed to be in the shadows of bigger, more established programs.

Brown starred in track and football at Los Angeles High School, but didn't get the attention he would have at nationally recognized powers such as Dorsey High School. Without a scholarship offer to a school he wanted, Brown enrolled at Los Angeles' Southwest Community College.

Two years later, he was a starting cornerback at TCU, which went 9-13 in his two seasons under coach Jim Wacker. As a senior, he had 75 tackles and 10 pass deflections and earned a spot in the Blue–Gray game, where he earned MVP honors.

But it didn't help his draft stock because he had been labeled a malcontent by the TCU coaching staff.

"I don't know who was spreading it, but it was definitely out there," said Scott Casterline, who represented Brown throughout his NFL career. "We figured he was going to be a late-round pick or a free agent.

He had really good speed and size, so we thought he'd get an opportunity somewhere."

The opportunity came with the Cowboys, who made him the 57th defensive back and 320th player selected in the 1991 draft. He almost didn't survive training camp.

"Jimmy [Johnson] was really riding him during two-a-days, and Larry Brown left camp," Casterline said. "I got a late-night phone call from [Cowboys personnel director] Bob Ackles, and he told me Larry had gone home to see his mother, who was sick."

Casterline and his partner, Vic Vines, drove to the Cowboys' training camp to meet with Cowboys officials.

"I got Larry on the phone, and he's talking about how Jimmy hates him," Casterline said. "Then we had a conference call with Bob, Jimmy, and Larry, and we're all telling him that Jimmy wouldn't be yelling at him if he didn't want him. We convinced him to come back to camp, and everything worked out."

Four weeks into his rookie season, Johnson replaced Manny Hendrix in the starting lineup with Brown.

"You don't do that with a guy who can't play," Brown said. "I was a 12th-round pick who wasn't supposed to make the team, and all of a sudden I'm not only the youngest player on the team, but the youngest starting cornerback in the NFL.

"A lot of people think I just had one good game—Super Bowl XXX—but I had a lot of good games and made a lot of big plays for the Cowboys."

As Larry Brown prepared for the 1995 season, the most important of his five-year NFL career, life intervened.

His pregnant wife, Cheryl, was having complications, and they weren't sure the baby was going to survive—if he made it to term. Kristopher Brown, born about three months early, weighed one pound and six ounces at birth.

The good news was that the Brown's first child, Kristen, had been born under similar conditions in 1993 and had survived with no complications.

Brown, who was going to be an unrestricted free agent at the end of the season, which meant he could sign with any team, spent hours at the hospital. He prayed for his son's life while the baby was hooked up to ventilators that helped him breathe because his lungs were underdeveloped. More than once, Brown slept at the hospital and went directly to practice.

"You get through it through love, prayers, family, and friends. I wasn't practicing much, and my diet was off," Brown said. "When you're going through a depression, you're not eating well, you're not sleeping much, and I was only practicing one day a week.

"It wasn't easy. A lot of times guys didn't know how I got out there and played. The players, the coaches—Dave Campo and guys like [Darren] Woodson and Deion—gave me anything I needed or wanted to help me get through that time."

Brown's teammates found strength in his perseverance. They also sent food to his house and made sure he didn't have to worry about anything but Cheryl and Kristopher.

"To see Larry go through that was painful," said Darren Woodson, a safety with the Cowboys from 1992 to 2004, "because I had kids and I know how much you love them. He couldn't really tell you what he was going through, but my heart was pouring out for him."

On November 16, three days before the Cowboys played Oakland, Kristopher died.

"I was on a plane when he told me, and it just floored me," Casterline said. "He had such a strong Christian faith, and he mentioned that to me when he told me about the baby. He said he didn't understand it, but he had faith in the Lord. Cheryl was the same way."

Brown didn't want to miss the game against Oakland, a team he rooted for as a child. But he wasn't sure he could arrive in time for kickoff because Kristopher's funeral was Saturday.

"I remember Larry telling me that he was going to play, and I just couldn't believe it," Woodson said. "I was telling him to just stay home with family, but he was going through so much that being around teammates was his way of trying to find a comfort zone."

Others, including Casterline and owner Jerry Jones, told him to take as much time as he needed. His wife encouraged him to play. Using Jones' private jet, Brown arrived in Oakland about 10:30 p.m. Saturday night.

"The best thing for him and the team was for Larry to play," Casterline said. "The whole team came to the funeral, and it wasn't just for show. That support made a tough time in Larry's life a lot better."

In the locker room on Sunday, Brown was surprised to find the players' helmets adorned with decals memorializing his son. Then the players dedicated their 34-21 victory to Brown.

"I didn't know they were doing it. I didn't expect it. They just did it," Brown said. "I learned there are a lot of things more important than your profession and what you do. I learned a lot of guys cared more about me the person than me the football player."

While Brown struggled with his grief, he also wondered about his future with the Cowboys once the 1995 season ended.

After all, the Cowboys had signed cornerback Deion Sanders to one of the most lucrative contracts in professional sports—a five-year, $35-million deal that included a $12.9-million signing bonus—and he wasn't sure where that put him in the eyes of Jones and the coaching staff.

That's because the Cowboys had a bevy of established stars such as Troy Aikman, Michael Irvin, and Emmitt Smith and a bevy of young up-and-coming players such as defensive tackle Leon Lett, cornerback Kevin Smith, and tackle Erik Williams, who were going to require big contracts to secure their services.

The Cowboys had already let significant contributors like linebacker Ken Norton Jr., center Mark Stepnoski, and receiver Alvin Harper leave via free agency. The NFL had adopted a salary cap in 1994, so now even if teams wanted to pay certain players, it had to work all of the players into a budget.

So Brown wasn't sure where he would be in 1996.

"A lot of guys felt Mr. Jones wouldn't keep the team together. Each year pieces kept falling off," Brown said. "When he paid Deion the money that he did, we figured the whole team, not just the defensive backs, would suffer.

"Whenever you get a chance to get a player like Deion Sanders, you have to get him, because he's a phenomenal talent, but I don't know if Mr. Jones calculated the real cost of signing him, because a lot of guys eventually had to leave the organization because we got Deion.

"Mr. Jones kind of felt that as long as he had Michael, Troy, and Emmitt, that was all he needed. Guys felt this would be the last run."

Whether he was in Dallas or somewhere else, Casterline figured Brown would be one of the most coveted cornerbacks in free agency, because he was a good bump-and-run cornerback, and the Cowboys were a high-profile team.

"Larry and I met every two or three weeks," Casterline said, "and I briefed him on what was going on. I had a pretty good feel for where he was going to go."

Although the team was winning, a chasm was forming in the locker room regarding coach Barry Switzer, who had taken over for Jimmy Johnson after the Cowboys won their second consecutive Super Bowl in 1993. Switzer, a longtime friend of Jones, didn't take the demanding approach Johnson did.

Players didn't worry about whether a mistake on Sunday would lead to their release on Monday. Switzer was a players' coach.

Larry Brown tries to escape John L. Williams of the Pittsburgh Steelers after a fourth-quarter interception in Super Bowl XXX. *Al Bello/Getty Images*

Players such as Aikman and Darryl Johnston, who thought Johnson's disciplined approach played an integral role in their championships, didn't like the way Switzer ran the team. They saw an overall attention to detail fading—and they didn't like it.

"I don't think the fans liked Barry, because they wanted a guy who was going to grab you and cuss you out after a bad play, but Barry treated us like professionals," Brown said. "He expected us to carry ourselves like professionals, and he gave us the freedom to do that. There were a few guys who didn't agree with his philosophy of doing things, but you have that on any team.

"Barry was an honest coach. He wasn't a bull-shitter. He'd shoot you straight. He'd let you know the decisions he was making and the ones that didn't come from him. Most of the guys respected him."

San Francisco had stopped Dallas' attempt to win an unprecedented third consecutive Super Bowl championship by beating the Cowboys 38-28 in the NFC championship game. The 49ers led 21-0 midway through the first quarter, and Dallas spent the rest of the game fighting back.

A 15-yard penalty against Switzer for unsportsmanlike conduct in the fourth quarter and a no-call on an apparent pass interference penalty that would've given Dallas the ball at the San Francisco 1-yard line also played a role in the Cowboys' demise.

Signing Sanders was designed to weaken San Francisco and give Dallas an edge in the NFC.

"A lot of guys felt they overreacted. We'd been to two Super Bowls and a championship game in three years. We just didn't play well against San Francisco in the 1994 game across the board," Brown said. "There were a lot of questionable calls. It was just one of those games. But Mr. Jones felt for whatever reason they were a better team than we were. A lot of the guys felt we were the better team. If we played our best game and they played their best game, we'd beat them any day."

With Sanders, Jones and Switzer felt confident in their ability to match up with San Francisco's receiver corps and quarterback Steve Young.

Sanders was expected to miss the first eight games because he was playing outfield for the San Francisco Giants, but the coaching staff wasn't worried because they figured Brown and Smith could handle both cornerback spots until Sanders arrived.

Then Sanders would play on the right side, Smith on the left, and Brown in the slot when teams used three-receiver formations.

But the plan never took shape because Smith ruptured his Achilles tendon in the first game, a 35-0 win over the New York Giants on *Monday Night Football.* The injury occurred the day after he signed a lucrative long-term deal. Suddenly Brown and Clayton Holmes were the top cornerbacks on the roster.

"They used me like Deion," said Brown, "putting me on the best receiver every game—and I loved it."

Brown tied free safety Brock Marion for the team lead with six interceptions as Dallas finished ninth in the NFL in total defense and eighth against the pass. The Cowboys won their fourth straight NFC East championship and earned home-field advantage throughout the playoffs.

Brown's interception with 9:24 remaining and Dallas holding a 31-27 lead helped propel the Cowboys over Green Bay in the NFC championship game and into Super Bowl XXX. Brown intercepted two passes by Neil O'Donnell in the second half, allowing Dallas to win a then-unprecedented three Super Bowl championships in four seasons.

GAME OF MY LIFE
By Larry Brown

We felt we would beat Pittsburgh and beat them handily. We had played in so many big games—everyone wanted to knock off the Cowboys every week—that a lot of times we played to the tempo of our opponent.

The first part of the game we were kicking their butts and getting after them. We got comfortable when we got ahead 13-0 in the second quarter, and we didn't have that killer instinct.

The first interception basically slipped out of Neil O'Donnell's hand and got away from him. We were leading 13-7, and I was thinking, "Let me see if I can get into the end zone." But I didn't want to drop it.

All week, the defensive coaching staff had been talking about turnovers. Turnovers, turnovers, turnovers. That's all they focused on all week. They also talked about taking advantage of opportunities to make a play. When you get an opportunity to make a play, make it.

Every week you see guys who drop interceptions or don't pick up a fumble, and it comes back to haunt them late in the game. We didn't want that to happen to us, so I wanted to make sure I caught the ball.

That was the most important thing.

We were in the zone, and I was looking for crossing routes. Neil tried to hit one, but the pass slipped. It didn't have a lot of velocity, and it came right to me. The easy interceptions are the hardest ones to catch.

In the fourth quarter, they got an onside kick and scored a touchdown to make it 20-17, and the game's momentum changed. Once they got the onside kick, we said, "OK, let's go play." There was no panic. They made a good play. It was a trick play, and they got it. That was our fault, because we weren't ready. Give them credit. Then we picked the tempo back up and started making plays like we normally did.

The second interception occurred on a blitz, where we didn't have any safety help. We wanted to be more aggressive after Pittsburgh got close, and we started blitzing like crazy.

We wanted to attack them, and we had practiced all week that when we blitzed, all we had to do was count, "A thousand one, a thousand two," and the ball was going to be gone. The coaches wanted us to be aggressive, especially when we blitzed.

I saw the receiver run a slant, and I jumped it and beat him to the spot. When you look at the tape, you can't tell he's running a hot route because I jumped it, and he ended up breaking behind me after I jumped the slant. Neil was throwing to a spot, and he threw it to me.

According to our film work, there were two or three routes—a slant, a fade, or a quick stop—their receiver was going to run based on the blitz we used. If we were in bump-and-run, he was going to run a fade or the slant. If we were playing off coverage, he was going to run the stop or slant.

When the ball was snapped, I peeked in the backfield and saw O'Donnell's shoulders. The way they were turned I could tell he was going to throw the slant, not the stop. I came out of my backpedal real slow—then boom—I went and got the ball.

We were so happy. I remember Troy jumping on me. It seemed like the offense was more excited than we were on defense. They drove for a touchdown, and that clinched the game.

The game was over, and I was ready to go in the locker room, when Brock Marion ran up to me and told me that I was named MVP. I couldn't believe it. We all know there are politics surrounding an award like that. None of us was even thinking about the MVP, because we just figured Troy, Michael, or Emmitt would get it no matter how anybody else played.

Winning the Super Bowl was great, but it was different than the first time we won it. There was no feeling like the first one, because we didn't know we could do it. We expected to win the second one, but we also wanted to prove the first one wasn't a fluke. And we expected to win the third one as long as we played our game. It was nice, but we didn't appreciate it the way we did the others.

In 1995, Larry Brown earned $502,000.

After intercepting two passes in the Super Bowl and earning the MVP award, his agent, Scott Casterline, expected that figure to quadruple—at the least.

And that didn't include all of the endorsement opportunities that could set up Brown and his family with enough money to last a lifetime. The Raiders were the early favorite, though he visited several teams.

Brown wasn't a big-time recruit in high school, and as a 12th-round pick in the NFL, he had always been fighting for a roster spot. This time he enjoyed being coveted.

"The Raiders were most intriguing. I'm from California. I'm going home. It's on grass and we practiced against them, so I knew a lot of guys on the team," Brown said. "On paper, they had one of the best teams. I grew up a die-hard Raiders fan, and I thought they had turned the corner."

Brown signed a lucrative five-year deal that included a $3.6-million signing bonus. He assumed the best part of his career was about to start.

It wasn't.

"It was a new environment. These aren't guys who scouted you out of college. These aren't the guys who drafted you. These aren't the guys you played with, and when you're young, you don't think about management and the direction of an organization," Brown said. "I thought every organization had the same commitment and stability the Cowboys had, and it wasn't like that."

Brown never lived up to the hype with the Raiders. In his first preseason with the Raiders, he suffered from plantar fasciatis, an inflammation of the tendon that runs along the base of the foot.

"The doctor said I needed to be in a cast for six weeks. They wanted me to play through it," Brown said. "I practiced once a week. Then I started taking cortisone shots and it didn't get better, so I ended up playing hurt.

"I couldn't walk. I'd be on crutches during the week. Ultimately, they put me in a cast. If they had done that in the preseason, I would've been ready one to two weeks into the season, but they didn't. When I got back, the season was wrecked and the team was in disarray."

The Raiders finished the season 7-9. Brown lasted just one more season before the Raiders released him.

"He had injury problems, and the Raiders had a very unstable coaching staff. Larry was also stepping into a situation where there was some jealousy," Casterline said. "There's always some resentment anytime a player moves into a situation like that, and it's tough for anyone to succeed."

Brown signed with the Vikings in 1998 and lasted less than a season.

An injury to Sanders later that year brought Brown back to Dallas for a few games. You can't reinvent the past. The Cowboys were no longer a championship team. The energetic youngsters who helped Dallas become the first team to win three Super Bowls in four seasons were now grumpy veterans.

"When I got back, Michael Irvin told me it wasn't the same," Brown said. "It was a different organization. It wasn't like the great old days. The camaraderie, the friendships... they just weren't the same."

When the season ended, Brown decided he was tired of professional football.

"My foot still wasn't where it needed to be, and I made the decision to walk away. I started on three teams that won the Super Bowl," he said. "I was happy to play in an era that was a part of history."

The transition from football star to suburban father has been difficult for Brown, just as it has been for countless other athletes.

He's owned businesses that failed, been in debt to casinos in Las Vegas, and filed for bankruptcy.

"When you're young and in business, I had some people who talked me into getting into business. I put up money, and when things don't work out, they want to come after whomever they think has the most money," Brown said. "I learned a lot about the people who are around you. Everyone around you does not like you, but you don't know any better. You don't know how to distinguish between the vultures and the people who genuinely care about you."

But he's fought through the adversity and found something he loves to do: talk about football on radio and TV. That passion has given him an opportunity to stay close to the game.

He's done some color commentary on college football games on radio and been part of ESPN's college football radio coverage.

"I knew I wanted to be part of the game," he said. "I loved the broadcasting, but if you're not a big name like Troy [Aikman] or Michael [Irvin], people tend to minimize what you've accomplished.

"I believe guys like myself represent the average player and the average fan. You provide a whole different perspective on the game, when you've been at the facility on cut day wondering if you were going to make it."

The flexibility of Brown's radio schedule also affords him the opportunity to be actively involved with his children—daughters, Kristin and Kayla, and son, Kameron—and their athletic schedules.

CHAPTER 25

DEION
SANDERS

Deion Sanders has always been a star. The sport never mattered: football, baseball, basketball, track. Put a ball in his hand, and he was guaranteed to do something special. It's not that he planned to do something special. It just seemed that every time he played a sport, he did something magical.

"I was never good. I was always great," he said. "My first year of football, I played offensive guard—and I did it with everything that I had. The next year they let me dot that 'I,' and it was on.

"I've never felt any pressure. It's always been a child's game to me, and when you play a game, you dance and have a good time. Sometimes you are gifted so much and make it look so easy that other people take for granted what you do. They allow you to go, and after you leave, they find out there's no replacement for what you do."

Sanders, the most successful two-sport professional athlete of his generation, created the foundation in the youth leagues of Fort Myers, Florida, where his mother always made sure he had the best equipment and played against the best competition.

At North Fort Myers High School, Sanders earned All-State honors in football, basketball, and baseball. He picked Florida State over the universities of Florida and Georgia because defensive coordinator Mickey Andrews made it clear that he would play and contribute as a freshman, if he was ready.

That's all the incentive Sanders needed. By the time his career at Florida State ended, he was a legend.

He won the Jim Thorpe Award as the nation's best defensive back as a senior and ended his career as the school's all-time leader in punt return yards. He also scored six career touchdowns—three interception returns and three punt returns—for the Seminoles, who went 4-0 in bowl games. Sanders also played center field for Florida State's nationally ranked baseball team, which advanced to the College World Series, and he won the Metro Conference's 100-meter and 200-meter dash titles as a freshman.

But that's not what gave him legendary status.

Once he played in the first game of a Metro Conference tournament baseball game, ran a leg on the 400-meter relay team while wearing his baseball pants, and then returned to the tournament and delivered the game-winning hit in the Seminoles' second game of the day.

The Yankees drafted Sanders in the 30th round of the 1988 amateur baseball draft because they knew football was his top priority. Baseball, though, always tugged at Sanders because he never mastered the game. You can't. Not when a 70-percent failure rate at the plate makes you a star.

The Atlanta Falcons made him the fifth pick of the 1989 draft, but he didn't reach a contract agreement until September 7. He did, however, make a memorable debut.

Sanders returned his first career interception 68 yards for a touchdown. In the process, he became the only athlete in modern history to score an NFL touchdown and hit a home run in a Major League Baseball game in the same week. (Five days earlier, Sanders had homered for the Yankees.)

"Other people think what you do is extraordinary, but you're just doing what you do," he said. "You're doing what you were blessed to do."

The Falcons, though, couldn't quench Sanders' desire to win. Sanders' ability at cornerback and as a kick returner excited the fans and helped increase attendance, but had little impact on the team's win-loss record. Atlanta went 30-50 in Sanders' five seasons, with one trip to the playoffs in 1991. The Falcons followed that 10-6 season with two 6-10 records.

That wasn't nearly good enough for Sanders, whose teams at Florida State had played in bowl games each of his four seasons, finished 11-1, and ranked among the top five in each of his last two years.

As a free agent, Sanders signed a one-year deal with San Francisco in 1994 and was promptly named Defensive Player of the Year after intercepting six passes and tying the franchise's single-season record for interception returns with touchdowns of 74, 93, and 90 yards.

He also became the first person to compete in the World Series and a Super Bowl. Sanders capped off a fantastic season with four tackles and an interception as San Francisco beat San Diego to win Super Bowl XXIX.

Dallas owner Jerry Jones, whose team had won two of the previous three Super Bowls, took notice. He figured the best way to push Dallas past San Francisco was to take the 49ers' best player. Sanders joined the Cowboys in September 1995, when he signed a seven-year, $35-million deal.

"Our locker room was so strong that I didn't think one player could disrupt our core," said Joe Avezzano, the Cowboys' special teams coach from 1990 to 2002. "Not only did we have a talented team, but we were like a traveling circus, and one player wasn't going to affect that.

"When a guy like Deion is on the other team and he goes through his antics and showboating, you tend not to like him. When he gets on your team and you see that it's just part of his personality and you get to know the person—not just the player, then you find out what a good person and teammate he is."

Three games into the 1998 season, the Cowboys found themselves at a crossroads, heading into a *Monday Night Football* game against the rival Giants.

The Cowboys had a new coach, Chan Gailey, who was about as anonymous as an NFL offensive coordinator could be in the era of sports talk radio and ESPN, and they were coming off their first losing season since 1990. A franchise, saluted for years because of its stability, suddenly had none.

The Cowboys had employed the same coach, general manager, and scouting director for the franchise's first 29 years. That triumvirate had produced five Super Bowl appearances, two world championships, and a legacy as one of the best franchises in any sport after a record 20 consecutive winning seasons from 1966 to 1985, one of the longest streaks in professional sports.

But cracks had begun forming in the foundation.

After a 6-10 season in 1997 that resulted in the Cowboys missing the playoffs for the first time since 1990, owner Jerry Jones fired coach Barry Switzer. After a lengthy search that lasted 34 days (January 9 through February 12) and almost resulted in UCLA coach Terry Donahue reuniting with Troy Aikman, Gailey became the Cowboys' third coach since 1993.

Gailey, a deeply religious man, tried to bring discipline to a club that had been spiraling out of control almost from the day the free-wheeling Switzer replaced the highly structured Jimmy Johnson as head coach. For example, in training camp, Johnson penalized those who committed penalties with post-practice laps around the practice field.

No one—even Aikman—was spared.

"He wasn't a very public person or a colorful character, but Chan Gailey was a very good football coach and he ran the team in an efficient manner," said Avezzano, "But most people—coaches, players, media, and fans—knew very little about him in the two seasons he was there."

Gailey won his debut in one of the most exciting games in franchise history, a 41-35 win over Washington. Dallas had trailed 35-14 in the third quarter. The Cowboys weren't as fortunate the next week.

Denver blew out the Cowboys 42-23 at Mile High Stadium as Terrell Davis ran for 191 yards and three touchdowns. More importantly, Aikman fractured his collarbone in the game, forcing him to miss the next five weeks.

So the Cowboys were facing a division rival on the road without their superstar quarterback. The talk that week centered almost entirely on how the Giants, the defending NFC East champions, were going to attack Jason Garrett, who had spent the bulk of his career as a third-string quarterback and had thrown just 91 career passes.

In the Cowboys' locker room, individuals talked about stepping up their performance to take pressure off Garrett and holding the fort until Aikman returned under center.

Sanders did just that.

He returned a punt and an interception for touchdowns, extending his NFL record for touchdown returns to 16. He also caught a 55-yard pass that set up another touchdown. He finished the evening with 226 yards in returns and receptions, as the Cowboys whipped the Giants 31-7.

"There are certain people, because of their athletic ability and personality, who can seize the opportunity and take over a game being played on a big stage," Avezzano said. "There's no greater stage in professional football—aside from the Super Bowl—than *Monday Night Football.*

"That was an unbelievable performance that few could imagine doing and even fewer could pull off, but that's what made him a great player."

GAME OF MY LIFE

By Deion Sanders

Troy had gotten hurt the week before, so we knew he wasn't going to play, but we believed in Jason Garrett. He was smart. He knew the game. And he was just so good in the huddle.

Deion Sanders celebrates in the end zone after making a touchdown against the New York Giants at Giants Stadium. *Al Bello/Getty Images*

He would tell receivers to make sure they get off the jam. Or he would say, "Guys, we really need this." Or he would say, "Prime, I need you." He was just like that. He had presence, and we thought he could do the job.

People talk about that game, but I don't rank games. I've never really been a person who looked back. The stats will tell you whether a game was good or not.

The one thing I remember about that game is being so tired. I was heavy and overweight because I had broken a rib in training camp and I couldn't run. So I had put on about 10 pounds. I think I was 200 and some change in that game. I usually play bump-and-run all game, but I played off some in that game.

I scored my first touchdown on a punt return.

Joe Avezzano would always ask me on a punt return whether I wanted it left or right, but I always like middle returns because it's the quickest way to the end zone. Besides, I didn't want to have to wait for a wall.

Most of the time, coaches want you to get a first down—10 yards—on a punt return. That's their goal. But that's not me. I never thought like that. I'm looking to score. Every time. Sometimes, I would sacrifice yards to try to get a big play, but I don't want the coach looking at me crazy when I get to the sidelines because I got tackled.

I'm looking at the big picture. They allowed me to have that leeway, and it worked well that season. We had so much confidence and camaraderie. Guys thought we were going to score on every punt return.

The punt return was a left return that went right for a touchdown.

When I got back to the sideline, I threw up. I just lost it. After returning the punt, people crowd around you and it takes away your air. I was like, "Let me breathe."

Here's something funny. My mama was watching the game and saw me throwing up.

My mama called my girlfriend and went off on her, "What did you do to my baby? What did you do to my baby?"

I'm serious, that's what she kept asking her.

I played a lot of offense in 1996. I didn't get many opportunities in 1998, but I was always trying to get some offense. I'm always trying to help the team and create situations. If I'm out there, obviously I'm going to draw some attention. It wasn't about me saying, "Throw me the ball. Throw me the ball."

It's fun to play whether it's offense or defense, but I got to the point where I got bored defensively because no one was throwing at me. You get to the point where you feel like you're not helping your team, even though you are. You want to feel like an asset, so you're always looking for a way to stay involved in the game.

Playing offense was a way to do that.

When we broke the huddle, I usually said something to the quarterback, so I'd be the last thing on his mind when he walked up to center.

"Holler at me, Red."

"Prime, I'm coming to you."

"All right, just put it up there."

I got the touchdown on the interception because of Kevin Mathis. We had taken the defense out of the game because we were up by quite a bit. "Little Fella" was playing cornerback, and they caught a couple in a row on him, so I said, "Young corner, you want me to show you how to do this thing?"

I said, "Come here, man."

So I ran on the field and he ran off.

The dude tried to throw an in, and I got it and went to the house.

"Little Fella" was screaming when I got to the sideline. He couldn't believe that mess. That's exactly what happened. It's funny because I was out of the game.

———————

A day after Sanders' dazzling performance, the NFL named him Prime Time Player of the Week. It's the only time the NFL has ever created an award to honor a player for his performance in a game.

"It was such an unusual performance that we were trying to decide whether he should be on special teams or defense, and he also caught a long pass that we just said why not just come up with a special award," said Greg Aiello, the NFL's director of communications. "He didn't fit any of the categories. It was in a prime-time game. His nickname was 'Prime Time.' It all fit together, so we gave him his own category. We were just trying to have some fun in recognition of a noteworthy and unique performance. We couldn't resist."

Sanders' performance against the Giants was merely a harbinger.

He finished the season with five interceptions, caught seven passes for 100 yards, and averaged an NFL-best 15.6 yards on punt returns with two touchdowns. And there's no reason to think his numbers wouldn't have been even better if he hadn't suffered a serious toe injury against Arizona in November.

Sanders injured his toe in the first quarter against Arizona and didn't return until the fourth quarter as the Cowboys held on to beat the Cardinals 35-28 in Sun Devil Stadium. The next week Sanders managed just 15 plays against the Seahawks before the pain forced him out of the game.

He didn't get on the field again until the Cowboys met the Cardinals in an NFC wild-card game at Texas Stadium. During the six weeks that he missed, fans and media had plenty of skepticism about the injury and skepticism for why a toe injury had forced Sanders out of the lineup.

"Most of the people who question the injury have never had the injury," Sanders told the *Dallas Morning News* the week before the play-off game. "If you want to feel how I feel, hit your toe with a hammer 10 times, slam it in your car door, then break it backwards.

"Then, go out there and run a 40-yard dash and try to cover Jerry Rice. That's how it feels."

The injury cost Sanders more than playing time. It cost him money.

Sanders was so dominant during the first half of the season that Jones opened negotiations with Sanders' agent, Eugene Parker, and talked publicly about making Sanders a Cowboy for the rest of his career. It seemed like a good idea.

Sanders, then 31, was still the best cornerback in the game, and opposing quarterbacks rarely challenged him. That meant the Cowboys could double-team the receiver on the other side of the field or use an extra defender against the run. And he remained a force on special teams.

No one rushed to the Texas Stadium concession stands on fourth down when the Cowboys forced a punt, because they never knew what Sanders might do. He had returns of 60, 59, 43, and 39 in the season's first six weeks. A holding penalty nullified a 71-yard return for an apparent touchdown.

"For any top returner, the element that makes the biggest difference is a burst of speed, and Deion was the fastest football player I've ever seen on the field," Avezzano said. "Sometimes he would make business decisions and avoid contact, but when he had an opportunity to make a big play, he always took it. He was always looking to make something happen when he had the ball in his hands. He wasn't interested in fair catches."

It was Sanders' superstar status, his ability to change a game in an instant, and his full-time commitment to football—he told the Cowboys he would give up baseball after the 1997 baseball season with the Cincinnati Reds—that convinced Jones he needed to extend Sanders' contract.

The sides had settled on a $20-million signing bonus and were haggling over the yearly salary. Sanders wanted to average $10 million per season, while the Cowboys were at $9 million.

"Then I hurt my toe," he said. "It was over after that. That's why I tell young guys today not to be greedy. Sometimes you have to compromise."

Sanders played one more season with the Cowboys, but it was clear his toe was still bothering him. Opposing quarterbacks didn't pick on him, but they no longer avoided him at all costs. At the end of the 1999 season, which ended with a 27-10 loss to Minnesota in an NFC wildcard game, Sanders figured he had played his last game for the Cowboys.

He was right.

He signed a free-agent deal with Washington that included an $8-million signing bonus and intercepted four passes in his only season. Then he retired. Three years later, Sanders ended his retirement to play with some of his best friends, including middle linebacker Ray Lewis, in Baltimore.

"I didn't allow somebody to tell me who I was," he said. "I told them who I was. I never cared about the Hall of Fame or what you were going to write or what you were going to say, because I know me. My critics have critics, so why would I listen to them?"

Deion Sanders' entrepreneurial spirit first surfaced in Fort Meyers, Florida, where the baby-faced businessman occasionally skipped classes to make money at the Kansas City Royals' spring training complex.

"It was a two- to three-mile walk to their complex, but I'd go there and shag the home run balls and put them in a sock. Then I'd sell the balls for two or three dollars to fans. If I got an autograph, then I'd sell them for more," he said. "A cracked bat might get me five or ten dollars, especially if I got it signed.

"That was my hustle at seven or eight years old. I can't imagine any of my sons missing school to do something like that."

Sanders had the opportunity to create his own collectibles business because his mother, a single parent, worked long hours to give her son a better life. Sometimes that meant she had to leave home before dawn.

"The things we did then would be called child abuse now. My mom would leave me at the crib and go to work," Sanders said. "I'd get up, eat some cereal, and go to school. Instead of calling the child custody people, the neighbors would check on you and make sure you were all right."

Deion Luwynn Sanders lived in a housing project until he was about seven and became a star football, basketball and baseball player at North Fort Myers High School. One of the most highly recruited athletes in the nation, he signed with Florida State.

A few years later, "Prime Time" was born.

"I looked at a sheet that showed defensive backs were one of the lowest-paid positions in football next to offensive linemen," he said matter-of-factly. "That's when I created 'Prime Time.'"

You see, it has always been about dollars and cents for Sanders. The more he talked and backed it up on the football field, the more endorsement opportunities he was going to have. And the bigger star he was going to become.

A similar approach worked for Muhammad Ali, whose poetic prose predicting when he would knock out his foes made the former heavyweight champion one of the most recognized men in the United States and the world.

Such an approach, though, does come at a price. Critics called him arrogant. And brash. And cocky. Sanders didn't care.

His athletic ability answered every critic.

Sanders retired after the 2005 season to focus on his television and radio broadcast career. He also owns a real estate development company that's building affordable housing for inner-city families throughout cities in Florida.

"I approach TV and business the same way," he said. "I work hard and I study, because I'm trying to perfect my craft. I want to be the best at whatever I'm doing."

Celebrate the Heroes of Texas Sports
in These Other NEW and Recent Releases from Sports Publishing

Captain Crash and the Dallas Cowboys
by Cliff Harris
- 5.5 x 8.25 hardcover
- 192 pages
- photos throughout
- $19.95
- 2006 release!

Legends of the Dallas Cowboys
by Cody Monk
- 8.5 x 11 hardcover
- 180 pages
- color-photos throughout
- $24.95

Cliff Harris's and Charlie Waters's Tales from the Dallas Cowboys
by Cliff Harris and Charlie Waters
- 5.5 x 8.25 softcover
- 250 pages
- photos throughout
- $14.95
- 2006 release! First time in softcover!

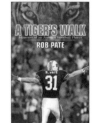

Longhorns for Life
by Whit Canning
- 6 x 9 hardcover
- 256 pages
- photos throughout
- $24.95
- 2006 release!

Longhorns' Perfect Drive: Texas' 2005 National Championship Season
by the *Austin American-Statesman*
- 8.5 x 11 hardcover and softcover
- 128 pages • color photos throughout
- $19.95 (hardcover)
- $14.95 (softcover)
- 2006 release!

Tales from the Texas Longhorns
by Steve Richardson
- 5.5 x 8.25 hardcover
- 200 pages
- photos throughout
- $19.95
- Updated 2005 edition!

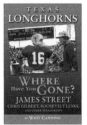

Texas Longhorns: Where Have You Gone?
by Whit Canning
- 6 x 9 hardcover
- 192 pages
- photos throughout
- $19.95

More Tales from Aggieland
by Brent Zwerneman
- 5.5 x 8.25 hardcover
- 192 pages
- photos throughout
- $19.95

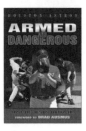

Houston Astros: Aces in Orbit
by Jesus Ortiz
- 6 x 9 softcover
- 300 pages
- eight-page b/w photo insert
- $16.95
- 2006 release!

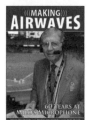

Making Airwaves: 60 Years at Milo's Microphone
by Milo Hamilton and Dan Schlossberg with Bob Ibach
- 6 x 9 hardcover
- 252 pages
- photos throughout
- $24.95
- 2006 release!